1,001 Facts Everyone Should Know about Israel

1,001 Facts Everyone Should Know about Israel

Mitchell Bard
and
Moshe Schwartz

ROWMAN & LITTLEFIELD PUBLISHERS, INC.
Lanham • Boulder • New York • Toronto • Oxford

ROWMAN & LITTLEFIELD PUBLISHERS, INC.

Published in the United States of America
by Rowman & Littlefield Publishers, Inc.
A wholly owned subsidary of The Rowman & Littlefield Publishing Group, Inc.
4501 Forbes Boulevard, Suite 200, Lanham, Maryland 20706
www.rowmanlittlefield.com

PO Box 317
Oxford
OX2 9RU, UK

British Library Cataloguing in Publication Information Available

Library of Congress Cataloging-in-Publication Data

Bard, Mitchell Geoffrey, 1959–
    1001 facts everyone should know about Israel / Mitchell Bard and Moshe Schwartz.
       p. cm.
    Includes bibliographical references.
    ISBN 0-7425-4357-9 (cloth : alk. paper) — ISBN 0-7425-4358-7 (pbk. : alk. paper)
    1. Israel—Handbooks, manuals, etc. I. Title: One thousand one facts everyone should
know about Israel. II. Title: One thousand and one facts everyone should know about
Israel. III. Schwartz, Moshe. IV. Title

DS102.95.B373 2005
956.94—dc22   2005012466

Printed in the United States of America

♾™ The paper used in this publication meets the minimum requirements of American
National Standard for Information Sciences—Permanence of Paper for Printed Library
Materials, ANSI/NISO Z39.48-1992.

"And the streets of the city Jerusalem will be filled with boys and girls laughing in its alleyways"

Zechariah, 8:3–5

In memory of those people who sacrificed their lives so that the laughter of Jewish children can be heard echoing through the alleyways of Jerusalem.

Mitchell Bard would like to dedicate this book to his extraordinary wife, Marcela Kogan, and to his children, Ariel and Daniel, who he hopes will grow up to share his love of Zion.

Moshe Schwartz would like to dedicate this book to his wonderful children, Elyana and Daniella, whose laughter is the sweetest sound he has ever heard.

Contents

Preface

$\mathcal{W}$e have had a long-standing interest in education and often find ourselves frustrated by the lack of knowledge many people have of some of the most basic facts about Israel. Given the intense press coverage of the Middle East, it is crucial that Jews and non-Jews have a working knowledge of the history of Israel to appreciate and understand current events.

While Mitchell has been publishing books and articles on Middle East topics for about fifteen years, the idea for this book arose while Moshe was teaching an elective history course on Israel and Zionism at Yeshiva University High School for Boys. Moshe found that the students opted to take the course out of an abiding love for, and interest in, the Jewish State. Moshe was shocked to discover, however, their ignorance of basic Israeli history. On the first day of class, for example, Moshe asked the seniors if they knew who Menachem Begin was. Only one of the seventeen students correctly identified him (see fact 228 if you do not know—and take Moshe's class next time). As the year wore on, it became clear that there was an endemic problem in the Jewish community: although the older generation knew Israeli history because they had lived through it and been raised with a love of Zion, Israel was still an abstraction for their children. While parents remember the events leading up to the 1967 Six-Day War, the surprise of the 1973 Yom Kippur War, and the tragedy of the 1982 Lebanon War, the younger generation is too young to remember any of these events.

To build a knowledge base for his students, Moshe began to ask them to research names and events each week and present their findings to the class. The project became a popular success, and students started collecting facts that we believe everyone should know about Israel.

ix

After reviewing some of the assignments at home, Moshe stumbled across a book of facts about American history and had an epiphany: Why not compile a book of essential facts about Israel to educate the next generation?

Deciding that researching, writing, and collating 1,001 facts about Israel was a monumental task, Moshe sought help and quickly turned to Mitchell, whom he knew from his reputation as one of the country's leading experts on U.S.–Middle East policy.

Together we have sifted through mountains of information from a wide variety of sources. We have asked friends and colleagues for suggestions, perused published and unpublished sources, and developed a collection of facts that will provide the knowledge you need to begin to understand Israeli history.

As with any list, the choices for inclusion are largely subjective. In the biography section, for example, hundreds of other figures could have been listed from the fields of business, the arts, politics, religion, and the military. We have not intentionally left any facts out for political, ideological, partisan, or any other reason. We simply tried to pick those facts that we deemed most important in understanding Israeli history, those we found interesting or amusing, and those that were simply fun bits of trivia.

Make no mistake, this book was written by two avowed and proud Zionists who firmly believe in Israel as a Jewish State. This book is not meant, however, to be a propaganda piece for Israel. Rather, we wrote what we believe is an accurate, honest, and comprehensive compilation of facts that tell the story of Israel, warts and all, from its humble origins in the days of the pioneers to the twenty-first-century high-tech society of today.

So sit back and enjoy these 1,001 facts and then amaze your colleagues, friends, and family with your knowledge of Israel.

Acknowledgments

The authors would like to thank all the people who contributed to the research, suggested facts for inclusion in the book, and checked the accuracy of our work. We are particularly grateful to fact writer/checker extraordinaire Rebecca Weiner, Dr. Rafi Danziger, and David Shyovitz. We would also like to thank Dr. Bernard J. Firestone, dean of Hofstra College of Liberal Arts and Sciences, for his input and guidance.

1,001 Facts

ZIONISM

1. Zionism   The national movement for the return of the Jewish people to their homeland and the resumption of Jewish sovereignty in the Land of Israel. Zionists advocate tangible as well as spiritual aims. Jews of all persuasions, left and right, religious and secular, joined to form the Zionist movement and worked together toward these goals. Disagreements led to rifts, but ultimately the common goal of a Jewish state in its ancient homeland was attained.

2. Magen David (Shield of David)   A six-pointed star formed by two overlying triangles, the Magen David emerged as a Jewish and Zionist symbol. The Magen David was placed on the cover of the first issue of Theodor Herzl's journal, *Die Welt*. The symbol is at the center of the flag of Israel and is also used by the Magen David Adom, Israel's "Red Cross."

3. Autonomism   A non-Zionist ideology first enunciated in the early twentieth century by Simon Dubnow, autonomism crystallized in Eastern Europe. Its adherents believed in the future viability of Jewish life in the Diaspora as long as Jewry continued to maintain self-rule in community organizations, sustain its educational and mutual-assistance institutions, and develop its "spiritual nationhood." The Holocaust put an end to the foundation of autonomism; today it has no practical impact on Jewish life and philosophy.

4. Jewish Anti-Zionism   Until the Nazi Holocaust, many Orthodox Jews opposed the Zionist aspiration of establishing a national home for the Jewish people in the Land of Israel. This opposition stemmed in part from distaste for the Zionist activists who were secularists and who rejected the traditional authority of the rabbis in favor of "foreign" ideologies such as socialism and nationalism. As a theological justification for their position, anti-Zionists cite various rabbinic traditions that forbid the hastening of the Redemption. The most intransigent and extreme of the Orthodox anti-Zionist parties is the Naturei Karta movement, a small but vocal organization that broke off from Aguddat Israel in 1935 because of Naturei's insistence on total separation from the Zionist Jewish community in Jerusalem.

5. Old Yishuv   The term used to denote the Jewish community in Israel prior to the Zionist Jewish community that began with the First Aliyah in 1882. The Old Yishuv was predominantly Orthodox and resistant to modern, secular concepts.

6. New Yishuv   The Zionist Jewish community beginning with the onset of the First Aliyah. The Zionists were overwhelmingly secular and socialist.

7. The Dreyfus Affair   In 1894, in the aftermath of military defeat at the hands of Prussia, Alfred Dreyfus (1859–1935), an assimilated Jewish captain in the French military, was tried for selling military secrets to Germany. He was found guilty and sentenced to internment in Devil's Island, the infamous prison in French Guiana. During the controversy surrounding the trial, anti-Jewish riots broke out in various French cities. French intellectuals recognized that Dreyfus, because he was a Jew, was being used as a scapegoat for France's military defeat. The French government retried Dreyfus and sentenced him to time served. Eventually, Dreyfus was fully exonerated and reinstated as a major in the army. Jews worldwide were shocked that enlightened France and much of her citizenry could act in such a blatantly anti-Semitic manner. The lesson learned by many was that assimilation is no defense against anti-Semitism. As a result of the anti-Semitic overtones of the trial and much of the French press, Theodor Herzl, a reporter covering the trial, involved himself with the Zionist movement. On September 13, 1995, 100 years after the fact, the French army officially admitted that Alfred Dreyfus was framed.

8. Russian Pogroms   In 1881, a series of attacks on Jews in Russia persuaded many that it was necessary to establish an independent Jewish homeland. The large number of Russian Jews who became Zionists because of the riots helped fuel aliyah and the worldwide growth of Zionism.

9. Hibbat Zion (Love of Zion)   This pre-Zionist movement began in 1882 and was most active in Russia. Its adherents advocated reviving Jewish life in the Land of Israel by working toward the physical development of the Land and founding agricultural settlements in Palestine. By the time the First Zionist Congress met in 1897, they had already begun to transform the face of the Land. Theodor Herzl, though, saw the aim of the Zionist movement as a charter for a Jewish national entity in the Land of Israel rather than its development through piecemeal settlement.

10. Po'alei Zion (Workers of Zion)   Emerging as a movement in the late 1800s, Po'alei Zion fused the ideologies of Zionism and socialism based on a Jewish proletariat. By 1907, a world Union of Po'alei Zion was founded, representing chapters in Russia, the Austrian Empire, America, Britain, Argentina, Rumania, and Palestine. After a 1920 split, one faction failed in its bid to affiliate with the Third International (Comintern). The other faction helped found the World Labor Zionist Movement.

11. Bund (abbr. of General Jewish Workers' Union in Lito, Poyln un Rusland)   The Bund was founded in 1897 as a Jewish socialist party and achieved a membership of 25,000–30,000. The organization passed a resolution in 1901 barring membership in the Zionist Organization. As a result, many Jewish members resigned from the Bund and, necessarily, from the affiliated trade unions. This resolution helped spur the growth of the Po'alei Zion trade union in Russia.

12. BILU (*Beit Ya'acov Lekhu Ve-Nelkhah*—House of Jacob Come and Let Us Go)   This organization was created by Russian Jews intent on moving to Israel in response to the numerous pogroms that took place in Russia during the 1880s. One of the first members of the organization to reach Palestine was Moshe Sharett.

13. World Zionist Organization (WZO)   The WZO was founded at the First Zionist Congress in 1897 by Theodor Herzl, the father of Zionism. Its aim was to facilitate the return of the Jewish people to the Land of Israel and revive Jewish life in the country. Membership grew from 164,333 in 1907 to 2,159,840 in 1946. Today, the WZO works primarily in the Diaspora to promote Zionism, strengthen Israel, and defend Jews everywhere. The World Zionist Congress, the main body of the WZO, meets every four years to discuss policies and elect executive committees.

14. Zionist Congress   Theodor Herzl established the Congress as the authoritative body of the Zionist Organization. The aim of the Congress, as stated by Herzl, was to "close the Zionist ranks . . . and to unify their endeavors." Each Congress consisted of the leading Zionist leaders and authorities from around the world. The Congress was held yearly from 1897 to 1901 and every other year from 1903 to 1939 (interrupted by World War I). After the establishment of Israel the Congress was held every four to six years. German was the official language of the Zionist Congress until the early 1930s when English became the tongue of choice. Starting with the Twentieth Congress, all official records have been kept exclusively in Hebrew. The Congress meets approximately every five years in Israel.

15. The Jewish Agency (*Ha-Sokhenut ha-Yehudit le-Eretz Israel*)   The Agency serves as the executive for the World Zionist Organization. Headquartered in Jerusalem, this nongovernmental body received its name from article four of the League of Nations Mandate for Palestine, which stated "an appropriate Jewish agency shall be recognized as a public body for the purpose of advising and cooperating with the administration of Palestine in such economic, social, and other . . . matters as may effect the establishment of the Jewish National Homeland and the interests of the Jewish population in Palestine." To this end, the Agency became the principal body responsible for Jewish immigration to Palestine, absorption, settlement, development, economic growth, and foreign relations. The Agency was also involved with education and cultural life. With the establishment of Israel, numerous functions of the Agency were transferred to governmental bodies. The Agency continues to function in the realms of immigration, settlement, youth activities, and projects funded through private donations.

16. Jewish Colonial Trust   The Trust was incorporated on March 20, 1899, pursuant to the decision of the First and Second Zionist Congress to establish a bank for the movement. A necessary reorganization took place in 1933; the Trust became an Israeli company, *Ozar Hityashevut ha-Yehudim*, in 1955.

17. Jewish National Fund (*Keren Kayemeth Leisrael*)   The JNF is the arm of the Zionist Organization through which land in Israel is purchased and developed. The Fifth Zionist Congress created the JNF on December 29, 1901. The name is derived from the Mishnaic tract (Pe'ah 1:1) that reads: "the fruits of which a man enjoys in the world, while the capital abides (*ha-keren kayemeth*) for him in the world to come." JNF leases run for a term of forty-nine years (equivalent to the Jubilee year recounted in the Bible) and may be renewed as long as the leaseholder or his heirs adhere to the utilization scheme set forth in the lease. By 1947, the JNF owned more than half of all Jewish holdings in the region. After Israel gained independence, the JNF shifted its goals to land improvement and afforestation.

18. First Land Deal   In April 1903, the Jewish National Fund acquired its first parcels of land in Palestine in the lower Galilee and Judea.

19. First Bank   The first Zionist bank, the Anglo-Palestine Bank, opened in Jaffa in 1903. Later, it would become known as Bank Leumi.

20. Keren Hayesod (Palestine Foundation Fund)   Since its inception in 1920, this institution has served as the financial wing of the Zionist Organization and has carried the burden of funding the Zionist agenda. It raised approximately $143,000,000 prior to Israel's independence. In the United States, monies are raised through the United Jewish Appeal.

21. First Zionist Conference (Basle, Switzerland, August 29–31, 1897) This meeting was an attempt to unify the Zionist movement. Theodor Herzl, responsible for the success of the conference, served as chairman. Some 200 participants discussed issues including Zionist (Jewish) communities outside of Palestine, settlements in Palestine, and questions pertaining to Jewish culture. The Conference marked the first step in creating the political and structural mechanisms responsible for the eventual emergence of modern Israel. The event was marked by the formulation of the Basle Program and the establishment of the Zionist Organization.

22. Second Zionist Congress (Basle, August 15–18, 1898)   Theodor Herzl presided over the meeting, which began work on the Jewish Colonial Trust. Zionist Socialists, absent from the first Congress, were present. In this Congress, Herzl sought to galvanize the fledgling Zionist movement to assert itself in the face of active opposition within the Jewish community.

23. Third Zionist Congress (Basle, August 15–18, 1899)   Theodor Herzl reported on his meetings with Kaiser William II of Germany in Constantinople and Jerusalem. Despite the fact that these meetings produced no practical results, the fact that they took place was of considerable symbolic value. The Congress worked primarily on the political cause of Zionism and ignored the planning of practical steps to create a Jewish state.

24. Fourth Zionist Congress (London, August 13–16, 1900)   The meeting was held in England because Theodor Herzl believed that England would be highly sympathetic to the Zionist plight. The Congress met in an atmosphere of growing concern over the situation facing Rumanian Jewry: many thousands had been forced to leave, and the remainder were subject to persecution.

25. Fifth Zionist Congress (Basle, December 26–30, 1901)   Theodor Herzl reported to the Congress on his meeting with Sultan Abdul Hamid II of Turkey and on the progress of the Jewish Colonial Trust. The Jewish National Fund was created. Meanwhile, a group led by Leo Motzkin, Martin Buber, and Chaim Weizmann called on the Zionist movement to adopt a program of Hebrew culture and a greater degree of democracy within the organization.

26. Sixth Zionist Congress (Basle, August 23–28, 1903)   The last Congress attended by Theodor Herzl met with the pall of the Kishinev pogrom (in Russia) hanging over the gathering. Herzl introduced for discussion the British offer of establishing a Jewish homeland in Uganda. Herzl supported the Uganda Plan in light of recent pogroms as a temporary solution, with the ultimate goal being the establishment of a Jewish state in Zion. The debate was marred by divisiveness, bitterness, and a walkout staged by opponents of the measure. Herzl, pleading not to irreparably destroy the Zionist Organization, coaxed the objecting delegates to return. The proposal to examine the possibility of Jewish settlement in East Africa passed by a vote of 295 in favor, 178 opposed, and 98 abstentions.

27. Seventh Zionist Congress (Basle, July 27–August 2, 1905)   Max Nordau, the new president, opened the Congress by delivering the eulogy for Theodor Herzl. Debate over the Uganda Plan ensued and preoccupied the gathering. A negative report by the commission of inquiry investigating the conditions in Uganda fueled opposition to the proposal. The Uganda Plan was rejected; a small group of dissenters withdrew from the Congress and the Zionist Organization in protest. A resolution was passed supporting the immediate initiation of efforts to settle Palestine without waiting for securing political rights to the region.

28. Eighth Zionist Congress (The Hague, August 14–21, 1907)   The meeting was held in The Hague to coincide with the Second International Peace Conference, held at the same location, with the intent of keeping a high public profile for the Zionist movement. The Congress was presided over by David Wolffsohn. Chaim Weizmann delivered a famous speech in which he wove together the aspirations of the political Zionists, who sought to first secure political recognition for a Jewish homeland, and practical Zionists, who sought to concentrate on fostering immigration to and establishing settlements in Palestine. He argued for a synthetic Zionism, saying, "We must aspire to a charter, but our aspirations will be realized only as a result of our practical work in Eretz Israel."

29. Ninth Zionist Congress (Hamburg, December 26–30, 1909)   This was the first Congress held in Germany. Participants David Wolffsohn and Max Nordau looked to the success of the Young Turk Revolution in Turkey as a beacon of hope for the fortunes of the Zionist movement. Meanwhile, the delegates were unable to agree on how to implement the Zionist agenda. Though Wolffsohn was reelected president, a rival leadership that included Menachem Ussishkin, Chaim Weizmann, and Nahum Sokolow emerged with support from the representatives of the workers' movement in Palestine.

30. Tenth Zionist Congress (Basle, August 9–15, 1911)   Nicknamed the Peace Congress, this conclave marked the end of the friction between the practical and political Zionists and the emergence of the synthetic approach espoused by Chaim Weizmann. Wolffsohn, in his address opening the Congress, resigned his post. For the first time, a session, led by Menachem Ussishkin, was held exclusively in Hebrew. Otto Warburg, a German Jew and distinguished scientist who was identified with the practical Zionist camp, succeeded Wolffsohn as president of the organization.

31. Eleventh Zionist Congress (Vienna, September 2–9, 1913)   The attendees of the meeting discussed settlement efforts in Palestine. Also, at the urging of Weizmann and Ussishkin, delegates agreed to establish a Hebrew University in Jerusalem. Max Nordau boycotted the gathering as a protest of the perceived abandonment of Herzl's philosophy by the Zionist Organization.

32. Twelfth Zionist Congress (Carlsbad, September 1–14, 1921)   The first gathering after World War I convened in the aftermath of the Balfour Declaration, the British occupation of Palestine, the Bolshevik Revolution, numerous deadly pogroms in the Ukraine, and the establishment of Keren Hayesod. The Congress also addressed the question of Zionism's relations with the Arabs, an issue that had become serious as a result of Arab riots in Jerusalem (1920) and in Jaffa (1921). The Congress passed a resolution declaring that Zionism seeks "to live in relations of harmony and mutual respect with the Arab people" and called for finding a "sincere understanding with the Arab people." The Congress also marked the emergence of a dynamic American contingent of Zionists led by Louis Brandeis. England became the epicenter of the Zionist movement, and Englishman Chaim Weizmann was elected president.

33. Thirteenth Zionist Congress (Carlsbad, August 6–18, 1923) This was the first Congress to convene after the League of Nations sanctioned the British Mandate of Palestine and the Zionist Organization was renamed the Jewish Agency for Palestine. The delegates debated permitting non-Zionist representation in the Jewish Agency and reelected Weizmann as president.

34. Fourteenth Zionist Congress (Vienna, August 18–31, 1925) Chaim Weizmann presided over the meeting, which focused on supporting and encouraging the economic growth and increased settlement construction that began as a result of the Fourth Aliyah. The Revisionists, led by Ze'ev Jabotinsky, debuted at this Congress and pushed for a more active Zionist movement and a more ambitious policy for the movement.

35. Fifteenth Zionist Congress (Basle, August 30–September 11, 1927)   Martin Buber delivered a eulogy for Ahad Ha'am. The Congress discussed the economic downturn afflicting Palestine and the slowdown in aliyah. It would turn out that 1927 was the first and only year in the pre-State period when more Jewish emigrants left the country than arrived. Chaim Weizmann was elected for a fourth presidential term. Henrietta Szold was elected to the Zionist Executive. She was the first women to serve on the Zionist Executive.

36. Sixteenth Zionist Congress (Zurich, July 28–August 10, 1929) President Weizmann reported on the inclusion of non-Zionists in the Jewish Agency. Attending the Congress were such notables as Herbert Samuel, Albert Einstein, Lord Melchett, and Sholem Asch. Meanwhile, the situation in Palestine had improved with the economy recovering and immigration increasing.

37. Seventeenth Zionist Congress (Basle, June 30–July 15, 1931) Shortly after the Sixteenth Congress ended, violence erupted in Palestine. Both the Shaw Commission and British official Sir Hope-Simpson criticized the Zionist movement's activities in Palestine. The Passfield White Paper adopted the recommendations of the Shaw Commission. As a result of Britain's new policies and its criticism of the Zionist movement, Weizmann resigned as president of the WZO. The Seventeenth Congress opened with opposition to Weizmann's pro-British philosophy. The Revisionists demanded a course of action aimed at guaranteeing a Jewish majority in Palestine and a proclamation stating that the ultimate goal of the Zionist movement was the establishment of a Jewish state. These demands were voted down. Weizmann refused to retract his resignation in light of the opposition to his policies and the demands of the Revisionists. Nahum Sokolow was elected president.

38. Eighteenth Zionist Congress (Prague, August 21–September 4, 1933)   Delegates saw the Nazi rise to power. The conflict between the Revisionists and the labor movement intensified, provoked in part by the mysterious murder of labor activist Chaim Arlosoroff. Sokolow was reelected president of the Zionist Organization. Representation by the labor movement grew as notables such as David Ben-Gurion and Moshe Sharett became involved.

39. Nineteenth Zionist Congress (Lucerne, August 20–September 4, 1935)   Thanks to the support of labor, the largest faction present, Chaim Weizmann returned to power as president of the organization. Much of the discussion focused on the efforts to bring German Jews to Palestine. Henrietta Szold reported on the role of Youth Aliyah in saving young Jews. David Ben-Gurion became an influential personality as he joined the Executive of the Jewish Agency, while the Revisionists dropped out of the movement and formed the competing New Zionist Organization.

40. Twentieth Zionist Congress (Zurich, August 3–16, 1937)   This meeting was devoted largely to responding to the Peel Commission and its partition plan. Delegates were deeply divided but ultimately issued the following statement: "The field in which the Jewish National Home was to be established was understood, at the time of the Balfour Declaration, to be the whole of Palestine, including Transjordan." Instead of an outright rejection of the plan, the Executive was charged with the task of seeking a more favorable partition from the British. Menachem Ussishkin presided over the gathering.

41. Twenty-first Zionist Congress (Geneva, August 16–26, 1939) Delegates met as the world teetered on the brink of war. They openly and vigorously took issue with the most recent British White Paper, the effect of which was to close the gates of Palestine to Jews fleeing the Nazi slaughter of the European Jewish community. Britain took a clear pro-Arab position, with Prime Minister Chamberlain being quoted as saying, "Let us offend the Jews rather than the Arabs." At the end of the proceedings, Chaim Weizmann said, "I have no prayer but this: that we will all meet again alive."

42. Twenty-second Zionist Congress (Basle, December 9–24, 1946) Meeting in the aftermath of the Holocaust, the Zionist movement was also suffering from heightened tension between the Jews and British in Palestine. The Congress met following the publication of the Morrison-Grady report that called for the creation of four districts (cantons) in Palestine that would disengage the local populations, and called for a Jewish-Arab conference. Chaim Weizmann encouraged delegates to adopt the Zionist platform that was formulated at conferences at the Biltmore Hotel in New York in 1942 and in London in 1945. The Biltmore program called for Palestine to be "a Jewish Commonwealth integrated in the structure of the democratic world." The Congress approved the program but rejected Weizmann's call for participation in the London conference. Weizmann resigned his position as president of the WZO.

43. Twenty-third Zionist Congress (Jerusalem, August 14–30, 1951) The first gathering held in Israel opened by the graveside of Theodor Herzl. The Congress debated the future of the Zionist movement in light of the establishment of the State of Israel. The Jerusalem Program, articulating the new goals of the movement, outlined plans for "consolidation of the State of Israel, the ingathering of the exiles in Eretz Israel, and the fostering of the unity of the Jewish people."

44. Twenty-fourth Zionist Congress (Jerusalem, April 24–May 7, 1956) Held prior to the Sinai Campaign amidst concern over the deteriorating security situation along the Israel-Egypt border, the Twenty-fourth Congress discussed aliyah, settlements for immigrants, and raising funds for Israel. A proposal to elect unified delegations from each Diaspora community instead of having party lines was rejected. Nahum Goldmann was elected president.

45. Twenty-fifth Zionist Congress (Jerusalem, December 27, 1960–January 11, 1961) In the wake of public criticism of the WZO by David Ben-Gurion, the Congress grappled with its strained relationship with the Israeli government. Jewish education in the Diaspora emerged as a major issue. Nahum Goldmann was reelected president.

46. Twenty-sixth Zionist Congress (Jerusalem, December 30, 1964–January 10, 1965) WZO President Nahum Goldmann opened the gathering with a call for the Zionist movement to fight assimilation by highlighting the diminishing role of spirituality in the Jewish communities of the Diaspora. The Congress focused attention on the plight of Soviet Jewry, calling on the Soviet Union to fight anti-Semitism and persecution. A resolution was passed calling on the countries of the world to stop arms sales to the region. Nahum Goldmann was reelected president for the third consecutive time.

47. Twenty-seventh Zionist Congress (Jerusalem, June 9–19, 1968) The Congress allowed for the first time participation by youth delegations and student groups. Delegates basked in the glow of the aftermath of the Six-Day War and the resulting tide of immigrants and volunteers that arrived from the Western world. The acceptance of the Israeli government's creation of the Ministry of Absorption ended the feud between the WZO and the Israeli government. The Jerusalem Program, enacted in 1951, was amended as follows:

"The aims of Zionism are: The unity of the Jewish people and the centrality of Israel in its life; the ingathering of the Jewish people in its historical home- land, Eretz Yisrael, through aliyah from all lands; the strengthening of the State of Israel founded on the prophetic ideals of justice and peace; the preservation of the identity of the Jewish people through the fostering of Jewish and He- brew education and of Jewish spiritual and cultural values; the protection of Jewish rights everywhere."

48.Twenty-eighth Zionist Congress (Jerusalem, January 18–28, 1972) Discussing the issues and concerns of the day, delegates addressed the issues of aliyah from Western countries, increasing immigration by Soviet Jewry, and concerns over Jewish education in the Diaspora. The payment of a shekel for membership in the WZO was eliminated, and Knesset elections were en- shrined as the method of determining the makeup of the Israeli delegation. A proposal was rejected requiring officers in the Zionist movement who have served for eight years to make aliyah.

49. Twenty-ninth Zionist Congress (Jerusalem, February 20–March 1, 1978)   Convening for the first time in six years, delegates debated religious pluralism within the context of the Zionist movement, resulting in the full ac- ceptance of the Reform and Conservative movements.

50. Thirtieth Zionist Congress (Jerusalem, December 7–17, 1982) Struggling to define its role vis-à-vis the State of Israel, attendees debated the Zionist movement's ideology and purpose in light of the Jewish Agency's en- trée into such areas as aliyah and Jewish education in the Diaspora. The issue of Jewish settlement construction in Judea, Samaria, and Gaza caused bitter debate, resulting in a resolution stating that delegates "agreed to disagree" on the issue.

51. Thirty-first Zionist Congress (Jerusalem, December 6–11, 1987) The gathering was marked by an inability to forge a consensus on many of the issues facing the Congress. No vision or statement of ideology was enunciated as the relationship with the Jewish Agency was left unresolved. Failed proposals included electing a president (a post left unfilled since the resignation of Nahum Goldmann in 1968) and the conferring of a special status to "Magishimim," of- ficers of the movement who undertook a commitment to make aliyah.

52. Thirty-second Zionist Congress (Jerusalem, July 26–30, 1992) Ideological issues took a backseat as delegates concerned themselves with the financial aid needed to assist the absorption of the waves of immigrants arriv- ing from the former Soviet Union and Ethiopia. Simcha Dinitz, reelected chairman of the Executive, became the subject of judicial proceedings, and new elections were held, resulting in the election of Member of Knesset Avraham Burg. A growing belief that the WZO has outlived its usefulness has margin- alized the activities of the Zionist Congress in many segments of the Jewish community.

53. Thirty-third Zionist Congress (Jerusalem, December 23–25, 1997)   This Congress struggled with the issue of religious pluralism within Judaism and passed a resolution requiring that all future Congresses have at least 25 percent of the delegates be between the ages of eighteen and thirty.

54. Thirty-fourth Zionist Congress (Jerusalem, June 17–20, 2002) Influenced by a younger leadership, the Congress focused on campus issues and passed resolutions calling for increased support for Jewish and Zionist education and Jewish youth movements. A resolution was also passed asserting the centrality of Israel in Jewish life.

55. Revisionist Zionism (Union of Zionist Revisionists)   Founded by Vladamir (Ze'ev) Jabotinsky, the Revisionists served as the major opposition to Chaim Weizmann and the World Zionist Organization during the 1920s and 1930s. Revisionists were critical of the small-scale immigration policy of the Zionist Organization, favoring immediate mass immigration. The Revisionists, through their New Zionist Organization, were instrumental in the creation of a large-scale illegal immigration network, bringing thousands of Jews to Palestine prior to 1940. The Revisionists opposed the Peel Commission Partition Plan. The Irgun adhered to Revisionist ideology and accepted Jabotinsky as its mentor. Revisionism is the ideological forerunner of the Likud party. The name comes from the notion of revising the policy of the Zionist movement in terms of the final goal of Zionism (the establishment of a Jewish state in all of Palestine) and the stages to reach that goal (e.g., free immigration and renewal of the Jewish battalions).

56. New Zionist Organization   The Revisionists formed their own organization after they seceded from the Zionist Organization in 1935 because of that group's adoption of a disciplinary clause aimed at preventing Revisionist political activity. The new body's elections involved some 713,000 voters. The New Zionist Organization sought the establishment of a Jewish majority state on both sides of the Jordan, the ingathering of all Jews to the new homeland, the revival of Hebrew, and the infusion of Jewish tradition in Jewish life. In 1946, after the establishment of an independent Jewish state and mass illegal immigration became the goal of the Haganah and mainstream Zionism, the Revisionists rejoined the Zionist Organization.

57. Betar   An Eastern European Revisionist Zionist youth movement that taught Hebrew, Jewish culture, and self-defense. The organization supported a Zionist ideal that included legal and illegal aliyah, pioneering the land of Palestine on both sides of the Jordan, and armed defense of Jewish settlements. Founded in 1923, chapters were soon established in more than twenty countries and throughout Palestine. These chapters trained with the Irgun, learning street-fighting, weapons use, and military strategy. By the late 1930s, Betar's almost 90,000 members were actively involved in illegally smuggling thousands of Jews into Palestine. Many Betar members joined Britain's Jewish Brigade during World War II. After the establishment of Israel, Betar played instrumental roles in establishing twelve Jewish settlements and populating Nahal units.

58. Madagascar Plan   A scheme first conceived in 1885 by German anti-Semite Paul de Legarde who sought to deport all Eastern European Jews to a French colony on the African coast. In 1937, a Polish commission traveled to Madagascar to explore the possibility of the removal of Jews to the island. In 1940, Adolf Eichmann drew up the Madagascar Plan, which called for the forced resettlement of four million Jews over four years, to be financed by seized Jewish assets. The proposal was leaked to the press, and the American Jewish Congress published a report arguing against the feasibility of the scheme. By this time, however, the Germans had already laid the groundwork for the "Final Solution."

59. Uganda Scheme   The British government proposed to establish a Jewish homeland in East Africa. After negotiations, Theodor Herzl tactically accepted the proposal in the belief that this was a stepping-stone to the eventual establishment of a state in Palestine. He raised the idea at the Sixth Zionist Congress, causing a bitter debate. The Uganda scheme was defeated during the Seventh Zionist Congress. The defeat resulted in the founding of the Territorialist Organization.

60. Territorialism   A twentieth-century political movement that sought to establish a majority Jewish state. Born after the Zionist Organization's rejection of the Uganda Scheme, the movement departed from traditional Zionism in its willingness to accept a location for a homeland other than Palestine. A handful of Jews moved to modern-day Kenya—then part of Uganda—to fulfill the territorialist vision.

61. The Balfour Declaration   The declaration was a letter written by British Foreign Minister Arthur James Balfour to Lord Rothschild on November 2, 1917. The letter reads, "His Majesty's Government view with favor the establishment in Palestine of a national home for the Jewish people, and will use their best endeavours to facilitate the achievement of this object, it being clearly understood that nothing shall be done which may prejudice the civil and religious rights of existing non-Jewish communities in Palestine, or the rights and political status enjoyed by Jews in any country." The Declaration was made public a week later and approved by the Allies at the San Remo Conference on April 20, 1920. The League of Nations incorporated the Declaration into Britain's Mandate on Palestine.

62. Revisionist Petition   In 1934, Revisionist Zionists successfully delivered to the British monarchy and parliament 600,000 Jewish signatures from twenty-four countries. The petition called for the establishment of a Jewish state in Palestine.

63. Ben-Gurion-Jabotinsky Agreement   In October 1934, arch rivals David Ben-Gurion and Vladimir Jabotinsky met in London and agreed to end the conflict between the Labor and Revisionist Zionists; however, the members of the Histadrut vetoed the agreement and the two groups remained at odds.

64. *New York Times* **Editorial**   In November 1938, the *New York Times* ran an editorial opposing the partition of Palestine, suggesting as an alternative settling Jews in Africa. In February 1948, the *Times* reported an unsubstantiated British charge that up to 1,000 communist agents were among the 15,000 Jews attempting to enter Palestine illegally.

IMMIGRATION

65. Aliyah (Ascent)   Refers to the act of immigrating to the Land of Israel. Aliyah is crucial to the realization of the Zionist dream; whoever makes aliyah contributes directly to the rebuilding of the Jewish homeland. In the early days of the modern Zionist movement, there were five distinct periods of aliyah, each of which contributed to the growth of the Jewish community in Palestine prior to the establishment of the State of Israel. These and subsequent waves of aliyah were primarily motivated by anti-Semitism or oppression in the country of origin.

66. Law of Return   Legislation enacted on July 5, 1950, marking the anniversary of the death of Theodor Herzl, which guarantees the right of all Jews to make aliyah and receive immediate citizenship. The law does not apply to Jews who pose a threat to the Jewish people, public health, or security. The definition of who qualifies as a Jew under the law has stirred much controversy. The religious parties in Israel insist that a Jew be defined as through strict matrilineal descent or Orthodox-sanctioned conversion. Conservative, Reform, secular, and other streams of Judaism argue for varyingly more expansive definitions of who is a Jew. The Law of Return grants rights to any child, grandchild, spouse of a child of a Jew, and even the spouse of a grandchild of a Jew. Under this law, a Jew is defined as "a person born of a Jewish mother or has been converted to Judaism and is not a member of another religion."

67. Yeridah (Descent)   The act of leaving the Land of Israel to settle elsewhere. It is estimated that there are approximately 700,000 Israelis living overseas, 200,000 of whom have emigrated since 1990.

68. Illegal Immigration (Aliyah Bet)   Jews first began to enter Israel illegally in 1888 when the Turks closed Palestine to Jewish immigration. In 1934, with Hitler's rise to power and British restrictions on the number of Jews who might enter Palestine, the Haganah and He-Halutz movements organized the first operation to smuggle Jews into Palestine by sea, succeeding in bringing approximately 350 pioneers to Palestine aboard the *Vellos*. In 1938, the Haganah established the *Mossad le-Aliyah Bet* to run all its clandestine immigration operations. Between 1945–1948, the Mossad ran sixty-five boatloads of immigrants to Palestine, most of which were intercepted by the British. Overall, some 115,000 Jews reached Palestine illegally; almost 800 illegal immigrants escaped the scourge of the Holocaust only to die fighting in Israel's War of Independence.

69. Cyprus   This island nation in the Mediterranean was discussed by Theodor Herzl and Neville Chamberlain as a possible place for Jewish settlement. Because of its proximity to Palestine, the British interned thousands of illegal Jewish immigrants in detention camps on the island. By 1948, more than 51,000 Jews attempting to reach Palestine would be interned in Cyprus. When the British Mandate ended, the camps were closed and all the Jews were brought to Israel.

70. No Refuge   In August 1939, the British announced that illegal immigrants who were caught would be imprisoned in Atlit prison. The prison was used for this purpose until the end of the British Mandate.

71. Youth Aliyah   Henrietta Szold, the founder of Hadassah, established Youth Aliyah in 1933 to rescue Jewish children from persecution and suffering and bring them to Palestine to be housed and educated. Some 5,000 teenagers were brought to Palestine before World War II and educated at Youth Aliyah boarding schools. Following World War II, an additional 15,000 arrived, most of them Holocaust survivors. Today, Youth Aliyah villages continue to play a vital role in the absorption of young newcomers, as well as offering thousands of disadvantaged Israeli youth a second chance.

72. First Aliyah (1882–1903)   The first large wave of immigrants came to Palestine following the pogroms in Russia in 1881–1882, with most of the *olim* (immigrants) coming from Eastern Europe; a small number also arrived from Yemen. Members of Hibbat Zion and Bilu, two early Zionist movements that were the mainstays of the First Aliyah, defined their goal as "the political, national, and spiritual resurrection of the Jewish people in Palestine." Most of the newcomers chose agricultural settlement as their way of life and founded *moshavot*—farm holders' villages based on the principle of private property. Nearly 35,000 Jews came to Palestine during the First Aliyah. Almost half of them left the country within several years of their arrival.

73. Second Aliyah (1904–1914)   Another 40,000 Jews immigrated during the Second Aliyah in the wake of pogroms in Czarist Russia and the ensuing eruption of anti-Semitism. Most of the newcomers were young people such as David Ben-Gurion and Yitzhak ben-Zvi, who were inspired by socialist ideals. It was during this period that the first kibbutz, Degania (1909), was established, as well as the first modern all-Jewish city, Tel Aviv (1909). The Hebrew language was revived as a spoken tongue, and Hebrew literature and Hebrew newspapers were published. Political parties were established, and workers' agricultural organizations began to form. Still, the harsh reality of life in Palestine caused nearly half of the immigrants to leave.

74. Third Aliyah (1919–1923)   Approximately 40,000 Jews arrived in Palestine during the Third Aliyah, which was a continuation of the Second Aliyah that had been interrupted by World War I. This group was stimulated by the October Revolution in Russia, the ensuing pogroms there and in Poland and Hungary, the British conquest of Palestine, and the Balfour Declaration. During this period the Histadrut was established and the Haganah was formed. Agricultural settlement expanded, and the first industrial enterprises were established. For the first time, relatively few newcomers returned to their countries of origin.

75. Fourth Aliyah (1924–1930)   The 82,000 Jews who immigrated to Palestine during the Fourth Aliyah came primarily because of the world economic crisis, anti-Jewish policies in Poland, and the introduction of stiff immigration quotas by the United States. Most of the immigrants belonged to the middle class and brought modest sums of capital with which they established small businesses and workshops. The economic crisis in Palestine and other hardships led 23,000 of the newcomers to leave.

76. Fifth Aliyah (1932–1939)   The Nazi rise to power and worsening plight of Jews in Germany prompted nearly 250,000 Jews to immigrate to Palestine. Many of the immigrants from Germany were professionals. Towns flourished as new industrial enterprises were founded and construction of the Haifa port and the oil refineries was completed. Throughout the country "stockade and watchtower" settlements were established. During this period, violent Arab attacks on the Jewish population took place and the British government imposed restrictions on immigration, resulting in a movement toward clandestine, illegal Jewish immigration. Though aliyah did not cease, the practice of numbering the waves of immigration was discontinued.

77. Wartime Aliyah (1940–1945)   Some 60,000 Jews immigrated to Palestine, most being refugees escaping Nazi Europe. During this period, the British White Paper severely restricted immigration and almost 3,000 Jews died in five major boating disasters while attempting to reach Palestine.

78. Aliyah to Israel   From 1948 to the end of 2004, 2,971,774 people immigrated to Israel. Of these, 105,179 came from the United States.

79. Aliyah May 1948–December 1951   Approximately 684,000 Jews arrived in Israel in roughly the first three years of statehood, bringing the total Jewish population of Israel to over 1.35 million. These immigrants came from Yemen, Aden, Algeria, Turkey, Libya, Poland, Rumania, Yugoslavia, Iraq, Bulgaria, and Central Europe.

80. Operation Magic Carpet   The code name for the massive Israeli airlift of Jews from Yemen and Aden to Israel. Beginning in December 1948 and ending in September 1950, roughly 48,000 Jews were airlifted to Israel on 378 flights. The oldest immigrant was a 108-year-old rabbi; twelve children were born en route to Israel.

81. Ma'barot   These were temporary absorption camps constructed to house the thousands of immigrants flocking to Israel in Israel's first decade. By the end of 1949, 100,000 arrivals were living in *ma'barot*. The use of *ma'barot* ended in 1954 as new immigrants went directly to towns and villages.

82. Jackson–Vanik Amendment   Legislation passed by Congress in 1975 that withheld most-favored-nation status to any country that did not allow free emigration of its citizens. The amendment was designed to pressure Russia into allowing Jews to emigrate by tying America's trade policy toward the Soviet Union to Soviet Jewish emigration policy. The amendment was named for its sponsors, Senator Henry "Scoop" Jackson and Congressman Charles Vanik. In the wake of the Jackson-Vanik Amendment, the Soviet Union issued 30,000 visas to Jews seeking to emigrate. Most Soviet Jews preferred to emigrate to the United States rather than Israel.

83. Operation Moses and Operation Sheba   The code name for the airlift of 7,800 black Jews from Ethiopia to Israel, rescuing them from famine and oppression. Operation Moses began on November 18, 1984, and was abruptly halted by the Sudanese on January 5, 1985, when news of the operation was leaked to the public. Almost immediately plans were made to resume the rescue, but the Sudanese president would agree only to a quick, one-shot operation carried out secretly by the United States. The CIA planned the operation code-named "Sheba" (also called "Joshua"), which began on March 28, 1985, with Ethiopian Jews from Israel working for the Mossad identifying the Ethiopian Jews in the camps and taking them by truck to an airstrip. Planes designed to hold ninety passengers each were prepared at the American base near Frankfurt, West Germany. These camouflaged U.S. Hercules transports landed at twenty-minute intervals to pick up their passengers. Instead of going to an intermediate destination, the planes flew directly to an Israeli air force base outside Eilat. The organizers had prepared to airlift as many as 2,000 Ethiopian Jews from the camps, but they found only 494, so three planes returned from Sudan empty.

84. Operation Solomon   On May 24, 1991, a total of thirty-four EL AL jumbo jets and Hercules C-130s—with seats removed to accommodate the maximum number of Ethiopians—began nonstop flights over a span of thirty-six hours to bring Ethiopian Jews from Addis Ababa to Israel before the

Ethiopian capital fell to rebel forces. A total of 14,324 Ethiopian Jews were rescued and resettled in Israel. The government authorized a special permit for the Israeli airline, EL AL, to fly on the Jewish Sabbath.

85. Aliyah, 1990–2004 Over one million new immigrants arrived in Israel, 85 percent of whom arrived from the former Soviet Union. Approximately 8.8 percent of immigrants from the former Soviet Union ended up emigrating from Israel. More immigrants have settled in Ashdod, a port city in the south, than any other location in Israel. Approximately 72,000 immigrants have settled in the city, making up more than one-third of its population. Haifa has the second-largest immigrant population with its almost 70,000 immigrants, representing over 23 percent of its total population. Jerusalem is the third most popular destination for immigrants. The 60,000-strong immigrant community is equal to 8 percent of the city's population.

86. Highest Aliyah since 1949 Nearly 200,000 immigrants arrived in 1990, the first year that the Soviet Union allowed open Jewish emigration. The number fell to 177,000 the following year and has not exceeded 80,000 since then.

87. Smallest Aliyah The fewest immigrants to the State of Israel in a single year took place in 1986, when only 11,298 people moved to Israel.

88. Oldest Immigrant The oldest immigrant to Israel was 111-year-old Tzippora Mataiyeva from Chechnya.

HISTORY

89. Black Thursday On December 17, 1914, the Turks decided to expel from Palestine anyone who refused to become "Ottomanized." Every Jew caught by the Turks was taken away, and hundreds were loaded onto a waiting Italian ship bound for Egypt. The decision provoked Jews to emigrate from Palestine.

90. Nili A Jewish, pro-British spying organization in Palestine during World War I, whose name is derived from the initials of the phrase in I Samuel 15:29, *Nezah Yisrael Lo Yeshakker* (The Strength of Israel Will Not Lie), which served as the password for the underground. The Turks learned of Nili's existence when they intercepted a carrier pigeon in September 1917 that was sent by the group to British forces in Egypt. Two members, Na'aman Belkind and Yosef Lishansky, were captured and executed by the Turks on December 16, 1917.

91. Tel-Hai (Hill of Life) A settlement established in the Galilee in 1918. It became known as the site of a heroic last stand led by Joseph Trumpeldor during the Arab revolt against the French in 1920. Trumpeldor was killed together with seven other defenders, and it is claimed that as he lay on his death bed, one of his final utterances was, "Never mind; it is good to die for one's country."

92. Palestine   The name is believed to come from the Philistines, the people who occupied the coastal region of Israel from around 1200 B.C.E. until around the time of Alexander the Great. Today's Israel was known as Judea until the Romans conquered the region and, seeking to remove Jewish identification with the land, renamed the province Palestina. The Arabic word *Filastin* is derived from this Latin name. This name was discarded with the fleeing Romans but was resurrected by the Crusaders when they established their dominion in the Middle East. After their demise, the name remained as the moniker of the Holy Land in some Christian circles. The Ottomans did not use the term Palestine; instead they divided the immediate and surrounding areas into a number of districts whose boundaries altered over the years. After World War I, the League of Nations granted Britain a mandate over Palestine. Starting in 1922, the British referred to the region west of the Jordan river as Palestine and the territory to the east as Transjordan.

93. Stamps in Palestine   The first post offices in Palestine were established by the European powers in the 1850s. The first was a French one in Jaffa that opened in 1852. Others were run by Austria, Russia, and Italy. After World War I, the British opened military post offices, but no services were offered to civilians, so Jews in Israel were unable to communicate by mail with their friends or relatives until late 1917. In 1927, the British issued a set of stamps that had pictures of the Dome of the Rock, Rachel's Tomb, the Old City of Jerusalem and the Tower of David, Tiberias, and the Sea of Galilee. The first Israeli stamps were issued in May 1948.

94. Feisal–Weizmann Agreement   Emir Feisal, representing the Arab kingdom of Hedjaz, and Chaim Weizmann, representing the Zionist Organization, signed an agreement on January 3, 1919, that called for the mutual realization of the national aspirations of Jews and Arabs. To this end, an Arab state (encompassing Syria, Iraq, and the Arabian Peninsula) and a Jewish homeland (in Palestine) were to be created, mass Jewish immigration permitted, religious worship guaranteed, and boundaries agreed upon. Pursuant to a reservation by Emir Feisal, the agreement was never realized because of the failure of Britain to fulfill its wartime promises to the Arabs.

95. Sykes–Picot Agreement   Anticipating the Turk's defeat, Britain and France, with the assent of Russia, signed a secret treaty during World War I dividing the Ottoman territories in the Middle East between them. Forged by Frenchman Georges Picot and Englishman Sir Mark Sykes, the understanding left no room for the establishment of a Jewish homeland. In 1917, the new Russian government allowed the treaty to become public. Intense opposition from Zionist and Arab quarters, coupled with pressure by the American government, forced the scrapping of the agreement and the redrawing of the borders along the lines of the League of Nations mandates.

96. Mandates In the aftermath of World War I, the victorious Allied powers met in San Remo, Italy, on April 19–26, 1920, to decide the future of the former territories of the Ottoman Empire. As a result of the meeting, France gained control over Syria and Lebanon, and Britain was given authority to govern Iraq and Palestine. The League of Nations formalized these arrangements, which were called mandates.

97. Palestine Mandate On April 25, 1920, at San Remo, the British were authorized to govern Palestine. The mandate was formalized by the fifty-two governments of the League of Nations on July 24, 1922. The British were charged with the task of creating a homeland for the Jewish people based upon the principles enunciated in the Balfour Declaration. The mandate called for a "Jewish Agency" to cooperate with British authorities in establishing a homeland. The original mandate included all the territory lying between the Mediterranean and the Jordan River (today's borders of Israel and the territories excluding the Golan Heights) as well as all of what is today Jordan. In 1922, Britain created a new country, Transjordan, by severing four-fifths of historic Palestine from the mandate. The mandate ended on May 14, 1948, with the British withdrawal from Israel.

98. High Commissioner for Palestine The head of Britain's administrative government in Mandatory Palestine. The first high commissioner was Sir Herbert Samuel (1920–1925), the only Jew to hold the post, followed by Field Marshall Herbert Onslow Plumer (1925–1928); Sir John Herbert Chancellor (1928–1931); Sir Arthur Grenfell Wauchope (1931–1938); Sir Harold MacMichael (1938–1944), whom the Irgun attempted to assassinate; Field Marshal John Standish Surtees Prendergast Vereker; Viscount Gort (1944–1945); and Sir Alan G. Cunningham (1945–1948).

99. British White Papers Statements of British policy presented to Parliament. Six White Papers dealing with Mandatory Palestine were issued between 1922 and 1939. Two were issued in 1937.

100. Churchill White Paper (1922) Authored by Winston Churchill during his stint as colonial secretary, the 1922 White Paper was the first significant statement of policy since the Balfour Declaration. The paper stated that Palestine would become "as Jewish as England is English" without impinging upon the culture or language of the Arab population. Significantly, the paper asserted that the Balfour Declaration intended that a Jewish homeland be established within Palestine but not consist of the entire Palestinian mandate.

101. Passfield White Paper (1930) Issued in the wake of the 1929 Arab riots, this document stated that the purpose of the mandate was not to establish a Jewish homeland. The paper criticized the policies of the Jewish community in Palestine.

102. The 1937 White Papers The first paper, presented simultaneously with the findings of the Peel Commission in July 1937, supported the implementation of the commission's partition plan, restricted land transfers "which might prejudice such a scheme," and restricted immigration to 8,000 Jews between the period of August 1937 and March 1938. In December 1937, the British issued another White Paper announcing the appointment of the Woodhead Commission to explore how to implement partition.

103. The 1938 White Paper This document adopted the Woodhead Commission's report acknowledging that partition was no longer British policy. The paper outlined British intentions to forge an understanding between the Jewish and Arab communities.

104. The McDonald White Paper (1939) The British declared "unequivocally that it is not part of their policy that Palestine become a Jewish State" but would attempt "the establishment within ten years of an independent Palestinian State" that would protect both Jewish and Arab interests. Immigration was restricted to 75,000 Jews during the next five years, and no Jews were to be allowed into the territory after the five-year period without Arab permission. The restriction on Jewish immigration coincided with the beginning of the Holocaust and the attempt of thousands of Jews to flee the Nazis.

105. King-Crane Commission In 1919, at the behest of President Woodrow Wilson, this commission was jointly established by the United States, Britain, and France to determine public attitudes in Syria, Lebanon, and Palestine toward mandates. Due to French and British foot-dragging, only two Americans, Henry C. King and Charles R. Crane, proceeded in the fact-finding mission. Their report called for the establishment of a mandate under American or British control and wholly opposed an open immigration policy aimed at the eventual establishment of an independent Jewish state. The report stated that the Zionist argument, "that they have a 'right' to Palestine, based on an occupation of 2,000 years ago, can hardly be seriously considered." These conclusions were never submitted to an authoritative body nor acted upon.

106. Haycraft Commission of Inquiry In 1921, High Commissioner Sir Herbert Samuel asked for an investigation into the causes of Arab riots that occurred in Jaffa. The commission concluded that the "racial strife was begun by the Arabs." The report condemned the ambivalence, and in some instances encouragement and open support of the riots, by British police. It went on to say that Arab opposition to Jews was based on Jewish immigration and the aims of the Zionist movement.

107. Shaw Commission This commission explored the 1929 riots emanating from disputes over Jewish rights at the Western Wall. The violence resulted in the death of 133 Jews and the wounding of 339 by the Arabs; 116 Arabs were killed and 232 wounded, largely as a result of British police action. The commission found that the violence was simply "an attack by Arabs on Jews," with the Mufti of Jerusalem, Hajj Amin Husseini, a major instigator of the violence. The commission stated that Arab frustration with their economic and national outlook led to the attack. The proposed solution was an unambiguous British commitment to the safeguarding of non-Jewish rights in Palestine.

108. The Peel Commission In 1937, a British commission led by Lord Robert Peel reported on the question of Palestine, the validity of Arab and Jewish complaints, and the outbreak of riots in 1936. The commission's report, while stating that "the primary purpose of the Mandate is to promote the establishment of the Jewish National Home," concluded that due to the competing Arab and Jewish claims to Palestine, the only solution to the conflict was partition of the Jewish and Arab populations. The commission proposed a partition plan that allotted 20 percent of the British Mandate to a Jewish state (encompassing the Mediterranean shore line, upper Jordan valley, and entire Galilee region), reserved Jerusalem and its environs for the British (including Bethlehem and a corridor to the coast by Jaffa), and committed the remaining 75 percent to an Arab state. The British government accepted the recommendations regarding the partition of Palestine. Among the Jews, bitter disagreements erupted between supporters and opponents, while the Arabs rejected the proposal and refused to regard it as a solution. The plan was ultimately shelved.

109. Woodhead Commission In 1938, a commission led by Sir John Woodhead was appointed to explore the partition recommendation of the Peel Commission. The commission proposed a reduction of the Jewish share of Palestinian territory to about 400 square miles around Tel Aviv—the only area where the Jews constituted a majority. The Woodhead plan was rejected by the Zionists as inadequate; it was also rejected by the Arabs, who opposed granting sovereignty to Jews over any part of Palestine.

110. Anglo-American Committee Formally called the Anglo-American Committee of Enquiry Regarding the Problems of European Jewry and Palestine, this joint British–American venture was established in 1946 to consider the question of Jewish immigration to Palestine in light of prevailing economic, political, and social conditions in Palestine and the condition of Holocaust survivors still in Europe. The unanimous report concluded that Palestine alone seemed prepared to devote resources to absorb Jews leaving Europe and that 100,000 visas should be issued forthwith to allow Jews to immigrate to Palestine. Because of limited resources in Palestine, however, the committee urged the United States and Britain to find additional locations for Jewish resettlement. The committee urged that in the long term Palestine become dominated by neither Jews nor Arabs. America accepted and Britain rejected the report.

111. St. James Conference   Organized at the behest of the British, Jewish and Arab leaders gathered in London on February 7, 1939, to discuss Palestine. Arab representatives came from Iraq, Transjordan, Egypt, Saudi Arabia, and Palestine; the Jewish delegation included David Ben-Gurion, Moshe Sharett, Chaim Weizmann, and Stephen Wise. The Arabs refused to meet with the Jews, forcing British officials to run messages between the two groups. Both sides rejected a British proposal to create a single state that would represent and preserve the interests of Arab and Jew. The conference ended on March 17, 1939, two months before the issuance of the 1939 McDonald White Paper.

112. The Biltmore Program   Due to World War II, no Zionist Congress could be held in 1942. The Extraordinary Zionist Conference was called by Chaim Weizmann, David Ben-Gurion, and Nahum Goldmann to form Zionist policy. At the conference, held May 6–11, 1942, at New York's Biltmore Hotel, David Ben-Gurion, then chairman of the Jewish Agency Executive, argued that Britain had failed to live up to the commitments as spelled out in the Balfour Declaration. The joint statement issued at the end of the session was known as the Biltmore Program. It reiterated Zionist demands for unrestricted Jewish immigration to Palestine and that Palestine should serve as a Jewish commonwealth. This statement was the first in which non-Zionist organizations joined with their Zionist counterparts to publicly advocate the establishment of such a Jewish commonwealth.

113. Zion Mule Corps   Vladimir Jabotinsky proposed that a Jewish legion be formed to join the British in liberating Palestine from the Turks during World War I, but the British resisted the idea of Jewish volunteers fighting on the Palestinian front. Instead, they suggested the Jews serve as a detachment for mule transport at another location along the Turkish front. Joseph Trumpeldor subsequently formed the 650-strong Zion Mule Corps, of whom 562 were sent to the Galipoli front.

114. Jewish Legion   Military formation of Jewish volunteers in World War I who fought in the British Army for the liberation of Palestine from Turkish rule. The idea of a Jewish Legion was raised in December 1914 by Vladimir Jabotinsky, but the British military command opposed Jewish participation on the Palestinian front. Jabotinsky continued to lobby and, in August 1917, the formation of a Jewish regiment was officially announced. The unit was designated as the 38th Battalion of the Royal Fusiliers. It included British volunteers, members of the former Zion Mule Corps, and a large number of Russian Jews. In April 1918, it was joined by the 39th Battalion of the Royal Fusiliers, more than 50 percent of whom were American volunteers. In June 1918, the Jewish Legion was sent to Palestine. It was later disbanded.

115. Palestinian Jews in the British Army   At the outbreak of World War II, 136,000 Jews in Palestine, virtually the entire population of 18–50-year-olds, voluntarily registered for national service. By the end of World War II, 26,200 volunteers served with British forces, making up three Jewish infantry battalions.

116. Jewish Brigade   The only military unit to serve in World War II as an independent, national Jewish military formation. In September 1944, after six years of prolonged negotiations, the British government agreed to the establishment of a Jewish Brigade. It consisted of 5,000 soldiers assigned to infantry, artillery, and service units. The Jewish Brigade fought on the Italian front under the command of Canadian-born Jew Brigadier Ernest Benjamin. In the summer of 1946, the British authorities decided to disband the Brigade.

117. Haganah (Defense)   The main Jewish underground in Palestine from 1920 to 1948. After the 1929 riots, the need for a centrally organized defense organization became clear; the British were not adequately defending Jewish lives. During the 1936–1939 Arab riots, the Haganah adopted a policy of restraint, consisting of a purely defensive posture. By the end of the riots, the Haganah had armed its 25,000 members with 6,000 rifles and 220 machine guns. During World War II, a small arms industry began producing mortars, shells, and machine guns. In 1941, when the Irgun broke with Jewish Agency policy and began attacking British targets, the Haganah went as far as turning over Irgun members to British authorities. After World War II, when it became clear that the British were closing the gates of Palestine to Jewish immigration, the Haganah coordinated attacks on British rail systems, equipment, and bridges. In a spectacular attack on June 17, 1946, the Haganah blew up twelve critical bridges, including those on the Palestine border. After the British struck a blow on Black Saturday, the Haganah ceased attacking British targets and focused its activities on facilitating illegal immigration and defending Jewish communities from Arab attacks. When the War of Independence began in May 1948, Haganah forces numbered 45,000 and the Haganah became the backbone of the new Israel Defense Forces.

118. Palmach (*Peluggot Mahaz*—Assault Companies)   The elite striking force of the Haganah. Established by the Haganah's national command on May 19, 1941, the Palmach consisted of nine assault companies: three in northern Galilee, two in central Galilee, two in southern Galilee, and one in Jerusalem. The Palmach launched preemptive strikes into Syrian and Lebanese territory, frequently sending members fluent in Arabic and wearing Arab dress into Syria and Lebanon to scout and sabotage targets. The Palmach grew to twelve companies. Palmach leaders included Yigal Allon, Moshe Dayan, Yitzhak Rabin, Haim Bar-Lev, Uzi Narkiss, and Ezer Weizman.

119. Irgun Zeva'i Le'ummi (National Military Organization) Established by the merging of disenchanted Haganah leaders and armed members of Betar. The Irgun took a more activist, less defensive tack than the Haganah. In April 1937, in response to Arab riots, the Irgun accepted the philosophy of Revisionist leader Vladamir Jabotinsky, prompting 1,500 of the Irgun's 3,000 members to return to the Haganah. This philosophy prompted a policy of the Irgun responding to Arab assaults on Jews with a campaign of reprisals, including terrorist attacks. In response to the British White Paper of 1939, the Irgun targeted British installations and personnel in Palestine. Irgun activities included the destruction of British Military Headquarters located in the King David Hotel (July 22, 1946), the bombing of the British Embassy in Rome (October 31, 1946), the prison break at the Acre fortress (April 27, 1946), and the execution of two British officers in retaliation for the hanging of three Irgun members. After the establishment of Israel, Irgun units slowly merged into the Israeli army. Menachem Begin served as commander of the Irgun from 1943 until its integration into the army in 1948.

120. Lehi (*Lohamei Herut Yisrael*—Fighters for Freedom of Israel) Also called the Stern Gang after its founder, Avraham Stern, Lehi was the smallest of the three underground Jewish militias. The group splintered from the Irgun in June 1940 because Lehi members opposed serving in the British army or halting armed attacks against the British for the duration of World War II. Stern was killed by the British in 1942. After his death, the organization was named Lehi and run by a triumvirate, including Yitzhak Shamir, until the establishment of the Israel Defense Forces. Lehi members assassinated British Minister of State for the Middle East Lord Moyne. Lehi also attacked military and government installations and targeted British soldiers and police. In 1947, their campaign included letter bombs to British officials outside of Palestine. Upon Israel's independence, Lehi merged into the Israeli army. Lehi members formed a political party, Fighter's List, that captured one seat in Israel's first Knesset.

121. Jaffa Disturbances In 1921, violence broke out in Jaffa that resulted in the deaths of 48 Arabs and 47 Jews. The injured numbered 73 Arabs and 146 Jews. The violence began at competing May Day rallies by Jewish labor and Jewish communists. The Haycraft Commission was organized to explore the seeds of and possible prevention of violence.

122. First Political Assassination On June 30, 1924, Dr. Ya'akov Israel de Haan, a member of the ultra-Orthodox Aguddat Israel movement, was shot leaving his synagogue. It is believed he was killed by members of the Haganah because of his vocal anti-Zionist position. The killers were never found.

123. Hebron Massacre In 1929, Arabs of Palestine killed 133 Jews in riots sparked over Jewish access to the Western Wall that began on the Jewish fast day Tisha B'Av. The worst massacre took place in Hebron where 67 Jews were killed, including eight American students studying at the Yeshiva of Slobodka, which was destroyed during the riot. As a result of the attack, the Jewish community of Hebron was evacuated.

124. Sheikh 'Izz ad–Din al–Qassam   The leader of an Arab terrorist organization formed in Haifa in 1931. The Sheikh vigorously opposed the Zionist movement and the British occupation of Palestine. He organized armed attacks on British and Jewish targets. He was captured by the British and hanged in 1935. The armed wing of HAMAS is named after the Sheikh.

125. The Arab Revolt   On April 19, 1936, Jews who had just taken part in the funeral for two Jewish victims of Arab terrorism killed two Arabs in revenge. The British quelled the riots within two days, but only after sixteen Jews were killed and Jewish property was destroyed. The Arab community went on a six-month strike. During the strike, Arab bands attacked British targets and Jewish settlements, convoys, and buses, resulting in the death of eighty Jews. The British responded with large-scale counterattacks that employed light tanks, aircraft, and 16,000 troops. The revolt was eventually put down in the spring of 1939, but only after the Arabs had captured British police stations, killed a British district commander, and caused the death of 415 more Jews. In the end, the Arab revolutionaries killed more fellow Arabs than Jews and Englishmen. The revolt led to the appointment of the Peel Commission.

126. Stockade and Watchtower (*Homa-Umigdal*)   Between 1936 and 1947, when the Jewish National Fund sought to settle land it purchased far from Jewish populations, a major concern was the vulnerability of new settlements to Arab attacks. In response, Jews established the strategy of erecting stockade and watchtower settlements. At dawn, convoys of hundreds of volunteers carrying prefabricated dwellings and fortifications set out for the new location. Before nightfall, settlement construction, including a surrounding double wall filled with earth and stones, searchlights, and a central watchtower, was completed. All told, 118 settlements spanning the Jordan valley and Galilee were erected in this manner.

127. Af–Al–Pi–Chen (In Spite Of)   The Revisionists began the first illegal operations to bring Jews into Palestine. The first operation occurred when fifteen illegal immigrants were smuggled into Palestine in April 1937. The operation was known as *Af-Al-Pi-Chen*.

128. Haifa Bombed   In July 1940, Haifa was bombed by the Italians as World War II spread to Palestine.

129. The *Patria* Affair   Approximately 3,500 German, Austrian, and Czechoslovakian Jews gathered in Rumania on October 1, 1940, and boarded three ships—the *Atlantic*, the *Milos*, and the *Pacific*. The British intercepted the *Pacific* and the *Milos* and forced the 1,800 refugees to transfer to the 12,000-ton *Patria*. The *Atlantic* was also intercepted by the British, and 100 refugees were removed to the *Patria*. When the British government announced that the Jewish refugees were to be deported to Mauritius, Haganah leaders decided to sink the *Patria* in an attempt to force the British to "rescue" the passengers and permit them entry into Palestine. On November 25, 1940, Haganah operatives set off an explosion aboard the ship. The explosion created a larger-than-intended hole in the boat's hull, and there was not enough time to evacuate all those on board. Some 200 Jews and 50 British soldiers drowned. The survivors were allowed to remain in Palestine, but those aboard the *Atlantic* were sent to Mauritius until August 20, 1945, when they too were permitted to enter Palestine.

130. The *Struma* The *Struma,* an old ship that was used for transporting cattle, left Rumania on December 12, 1941, with 769 immigrants aboard. The vessel, the last to leave Europe in wartime, sailed to Turkey in the hopes of obtaining visas to Palestine. Turkish authorities refused to allow any of the passengers off the boat, fearing that the passengers might seek refuge in Turkey. For more than two months, the ship remained off the coast of Turkey. The British refused to grant the Jewish refugees entry into Palestine and eventually they sailed into the Black Sea. The day after the ship set sail, a Russian submarine sank the *Struma*. Only one passenger survived the attack.

131. The King David Hotel Bombing Overlooking the Old City of Jerusalem, the King David was the site of the British military command and the British Criminal Investigation Division. The Irgun targeted the King David after British troops invaded Jewish Agency headquarters on June 29, 1946, and confiscated large quantities of documents that detailed Jewish Agency operations, including intelligence activities in Arab countries. These documents were taken to the King David Hotel. At about the same time, more than 2,500 Jews from all over Palestine were placed under arrest. In targeting the hotel, Irgun leader Menachem Begin stressed his desire to avoid civilian casualties and three telephone calls were placed on July 22, 1946, one to the hotel, another to the French Consulate, and a third to the *Palestine Post*, all warning that explosives in the King David Hotel would soon be detonated. The call into the hotel was received and ignored. When the bombs exploded, a total of ninety-one people were killed and forty-five injured. Among the casualties were fifteen Jews. The Jewish National Council denounced the bombing. The commander of British forces in Palestine subsequently forbade British troops from socializing or having business ties with Jews.

132. Acre Prison Break During the British Mandate, the Al Jazzar fortress, located in Acre, was transformed into a prison. The British held Arab and Jewish political prisoners (including Vladamir Jabotinsky and Moshe Dayan) and hanged both Arab and Jewish fighters at Acre prison. On May 4, 1947, the Irgun masterminded a prison break designed to free forty-one Jews, including leaders of the Jewish underground. A total of twenty members of the

Irgun and seven from Lehi actually escaped, along with 182 Arabs who escaped in the commotion. Nine Jewish fighters were killed in clashes with the British army, six escapees and three members of the attacking force. Eight escapees, some of them injured, were caught and returned to jail. Also arrested were five of the attackers who did not make it back to base. In June, three Jews involved with the prison break were captured and hanged. The following day, the Irgun retaliated by hanging two British officers. Today, the prison is a museum commemorating those who were incarcerated and hanged at Acre for their participation in the fight to establish a Jewish state.

133. The *Exodus*   The *Exodus* set sail from Site, France, on July 11, 1947, with more than 4,500 Jewish refugees fleeing Europe for Palestine on board. When British soldiers boarded the ship in the Mediterranean Sea to prevent its entry into Palestine, a fight broke out, killing three and injuring thirty. The passengers were forced into three transport boats headed back to France. After being denied entry to France, the passengers were sent to Hamburg, Germany, where they were interned in a British-run displaced persons camp. This aroused world opinion against Britain, contributing in the short run to the British decision to transport illegal immigrants to detention camps in Cyprus rather than return them to Europe, and in the long run to the British withdrawal from Palestine. The novel *Exodus*, by Leon Uris, recounts the story of the *Exodus* and the Jewish struggle to establish the State of Israel. The book became a best-seller in 1958 and was for many Americans the first exposure to the history of the State of Israel. An even wider audience watched the sympathetic depiction of Israel's early history in the 1960 film of the same name. *Exodus* starred Paul Newman as a Haganah leader who falls in love with the non-Jewish American character played by Eva Marie Saint.

134. *Pan Crescent* and *Pan York*   The *Pan Crescent* (renamed *Atzma'ut*) and *Pan York* (renamed *Kibbutz Galuyot*) were the two largest ships used for illegal immigration to Palestine. They were bought in the United States in 1947 to bring some 15,000 illegal Jewish immigrants from Rumania to Palestine. The British persuaded Rumania to refuse to allow the boats to sail from the Port of Constanza. The United States threatened to withdraw its support of the UN Partition Plan if the ships brought Jewish refugees to Palestine. After much negotiation, the British allowed the ships to go to Cyprus, where they arrived on December 31, 1947.

135. Black Sabbath   In an attempt to cripple the Jewish underground, on Saturday, June 29, 1946, the British embarked on a two-week intensive campaign to arrest Jews involved in anti-British activities and unearth evidentiary documents. While a number of Jewish activists were arrested, no significant underground commanders were captured. The first day of the British campaign became known as "Black Sabbath."

136. Mount Scopus Massacre   On April 13, 1948, an Arab force ambushed a Jewish convoy on the way to Hadassah Hospital, killing seventy-seven Jews, including doctors, nurses, patients, and the director of the hospital. Another twenty-three people were injured. The attack took place in front of British soldiers who chose to watch the massacre and not intervene. A memorial listing the names of all who perished was erected at the site.

137. Moyne Assassination   Lehi members assassinated British Minister of State for the Middle East Lord Walter Moyne in Cairo in November 1944. In 1975, the two Lehi members executed in Egypt for the assassination were reinterred in Israel.

138. *Lino*   A ship hired by Syria to carry 8,000 rifles and 10 million rounds of ammunition. In March 1948, while en route to Beirut, Jewish frogmen sank the *Lino*. The Haganah salvaged the weapons and smuggled them into Palestine.

139. Deir Yassin   An Arab village located along the Tel Aviv-Jerusalem road used by Arabs to ambush Jewish convoys supplying Jerusalem with food, fuel, and ammunition. On April 9, 1948, in a combined Irgun-Lehi attack aimed at alleviating the siege of Jerusalem, many Arabs were killed, and a number of women and children were massacred. At the time, the dead were believed to number 250, but more recent research suggests the figure was closer to 110. The killing of innocent civilians was condemned by the Jewish leadership, including David Ben-Gurion, who apologized to King Abdullah ibn Hussein of Transjordan. The wide publicity given the attack in the Arab world was a contributing factor in the flight of thousands of Arabs from Palestine.

140. British Withdrawal   After ruling Palestine for nearly three decades, the British acquiesced to the UN partition decision and withdrew the last of their forces on May 14, 1948. Up until then, they did nothing to assist in implementing partition.

141. Israel Declares Independence   The Declaration of the Establishment of the State of Israel was approved by the People's Council, composed of representatives of the yishuv and the Zionist movement, on Friday, May 14, 1948, several hours before the British Mandate for Palestine came to an end. It was read by David Ben-Gurion, who subsequently became the nation's first prime minister.

142. The Declaration of Independence   The declaration signed on the day of Israel's independence gave the state its official name; asserted the right of the Jewish people to exercise self-determination in its sovereign state; established provisional institutions to govern; indicated an elected constituent assembly would formulate a constitution; set forth the principles of political rule; and called for peace and cooperation with the Arabs of Israel, the neighboring countries and their people, the Jewish people throughout the Diaspora, and the United Nations Organization. Chaim Weizmann, one of the key figures behind the creation of Israel and the state's first president, was not among the 37 people who signed the Declaration of Independence because he was in the United States during the signing.

143. Nameless Stamps   The first Israeli stamps were issued on May 16, 1948, but they did not have the word Israel on them because the name of the new state was not known until the Declaration of Independence, issued just one day earlier. Instead, the stamps, depicting ancient Jewish coins, had the words *Do'ar Ivri* (Hebrew Post).

144. *Altalena*   On June 21, 1948, the *Altalena* approached Tel Aviv carrying 900 Irgun volunteers, 4,000 tons of ammunition, and supplies for the Irgun. The Irgun had already agreed to be incorporated into the unified Israeli Defense Forces but refused to turn over the ship's cargo to the provisional government's military leadership, insisting that Irgun units get the bulk of the weapons. David Ben-Gurion viewed the Irgun activity as a threat, saying, "The state cannot exist until we have one army and control of that army." He ordered the ship destroyed to prevent the creation of armed militias outside the unified command of the IDF. The *Altalena* was destroyed by a Haganah force in Tel Aviv harbor led by Yitzhak Rabin; more than a dozen Irgun members were killed.

145. Attempt on Ben-Gurion's Life   In 1949, Avraham Zarfati, a recent immigrant from Tehran, entered the Knesset building and aimed a Sten submachine gun at the table where Prime Minister Ben-Gurion and other ministers were seated. Zarfati was overpowered by Knesset ushers before he was able to shoot.

146. Cairo Trial   In 1951, Avraham Dar went to Egypt to establish an intelligence-gathering operation. In 1954, the established cells were ordered to undermine Egyptian-English relations. Israeli agents set off incendiary devices in a post office in Alexandria and, two weeks later, set fires at American libraries in Alexandria and Cairo. Days later, an incendiary device ignited while being carried by Israeli saboteur Phillipe Nathanson. He and ten other people were quickly captured. While in custody, Israeli army officer Max Bennet committed suicide. The remaining ring members were tried on December 7, 1954. Two of the accused were hanged, two were acquitted, and the remaining six defendants were given prison sentences ranging from seven years to life. Avraham Dar escaped capture.

147. Lavon Affair   The botched intelligence operation in Cairo prompted an investigation, but the commission appointed by Prime Minister Moshe Sharett failed to establish what had happened. The controversy led to the resignation of Defense Minister Pinhas Lavon. In 1960, a district court, in an unrelated matter, ruled that one of the intelligence officers involved in the affair had lied to the investigative commission at the behest of a superior. The minister of justice led a seven-member panel investigation that reported Lavon had not ordered the Egypt operation. David Ben-Gurion led a vociferous attack on the panel's conclusions. A Mapai Central Committee meeting resulted in the dismissal of Lavon from his Histadrut post. The deep rifts within the party caused by the scandal started to weaken Mapai's grip on power and caused the Rafi party to break away from Mapai.

148. *Bat Galim*   Egypt, in violation of international law and in breach of Security Council Resolution 95, interfered with vessels sailing through the Suez Canal bound for Israel. On September 28, 1954, Egyptian forces detained the Israeli freighter *Bat Galim* as it sailed through the canal. The ship's crew was arrested, and the cargo was seized. Egypt charged that the Israeli crew fired on Egyptian fishermen. Under pressure from the United Nations, Egypt freed the Israeli crew on January 1, 1955.

149. Kasztner Trial   In 1955, Malkhiel Gruenwald, a Hungarian Jew who lost his family in Auschwitz, accused Dr. Israel Kasztner, a ranking government official and former leader of Hungarian Jewry, of having collaborated with the Nazis during World War II. The Israeli attorney general indicted Gruenwald for slander. The judge concluded that Kasztner "sold his soul to the devil" by collaborating with the Nazis, saving his friends and relatives, but failing to warn Hungarian Jews. Gruenwald was cleared of libel. In 1957, Kasztner was murdered. A year later, in a split decision, the Israeli Supreme Court held Gruenwald guilty of libel, but in a scathing decision, a plurality called for an investigation into Kasztner's role into the events that occurred in Hungary. Gruenwald received a one-year suspended sentence. *Perfidy*, a controversial book by Ben Hecht, details the events of the trial and other landmark events in Israeli history.

150. Kfar Kassem   Israel imposed a curfew on Arab villages in preparation for the Sinai Campaign. In Kfar Kassem, an Arab village located near the border with Jordan, the Israeli army imposed a curfew from October 29, 1956, at 5:00 p.m. until 6:00 a.m. the following day. All Arabs who violated the curfew were to be shot on sight. The order was issued at 3:30 p.m. while most of the Arab villagers were still at work. When Arabs, who were unaware of the curfew, began arriving home from work after 5:00 p.m., Israeli soldiers shot and killed 47 villagers. The incident was initially covered up by the Israeli government. Only weeks later did Prime Minister Ben-Gurion make the incident public when he revealed the results of a secret investigation. Eight soldiers were convicted of crimes. The harshest sentence meted out was three and a half years in jail.

151. Second Attempt on Ben-Gurion's Life   Moshe Dweika, a Syrian Jew who moved to Israel as a child, entered the Knesset building on October 29, 1957, and tossed a grenade at members of Parliament, injuring Prime Minister David Ben-Gurion, Foreign Minister Golda Meir, and others.

152. Colonel Nehemia Argov   A close aide and personal friend of David Ben-Gurion, Col. Argov committed suicide on November 2, 1957, following a car accident. Ben-Gurion was hospitalized at the time, and Israeli newspapers published a special edition for him omitting articles relating to Argov's death to shield the prime minister from grief while he was recovering from injuries sustained in a grenade attack.

153. Eichmann Trial   Adolf Otto Eichmann (1906–1962) served as chief of operations for the "Final Solution," the Nazi plan to exterminate the Jews of Europe. He was personally responsible for the deportation and extermination of all Jews within reach of Nazi Germany. After Germany's defeat in World War II, Eichmann escaped to Argentina and lived in Buenos Aires under the alias Ricardo Klement. Mossad agents kidnapped Eichmann and brought him to Jerusalem. On May 23, 1960, Prime Minister Ben-Gurion made the dramatic announcement in the Knesset that Eichmann had been captured. The UN Security Council recognized the need to bring Eichmann to trial, and the UN vote was the only time in Israel's first twenty-five years of existence that the United States and the Soviet Union joined in support of Israel. After a public trial in Jerusalem, Eichmann was found guilty and sentenced to death. On May 31, 1962, Eichmann was hanged at Ramleh prison and his cremated remains were scattered over the Mediterranean Sea. Eichmann remains the only person ever given the death sentence in Israel. Isser Harel, the Mossad chief responsible for Eichmann's capture, wrote *The House on Garibaldi Street*, a book recounting the kidnapping that was made into a TV movie.

154. Soblen Affair   In 1962, American Jew Dr. Robert Soblen, who was sentenced to life in prison in the United States for spying for the Soviet Union, escaped to Israel. He was arrested and deported. Soblen attempted suicide during the flight to the United States and was taken to a hospital in London where he died shortly thereafter.

155. Prime Minister's Marriage   While serving as prime minister, Levi Eshkol wed Knesset librarian Miriam Zelikovich on January 3, 1964.

156. Defection from Iraq   In August 1966, Iraqi Air Force pilot Munir Radfah defected, flying his MIG-21 to Israel. His defection gave a Western nation a MIG-21 for the first time and allowed Israel to help Western intelligence learn more about Soviet capabilities.

157. Peace Flight   In February 1966, Israeli activist Abie Nathan flew his single-engine plane, called "Shalom One," from Tel Aviv to Port Said, Egypt, on a one-man mission for peace. He was promptly arrested and sent back to Israel. The flight made world headlines.

158. The *Dakar*   The *Dakar* was a submarine purchased from England that left the United Kingdom heading to Israel on January 9, 1968. On January 28, 1968, all contact was lost with the *Dakar* and its crew of 69 Israel seamen. The sub was assumed to have sunk, but the only trace ever found was a buoy that washed up on a Gaza shore in February 1969. In 1999, more than thirty years later, a U.S. salvage team located the sub less than two miles beneath the surface southeast of Crete at a point along the vessel's original route.

159. Disappearing Boats   In 1968, Israel purchased five French missile boats, but they were impounded by France because the French were adhering to an arms embargo against Israel imposed during the 1967 war. Early on December 24, 1968, Mossad agents secretly sailed the missile boats out of Cherbourg harbor. The French awoke to find the boats gone; they arrived in Haifa on December 31.

160. Iraqi Executions   In January 1969, Iraq executed nine Jews accused of spying for Israel.

161. Swiss Spy   In September 1969, Swiss police arrested Alfred Frauknecht, a Swiss engineer, and accused him of passing plans for the French Mirage jet to Israel. The stolen blueprints helped Israel build the Kfir fighter plane.

162. Agranat Commission   Supreme Court President Shimon Agranat led an investigation into the cause of the intelligence failure and Israel's unpreparedness at the onset of the Yom Kippur War. An interim report released in April 1974 recommended that Chief of Staff David Elazar (along with three of his deputies) be dismissed and intelligence chief Eli Ze'ira be transferred. The commission also asked for the suspension of Shmuel Gonen, commander of the Southern Front. A public outcry ensued, criticizing the commission's decision to absolve Defense Minister Moshe Dayan from blame. Eventually, Prime Minister Golda Meir was forced to resign, bringing down the coalition government. The full report was issued in 1975 and was supposed to be declassified in 2005. The Knesset recently passed a bill that will allow for most of the content of the Agranat Commission to remain classified.

163. Peace Now Rally   The first Peace Now rally was held April 1, 1978. Later, on September 2, 1978, an estimated 100,000 people gathered in Tel Aviv and held the largest peace rally in Israel's history to that point, urging Prime Minister Menachem Begin to be flexible in the peace negotiations with Egypt.

164. Law of Jerusalem   On July 30, 1980, the Knesset adopted legislation unifying Jerusalem under Israeli jurisdiction. The law reads, "United Jerusalem, in its entirety, is Israel's capital. It is the place of residence of the state President, the Knesset, the Government, and the Supreme Court."

165. The Golan Heights Law   On December 14, 1981, the Knesset extended "Israeli law, jurisdiction, and administration" to the Golan Heights, but Israel did not annex the territory.

166. Activist Murdered In February 1983, Peace Now held a demonstration in Jerusalem against the war in Lebanon. A hand grenade was thrown into the crowd, killing Emil Gruenzweig.

167. Unity Government In the 1984 elections, for the first time in Israel's history, neither of the major parties won enough seats to form a coalition government. Labor and Likud agreed to form a National Unity Government, dividing up cabinet ministries and setting up a rotating premiership, with Labor's Shimon Peres serving the first two years and the Likud's Yitzhak Shamir serving the last two.

168. Demjanjuk Trial In 1986, the United States deported John Demjanjuk to Israel to stand trial for Nazi war crimes. Demjanjuk came to the United States from Germany shortly after the end of World War II. In April 1988, Demjanjuk was convicted of crimes against the Jewish people and sentenced to death by hanging. On appeal in July 1993, the Supreme Court acquitted Demjanjuk because it found plausible doubt that he was the prison guard known as "Ivan the Terrible." He was subsequently released and sent back to the United States.

169. No Confidence On March 15, 1990, the government fell for the first time on a vote of no confidence by a margin of 60 to 55. The result was due to members of the religious Shas Party absenting themselves from the vote to protest Prime Minister Yitzhak Shamir's opposition to a U.S. demand to hold peace talks with the Palestinians in the territories.

170. Rabin Assassinated On November 4, 1995, Prime Minister Yitzhak Rabin was assassinated by Yigal Amir in central Tel Aviv after attending a peace rally because Amir believed that Rabin betrayed the Jewish people by agreeing to the Oslo Accords. Rabin was laid to rest on Mount Herzl in Jerusalem. Amir was tried in December 1995 and convicted the following February. He was sentenced to life in prison. The square where Rabin was assassinated was renamed Yitzhak Rabin Square.

171. Spy Charges In 1996, Israeli Druze Azzam Azzam was arrested in Egypt and accused of spying for Israel. He was sentenced a year later to 15 years in prison. He was freed on June 11, 2004, as part of a prisoner exchange with Israel.

172. Finally at Peace Four soldiers in Napoleon's army finally received a proper burial in 1999, 200 years after they died trying to seize Acre from the Turks. The unsuccessful attack was a turning point in Napoleon's failed Middle East campaign. Napoleon withdrew from the Holy Land on May 20, 1799.

173. Disengagement In 2004, Ariel Sharon, in an attempt to break the stalemate in the Palestinian-Israeli conflict, proposed the Disengagement Plan. He began implementing the plan on August 15, 2005, when Israeli forces started evacuating Israeli inhabitants of the Gaza Strip. In eight days, some 8,500 Jews were removed, sometimes forcibly, from the 21 Jewish settlements that existed in the Gaza Strip. In addition, Israel evacuated four settlements from the northern West Bank and intends to remove additional settlements located in remote areas or within a large Arab population. At the conclusion of the implementation of the plan, no Israeli communities or military outposts should remain in the northern West Bank.

174. Protesting the Disengagement   On July 25, 2004, an estimated 130,000 people built a human chain of solidarity stretching from the Gaza Strip to the Western Wall. The chain stretched some 90 kilometers and was meant as a protest against the Disengagement Plan and a sign of solidarity with the Jews living in Gaza. Other protests that were held in August 2005, just prior to the disengagement, were attended by more than 150,000 people.

175. Israel's Security Fence   As a result of a rash of suicide bombings and terrorist attacks that has taken the lives of hundreds of Israelis and wounded thousands, Israel decided to erect a security fence running roughly along the border between the West Bank and Israel to thwart further terrorist infiltrations. Construction began on June 16, 2002. The first 85 miles of fence were completed in August 2003, and another 50 miles were erected by the end of 2004. In the areas where the fence is in place, the incidence of terrorist attacks has dropped some 90 percent. When completed, the fence is expected to extend some 400 miles, cost $1 billion, and extend its protection around some 7 percent of West Bank territory. In July 2004, the International Court of Justice, in a nonbinding opinion, ruled that Israel's separation fence violated international law and demanded that the fence be demolished. Israel rejected the findings of the ICJ.

PEOPLE

176. Richard the Lion-Hearted   In 1191, King Richard I of England (1157–1199) captured Acre from the Saracens. He executed 2,700 Muslim prisoners of war; nevertheless, because of his "valorous" behavior during the Crusade, he became known as Richard the Lion-Hearted.

177. St. Louis in Israel   King Louis IX of France—St. Louis—spent a year in Caesarea after being released from prison in Egypt in 1251. He helped build the city walls with his own hands. In 1265, the Mamelukes drove out the Crusaders and the Sultan tore down the walls, reputedly saying, "What a king has built, a king will destroy."

178. Moses Hess (1812–1875)   One of the early important German socialists, Hess was born to an Orthodox family but believed that Jews should assimilate, a path he pursued by marrying a Christian. Hess helped Karl Marx write the *Communist Manifesto* and coined the term "religion is the opium of the masses." Later in life he returned to Judaism and became a strong supporter of Zionism, arguing that the Jews must preserve their identity and forge a homeland in Palestine. He believed that religion could hold the Jews together until they could establish a society in Palestine, at which time religious laws could be adapted to society and the times. His early Zionist writings, including *Rome and Jerusalem; The Last National Question*, enjoyed a renaissance when Herzl invigorated the Zionist movement.

179. Leon Pinsker (1821–1891)   Pinsker led Hibbat Zion and authored *Autoemancipation*, a powerful and influential pamphlet articulating the Zionist cause. Born in Poland, he studied law at Odessa University but switched to medicine at the University of Moscow because his Jewishness barred his practice of law. He returned to Odessa, practicing medicine and becoming active in the Enlightenment and Haskalah movements. The 1881 pogroms had a great impact on Pinsker; believing that anti-Semitism would persist, he abandoned his fervor for enlightenment and Jewish acceptance in Russian society in favor of Zionism. Pinsker, who cared not whether Palestine served as the location of the Jewish state, led Hibbat Zion and Hovevei Zion and worked with Baron Edmond de Rothschild. His remains were reinterred on Mount Scopus.

180. Baron Edmond James de Rothschild (1845–1934)   Known as the father of the Yishuv, Rothschild used his personal fortune to bankroll Palestinian settlements at a time when financial difficulties threatened their existence. Rishon le-Zion, Zikhron Ya'akov, and Ekron were the first to receive his assistance. In total, he aided over twenty-five settlements (including Petah Tikvah and Rosh Pina) and purchased nearly 125,000 acres in Palestine. Of his work, Chaim Weizmann stated, "In my opinion he was the leading political Zionist of our generation." These sentiments, echoed by Ben-Gurion, led to Rothschild's election as honorary president of the Jewish Agency (1929). Rothschild, who supported Hebrew University and helped begin numerous business ventures in Palestine, is buried near Zikhron Ya'acov.

181. Max Nordau (1849–1923)   A cofounder of the Zionist Organization, Nordau was born in Hungary to an Orthodox rabbi. At eighteen he rejected Orthodox Judaism. His influential *The Conventional Lies of Society*, a critique of religious and political institutions, was translated into fifteen languages and banned in Russia and Austria. His later works, all highly controversial, catapulted him to a position of international prominence as a philosopher and writer. Nordau served as a correspondent of the Austrian *Neue Freie Presse* (the paper where Theodor Herzl served) and was a vocal critic of anti-Semitism. He authored the Basle program; served as president of the Seventh, Eighth, Ninth, and Tenth Zionist Congresses; and in 1911 predicted that if the status quo continued, six million Jews in Europe would perish. Nordau supported Herzl's Uganda plan and the establishment of Jabotinsky's Jewish Legion. Nordau retired from Zionist activity in 1921. He is buried in Tel Aviv.

182. Ahad Ha'am (1856–1927)   Born Asher Hirsch Ginsburg to a wealthy Hasidic family in the Russian province of Kiev, Ginsburg wrote about Zionism under the pen name Ahad Ha'am. He criticized Herzl and other Zionist leaders for being detached from Jewish values, and he fought against the plan to establish a Jewish state in Uganda. Ahad Ha'am helped secure the Balfour Declaration. He opposed the immediate settlement of Palestine in favor of first building a political and educational infrastructure that would emphasize Jewish values and spirituality. He did not settle in Israel until 1922. Ahad Ha'am was one of the important Zionist writers and thinkers, and his ideas on Zionism and Judaism remain influential.

183. Aharon David Gordon (1856–1922)   A. D. Gordon was born in 1856 in Podolia, Russia. At age forty-seven, Gordon decided to immigrate to Palestine and begin a life as a farmer. He eventually made his home in Degania, where the first kibbutz would be founded. Gordon had been a white-collar worker all his life; nevertheless, he became the foremost exponent of Labor Zionism, the idea that physical effort on the land would bring about the redemption of the Jewish people.

184. Eliezer Ben-Yehuda (1858–1922)   An early Zionist leader known as the father of modern Hebrew. Eliezer was born Yizhak Perelman in Lithuania, and he studied medicine in Paris. He suffered from tuberculosis and, as a result, left Paris and his medical studies for Palestine's more favorable climate. His fervent conviction that Jews could not become a single nation in their own land absent a unifying language led him to spearhead the movement to revive Hebrew as a living language. In 1890 he helped establish the Vaad Halashon, the forerunner of the Academy of the Hebrew Language.

185. Theodor Herzl (1860–1904)   The father of modern Zionism, Herzl was born in Budapest, Hungary. A secular Jew, Herzl grew sensitive to anti-Semitism while working in Paris as a correspondent for the *Neue Freie Presse,* a Vienna newspaper. It was not until the Dreyfus Affair that he began to direct his energies toward the Zionist movement. His charisma, political skill, and access to influential people (stemming from his career as a highly respected journalist) culminated in uniting and invigorating a fractured and weak Zionist movement. In 1897, Herzl chaired the first of six Zionist Congresses. Herzl's book, *The Jewish State,* argued for the necessity of a Jewish homeland and proceeded to outline how such a state could be formed. In his early years, Herzl was prepared to accept a British plan to establish Uganda as a temporary homeland for the Jewish people. Eventually, he espoused the belief that the land of Palestine was the only place that a Jewish state should be established. Herzl founded the World Zionist Organization and served as its president until his death. Herzl's remains were brought to Israel and reinterred on September 18, 1949, on Mount Herzl, Jerusalem.

186. Meir Dizengoff (1861–1936)   One of the founders of Tel Aviv, Dizengoff was the city's first mayor, serving in that capacity from 1911 until his death. The main street in today's sprawling city is named in his honor.

187. Abraham Menachem Mendel Ussishkin (1863–1941)   Born in Dubrovno, Russia, Ussishkin was motivated into Zionist activism while a student at the Technological Institute of Moscow by the Russian pogroms of 1881. By 1885, Abraham had been elected secretary of all the Hovevei Zion chapters in Moscow. He rapidly became a force in the world Zionist movement. He was a bitter opponent of the Uganda scheme and actively supported the revival of Hebrew and aliyah. His Zionist activities resulted in his being temporarily exiled from Russia. Ussishkin helped organize a 200,000-person rally in Odessa supporting the Balfour Declaration and was instrumental in the establishment of Hebrew University. In 1919, he settled in Palestine and became a leading figure in the yishuv, later serving as head of the Jewish National Fund (1923–1941).

188. Nathan Birnbaum (1864–1937)   Born in Vienna, Birnbaum independently formulated ideas similar to those of Leon Pinsker. In 1882, he published his first pamphlet opposing assimilation. Promulgating the ideas of the Hovevei Zion movement, Birnbaum coined the term *Zionism*. In 1893, he published a brochure in which he expounded ideas similar to those that Herzl was to promote subsequently. An early adherent of Herzl, Birnbaum played an important role at the First Zionist Congress (1897) and took a leading role at the Vienna headquarters of the Zionist Organization. Gradually, Birnbaum began to question the political aims of Zionism and to attach increasing importance to the national-cultural content of Judaism. In 1898, he left the Zionist movement and became a leading spokesman for Diaspora nationalism. He stressed the Yiddish language as the basis of Jewish culture and was one of the chief promoters of the Conference on Yiddish held in Czernowitz, Bukovina, in 1908, which proclaimed Yiddish as the national language of the Jewish people. He turned to religion, eventually embracing extreme Orthodoxy. He advocated taking steps to prepare for the coming of the Messiah and argued that Jews should embrace agricultural work. In his 1927 book, *Im Dienste der Verheissung* (In the Service of the Promise), he called on the Jewish people to work in and for Eretz Israel out of love for the land but without political aspirations. In 1919, Birnbaum became secretary-general of the World Aguddat Israel movement. After the rise of Nazism, he left Germany for the Netherlands, where he edited *Der Ruf* (The Call).

189. Sir Herbert Louis Samuel, First Viscount (1870–1963) Samuel was born to an Orthodox Jewish family in Britain. He was elected to

Parliament on the Liberal ticket in 1902. At the outbreak of World War I, Samuel began pushing the idea of a Jewish homeland in Palestine under the protection of Britain. He worked closely with Britain's political leadership, including the prime minister and his cabinet, to realize the Zionist dream and was instrumental in the issuance of the Balfour Declaration. He became the first Jew to rule Palestine in 2,000 years when, in 1920, he was appointed first high commissioner of Palestine. He returned to England in 1925 to continue his political career; he was knighted in 1920 and made viscount in 1927.

190. Aaron Aaronsohn (1876–1919)   Born in Rumania, Aaronsohn arrived in Palestine in 1882. His family was one of the founders of Zikhron Ya'akov. Aaronsohn became an agronomist and, in 1906, discovered specimens of wild wheat that catapulted him into worldwide prominence in his field. He subsequently established an agricultural experiment station at Atlit, near Haifa. In 1915, Aaronsohn helped create Nili, a secret intelligence group that assisted British forces fighting against the Turks. In 1916, he visited London and circulated a memorandum on the future of Palestine, which helped to make the idea of a Jewish national home in Palestine a part of British policy. Later he worked with Zionists at the Paris Peace Conference wrestling with the question of the Jewish homeland's boundaries. Aaronsohn was killed in a plane crash over the English Channel.

191. Vladamir (Zev) Jabotinsky (1880–1940)   Jabotinsky is the father of the ideology that gave birth to the Likud party. Born in Odessa, Russia, Jabotinsky joined a Jewish defense organization in 1903 to defend against anti-Jewish pogroms. He was instrumental in creating Jewish military units under British command during World War I. In 1920 he formed the Haganah unit in Jerusalem and was sentenced by the British to fifteen years in prison for these activities, only to be released by 1921. Jabotinsky resigned from the Zionist Organization in 1923 because he believed the movement was not pressuring Britain to adhere to its obligation to establish a Jewish homeland. He pushed for the creation of a Jewish legion and increased Jewish immigration to Palestine with the aim of creating a Jewish majority in the entire Palestinian Mandate. In 1935, his break with the Zionist Organization was complete when Zionist leaders representing 173,000 people voted Jabotinsky leader of the newly formed New Zionist Organization. Under his leadership, the New Zionist Organization played a leading role is assisting illegal immigration to Palestine during the 1930s. Jabotinsky adopted a philosophy of striking against the Arab civilian population in retaliation for Arab terrorist attacks against Jews. In 1937, Jabotinsky became leader of the Irgun but had little day-to-day control of the organization because he lived outside of Palestine. In addition to his Zionist activities, Jabotinsky was a newspaper journalist and served as a war correspondent during World War I. He signed his articles with his pen name, Altalena. Jabotinsky is buried on Mt. Herzl.

192. Joseph Trumpeldor (1880–1920)   Still a potent symbol of Jewish defense and pioneering spirit in Israeli folklore, Trumpeldor was born in Caucasus. He served in the Russian army and was highly decorated for his heroics during the Russo-Japanese War. Despite a war wound that resulted in the loss of his arm, Trumpeldor voluntarily returned to the front as an officer. He arrived in Palestine in 1912 and was deported for refusing to become a Turkish citizen during World War I. As an organizer and deputy commander of Britain's Zion Mule Corps, Trumpeldor fought against the Turkish army. He returned to Palestine in 1919 and was asked to organize a defense for the Jewish settlements in the Galilee. On March 1, 1920, Trumpeldor suffered a fatal wound while defending Tel-Hai from an Arab attack. Yetta Raphaelsky was the fiancée of Josef Trumpeldor. She left Moscow for Palestine to marry him in 1919 only to discover that he had been killed at Tel-Hai. A year later she attempted suicide by jumping off a building in Berlin and was paralyzed for the remaining eight years of her life.

193. Moshe Smoira (1888–1961)   Israel's first Supreme Court president, Smoira was born to a Hasidic family in Prussia. He served in the German army during World War I and settled in Palestine in 1922. He headed the Supreme Court from 1948 to 1954.

194. Yizhak Sadeh (1890–1952)   The founding commander of the Palmach, Sadeh was born in Poland and decorated for bravery in World War I by the Russian army. News of Joseph Trumpeldor's death at Tel-Hai prompted Sadeh to move to Palestine in 1920. During the 1936 Arab riots, Sadeh volunteered for the Haganah and initiated the strategy of taking a more offensive posture through the use of first strikes. He spearheaded the formation of the Palmach and was its commander until his appointment as chief of the Haganah's general staff in 1945. His duties included coordinating the joint resistance activities of the Haganah, Irgun, and Lehi. Sadeh originated and commanded Israel's first armored brigade and fought in crucial battles during the War of Independence. He retired after the war, leaving an indelible mark on the IDF's organization, strategy, and training.

195. Sarah Aaronsohn (1876–1919)   Along with her brother Aaron, Sarah was a member of the Nili group that helped the British in their war against the Turks. While on a secret mission to Egypt in 1917, her brother advised her not to risk her life further. She refused and returned to Palestine to lead the group. She was subsequently arrested by the Turkish military authorities and tortured for three days. She would not disclose any secrets and chose to kill herself to escape further torture.

196. Shemuel Dayan (1891–1968)   Dayan was born in the Ukraine to a Hasidic family. He immigrated to Palestine in 1908, where he helped establish Kibbutz Deganyah Aleph and Deganyah Bet and Moshav Nahalal. He served as the representative of the moshav movement in many Jewish and Palestinian forums. Dayan served in the first three sessions of the Knesset. He was the founder of the Dayan political dynasty, the only family to have three generations of Knesset members: Shemuel Dayan, son Moshe Dayan and granddaughter, Yael Dayan (daughter of Moshe Dayan).

197. Folke Bernadotte, Earl of Windsor (1895–1948)   A Swedish diplomat who was responsible for saving the lives of thousands of Jews during the Holocaust. On May 20, 1948, the United Nations Security Counsel sent Bernadotte to Palestine to broker Arab-Israeli negotiations. Deviating from his UN charge, he outlined a peace plan that would transfer Jerusalem and the Negev to Transjordan in exchange for the incorporation of the western Galilee into Israel. The UN did not support the proposal. Folke Bernadotte was assassinated in Jerusalem in September 1948; his killers, never apprehended, are believed to have been members of the Lehi.

198. Chaim Arlosoroff (1899–1933)   A leader of the socialist movement in Palestine. Born in Romny, Ukraine, Arlosoroff settled in Israel in 1924 after completing a PhD in economics at the University of Berlin. Arlosoroff was a strong supporter of Chaim Weizmann, became a leader of the Mapai party, and was elected to head the political department of the Jewish Agency at the Seventeenth Zionist Congress. Later in life he began to doubt British support for Zionism and questioned his earlier belief that Jews and Arabs could work together. In June 1933, Arlosoroff was assassinated on a beach in Tel Aviv. Two members of the Revisionist Movement, Abraham Stavsky and Zevi Rosenblatt, were tried for the murder of Arlosoroff. They were acquitted for lack of evidence, and the murder remains an unsolved mystery.

199. Mickey Marcus (1902–1948)   A West Point graduate and colonel in the United States Army during World War II, Marcus went to Israel to help the Jewish nation build a cohesive military capable of defending the fledgling state. Before World War II, Marcus was one of the federal prosecutors responsible for winning the conviction of Lucky Luciano. After the war, the U.S. War Department allowed Marcus, who was a reservist, to go to Israel on condition that he not use his name or rank. Thus, "Michael Stone" was the man who designed a command structure for Israel's new army and wrote manuals to train it, adapting his experience at Ranger school to the Haganah's special needs. When the Jewish section of Jerusalem was about to fall, Marcus ordered the construction of the "Burma Road" to break the Arab siege. In gratitude, Ben-Gurion named Marcus Lieutenant General, the first general in the army of Israel in nearly 2,000 years. Shortly thereafter, Marcus was killed by an Israeli soldier when, due to his inability to speak Hebrew, Marcus failed to respond at a checkpoint with the proper password. Mickey Marcus is buried at West Point. Hollywood later immortalized Marcus in the movie *Cast A Giant Shadow*, starring Kirk Douglas and costarring Yul Brynner, John Wayne, Frank Sinatra, and Angie Dickenson.

200. Charles Orde Wingate (1903–1944)   An officer in the British army, Wingate was transferred to Palestine with the rank of captain in 1936. He was instrumental in the fight against Arab terrorism during the 1936–1939 riots. Wingate forged close ties with the Jewish community and the Haganah. He trained an elite squad of Haganah fighters in counterterrorism and military techniques. This elite force became known as the Special Night Squads. His ardent support for and assistance to the Zionist cause resulted in his transfer out of Palestine. His passport was stamped with the following: "The bearer . . . should not be allowed to enter Palestine." Wingate was promoted to the rank of major general during World War II, died in a plane crash in Burma, and is one of the very few non-Americans buried at Arlington National Cemetery.

201. Pinhas Lavon (1904–1976)   Lavon was born Pinhas Lubianiker to an Orthodox family in East Galicia. He received a law degree from Poland's Lvov University and became a Zionist leader and organizer in Poland. In 1929 he immigrated to Palestine where he became a labor activist and led the effort to rebuild a Jewish settlement destroyed by Arab riots. Lavon served in the Knesset from 1941 to 1961. In 1949 he assumed the position of Histadrut general secretary. His appointment to defense minister in 1953 ended in disgrace when he was forced to resign as the result of a botched intelligence operation. The ensuing scandal is known as the Lavon Affair. Despite his resignation, he was continually reelected as general secretary of the Histadrut until his removal in 1961 as a result of renewed repercussions from the Lavon Affair.

202. Avraham Stern (1907–1942)   Stern established and led Lehi until his death. Born in Russian Poland, Stern immigrated to Palestine in 1925 and became an active member of the Irgun. He went to Poland to procure arms and coordinate Irgun training programs with the Polish authorities and spent a brief stint in a British prison for his anti-Mandate activities. Stern's opposition to the Irgun's suspension of military activity against the British during World War II led to the formation of Lehi, a splinter militia. Stern was killed during a British raid on his hideout.

203. Yosef Burg (1909–1999)   Yosef Burg was born in Dresden, Germany, in 1909, and received a doctorate in philosophy from the University of Leipzig in 1933. During his youth in Germany, Burg was active in the Mizrachi movement and in promoting immigration to Palestine. He was saved from arrest on Kristallnacht and immigrated to Palestine the following spring. After the war, Burg went to France and became the director of the Paris-based Central European section of Mizrachi and Ha-Poel Mizrachi, which aided Holocaust survivors and established institutions for homeless Jewish children.

He returned to Israel in 1949 and became a leader of the religious Zionist movement. He served in the Knesset until 1987 as the head of the National Religious Party. He also held numerous ministerial positions.

204. Teddy Kollek (1911–)   The longtime mayor of Jerusalem, Kollek was born in Vienna and actively participated in the He–Halutz movement in Czechoslovakia, Germany, and England from 1931 to 1934. In 1934 he settled in Kibbutz Ein Gev in Palestine. Prior to the outbreak of World War II, Kollek met with Adolf Eichmann and negotiated the release of 3,000 Jewish children. During the war he returned to Europe as a member of the Jewish Agency's political department and served as a contact for the Jewish underground in Istanbul. In 1947–1948 he represented the Haganah in the United States and in 1951–1952 served as Israel's Minister Plenipotentiary in Washington, D.C. In 1965, Kollek was elected mayor of Jerusalem, a post he held until 1993 when he was defeated by Ehud Olmert. Kollek was a founder and chairman of the Israel Museum. Kollek left a flourishing legacy, masterfully overseeing the growth and construction of modern Jerusalem. He was known for smoothing tensions between Arabs and Jews. Kollek's ability to raise money from world Jewry was a major factor in the creation of the network of parks existing throughout Jerusalem.

205. Israel Be'er (1912–1966)   After moving from Vienna to Palestine in 1938, Be'er joined the Haganah. He received the rank of lieutenant colonel and served on the General Staff during the War of Independence. In 1961, he was arrested for spying for the Soviet Union. A friend of Prime Minister Ben-Gurion, he died in prison while serving a fifteen-year sentence for treason.

206. Ruth "Aliav" Kluger (1914–1980)   Born in Kiev, Russia, Kluger immigrated to Palestine in 1934. She helped build *Mossad le-Aliyah Bet* and was so instrumental in rescuing European Jews from the Nazis that she was given the nickname Aliav—an anagram of Aliyah Bet. Her efforts in fighting the Nazis were so well known that General Charles De Gaulle awarded her the Croix de la Lorraine and the Legion d'Honneur for her work with French and other European resistance. Kluger wrote about her experiences in Rumania during World War II in her book *The Last Escape.*

207. Moshe Dayan (1915–1981)   Born in the Deganyah Alef Kibbutz in northern Israel, Dayan became involved with the Jewish paramilitary at age fourteen and was arrested by the British in 1939 for his involvement in illegal Haganah military training. He was released in 1941 and, during World War II, participated in the British invasion of Syria. He lost his left eye while fighting for the British against Vichy French forces in Lebanon. Dayan commanded the defense of Jewish settlements in the Jordan valley during the War of Independence. By 1953, Dayan was appointed commander in chief of the IDF. After leaving military life in 1958, Dayan was elected to the Knesset as a member of Ben-

Gurion's Mapai party. He held many cabinet positions over the course of his political career, including serving as defense minister during the Six-Day War. After the war, Dayan was charged with administering the territories captured by Israel. His trademark eye patch and impressive military leadership during the Six-Day War made Moshe Dayan one of Israel's most famous and popular leaders. His popularity waned, however, after the 1973 War when many Israelis held him responsible, as defense minister, for the nation being unprepared for the Arabs' surprise attack. He resigned his post but later became a figure in the peace negotiations with Egypt as foreign minister under Menachem Begin. In 1979, Dayan resigned because of policy disagreements with Begin, and he ceased to be a major player in Israeli politics. He died two years later of colon cancer.

208. Abba Eban (1915–2002)   One of Israel's most well-known diplomats, Eban was born in Cape Town, South Africa, and raised in London. Eban played an active role in the Zionist movement prior to the establishment of the State of Israel. Eban served in the British military, first as a major on the staff of the British minister in Cairo and later as an intelligence officer stationed in Palestine. His numerous political posts included Israel's first representative and ambassador to the United Nations (1948–1949), ambassador to the United States (1950–1959), deputy to the prime minister (1963–1966), and foreign minister (1966–1974). Eban left the Labor party in 1988 because he believed that his position on the Knesset election list was "not at the proper ranking." Eban was a prolific author and eloquent spokesman for Israel; his works include *The Voice of Israel* (1957), *The Tide of Nationalism* (1959), and a history of the Jews entitled *My People* (1969). He also hosted two critically acclaimed series: *Israel: A Nation Is Born* and *Heritage: Civilization and the Jews.* Abba Eban moved to New York later in life, making him one of the most famous emigrants from Israel.

209. Yigal Allon (1918–1980)   An army chief of staff and archaeologist, Allon was born in Jerusalem and studied at the Hebrew University and at Oxford. Allon joined the Haganah during the Arab riots of 1936–1939 and also participated in the Allied occupation of Syria and Lebanon. A founding member of the Palmach, Allon oversaw operations that included illegal immigration, establishment of Jewish settlements in regions deemed closed by the British, sabotage of military targets, and operations behind enemy lines. By the end of the War of Independence, Allon was commander of the southern front. In this capacity he drove all Arab forces from the Negev and parts of the Sinai. Elected to the Knesset in 1954 by the Mapai party, Allon was appointed minister of labor in 1961 and deputy prime minister in 1968. His military techniques and initiatives were utilized during the Six-Day War and remain influential to this day. He devised the famed "Allon Plan," designed to redraw the Israeli border in the West Bank with an eye toward maximizing security and minimizing control over Arab population centers.

210. Hannah Szenes (1921–1944)   Responding to anti-Semitism in her native Hungary, Szenes moved to Palestine in 1939. She fought for the Haganah in a special unit that parachuted behind German lines to rescue Allied prisoners and organize Jewish partisan activity. She worked with Josep Broz Tito's underground. Hannah was captured and tortured by the Hungarian police. She was tried by a secret court and executed by firing squad on November 7, 1944. Her body was reburied at Har Herzl in 1950. Her poems are still popular in Israel today.

211. Olei Ha-Gardom (Those Who Went to the Gallows)   The term refers to the twelve Jews sentenced to death by the British Mandatory Government for their underground activities against the British. Two of the twelve individuals escaped the hangman by taking their own lives while awaiting their fate on death row. The members of the group were affiliated with either the Irgun or the Lehi, with Shlomo Ben-Yosef, who was hanged prior to the establishment of the underground organizations, being the only exception.

212. Shlomo Ben-Yosef (1913–1938)   The first Jew executed by the British in Palestine. Ben-Yosef was hanged on June 29, 1938, at Acre prison for attempting to attack an Arab bus in reprisal for the murder of Jews at the hands of Arab terrorists.

213. Mordechai Vanunu (1954–)   An employee at Israel's nuclear reactor at Dimona, Vanunu leaked information and photographs detailing Israel's nuclear capability to England's *Sunday Times*. On October 26, 1986, shortly after publication, the Mossad drugged and kidnapped Vanunu in Rome, taking him to Israel where he was tried and sentenced to eighteen years in prison for leaking classified information and committing espionage. He was released from jail in April 2004. Terms of his release include not being able to leave Israel or talk to the media about Israel's nuclear program.

214. Eli Cohen (1924–1965)   Born in Alexandria, Egypt, Cohen, along with every other Jewish student, was expelled from Farouk University in 1949. Cohen settled in Israel in 1957 after being deported from Egypt after the 1956 Sinai Campaign. He worked for Israeli intelligence in Syria and provided an incredible amount of information over a period of three years. In 1967, the Israelis were able to conquer the Golan Heights in two days in part due to the intelligence he provided. Cohen was arrested for espionage in Damascus in January 1965. He was summarily tried and convicted without benefit of counsel. Even the combined intervention of French, Belgian, and Canadian heads of state and Pope Paul VI could not persuade the Syrian government to commute the death sentence. Cohen was hanged on May 18, 1965, in Damascus' city square.

215. Moshe Arens (1925–)   Born in 1925 in Lithuania, Moshe Arens later moved to the United States, where he remained until he immigrated to Israel in 1948. He studied mechanical engineering at the Massachusetts Institute of Technology and aeronautical engineering at the California Institute of Technology. Moshe Arens was an associate professor of aeronautical engineering at the Technion and then vice president for engineering at Israel Aircraft Industries until he entered politics in 1974, when he was elected to the Knesset as a member of the Likud. He served in numerous government posts, including ambassador to the United States, minister of defense, and minister of foreign affairs. He retired from political life in 1999.

216. Rabbi Meir Kahane (1932–1990)   Born and raised in Brooklyn, New York, as a young man Kahane joined the Revisionist Zionist Foundation of Youth. Because of his political activities, he served a total of three years in American prisons, first landing in prison at the age of fifteen. In the 1960s, Rabbi Kahane founded the Jewish Defense League. In 1971, Kahane moved to Israel and established the Kach Party, whose platform called for the removal of Arabs from Israel. He held the lone Kach seat in the 1981 Knesset. Rabbi Kahane remained active in politics after Kach's expulsion from the Knesset until he was assassinated in New York by Egyptian Said el Nossair.

217. Aharon Barak (1936–)   Born in Lithuania in 1936, Barak studied law, economics, and international relations at the Hebrew University in Jerusalem. Barak received an M.A. in law in 1958 and a doctorate in 1963. He was an associate professor of law at Hebrew University and participated in the preparation of an international treaty on bills of exchange in the framework of the United Nations Commission of International Trade Law. In 1972, he was appointed professor at the School of Law, Hebrew University, and one year later received the Kaplan Prize for excellence in science and research. He became dean of the law school in 1974 and was appointed attorney general in 1978. Shortly thereafter, he was appointed justice of the Supreme Court. In 1995, he was named president of the Supreme Court.

218. Shulamit Aloni (1928–)   Born in Tel Aviv, Aloni fought to defend Jerusalem during the 1948 War and was taken captive by Jordanian forces in the Old City. She became a teacher, writer, and commentator and founded the Israel Consumers Council. She was elected to the Knesset in 1965 as a member of Mapai. Excluded from Mapai's election ticket in 1969 because of her maverick tendencies, Aloni formed the Citizens' Rights Movement (CRM) to advocate electoral reform, separation of religion and state, and a basic law protecting human rights. She was elected to the Knesset in 1973 under their banner. In the 1992 elections, CRM became part of Meretz and Aloni became a minister in the Labor coalition. Known for her antireligious views, Aloni became a lightning rod for criticism from right wing and religious circles.

219. Anatoly Sharansky (1948–)   Born in the Ukraine in 1948, Sharansky was a human rights activist in the Soviet Union and worked with Andrei Sakharov. He received a degree in mathematics from the Physical Technical

Institute in Moscow. Sharansky became active in the Zionist cause and applied for a visa to immigrate to Israel in 1973. His visa application was rejected for "security" reasons, and he was convicted for treason and spying on behalf of the United States in 1977. While in jail, Sharansky became a symbol for the human rights movement in general and for the Soviet Jewry movement in particular. His wife, Avital, campaigned for his release, but even international pressure failed to secure his release until 1986, when Sharansky was released as part of an East-West prisoner exchange. He was given a hero's welcome when he arrived in Israel on February 11, 1986. In Israel, under the Hebrew name Natan, Sharansky worked to free other Soviet dissidents and then became involved in domestic politics in the hope of providing political representation to Soviet immigrants. In 1995, he created a new political party, Yisrael Ba'aliya, dedicated to helping immigrants' professional, economic, and social acculturation. He has held a number of government posts, including minister of industry and trade mninister (1996–1999), minister of the interior (1999–2000), and minister of housing and construction and deputy prime minister (2001–2003). In 2003, Sharansky assumed ministerial responsibility for Jerusalem and for Diaspora affairs.

220. Yossi Beilin (1948–)   Born in Israel, Beilin worked as a journalist and eventually joined the editorial board of *Davar*. He returned to school and received his PhD in political science from Tel Aviv University. Entering politics, Beilin served as spokesman of the Labor Party from 1977 to 1984, as government secretary from 1984 to 1986 and as director-general for political affairs of the Foreign Ministry from 1986 to 1988. He was elected to the Knesset in 1988, and served as deputy minister of finance from 1988 to 1990. He was a member of the Knesset Defense and Foreign Affairs Committee from 1990 to 1992. In 1992, with the support of Shimon Peres, Yossi Beilin began secret negotiations with the PLO. These talks led to the signing of the Oslo Accords. From 1992 to 1995 Beilin served as deputy minister of foreign affairs. In July 1995, he was appointed minister of economics and social development. In November 1995, he was appointed minister without portfolio in the Prime Minister's Office, serving until July 1996. From 1996 to 2001, Beilin served as minister of justice. He has published several books: *Sons in the Shadow of Their Fathers*, *The Price of Unity*, *Industry in Israel*, *Israel at Age 40 Plus*, and *Israel, A Concise Political History*.

221. Avraham Burg (1955–)   Born in Jerusalem, Avraham Burg is the son of Dr. Yosef Burg, one of the founders of the National Religious Party. Avraham Burg, an observant Jew, began his political career as one of the leaders of the movement protesting the Lebanon War. When Burg was thirty, Prime Minister Peres appointed him as his adviser on Diaspora affairs. By 1992, Burg finished third in the Labor Party list, with only Yitzhak Rabin and Shimon Peres receiving more votes. In February 1995, Burg resigned from the

Knesset after being elected chairman of the Executive of the Jewish Agency for Israel and the World Zionist Organization. Burg returned to the Knesset in 1999 and was elected speaker.

222. Ron Arad (1962–)   A navigator with the Israeli Air Force, Captain Arad parachuted out of his Phantom jet while flying over Lebanon on October 16, 1986. He was soon captured by members of the Islamic fundamentalist Amal Militia. Arad was brought to Beirut and personally held by the then head of Amal security, Mustafa Dirani. The leader of the Amal Militia, Nabi Berri, announced that he was holding Arad and proposed an exchange for Shiite and Lebanese detainees. In early 1988, Dirani severed his ties with Amal due to ideological differences and took Arad with him. Arad was held captive by Dirani's group until the beginning of 1989 and was then handed over to the Iranian "Revolutionary Guards" in exchange for a large sum of money. Today, Arad's whereabouts are unknown. He is the most famous of Israel's many POW/MIAs.

Prime Ministers

223. David Ben-Gurion (1886–1973)   Israel's first defense and prime minister, David Ben-Gurion was born in Plonsk, Poland, and spent his childhood years studying in a religious school (*heder*). He moved to Palestine in 1906 at the age of 20. After a brief stint in the Russian army, he returned to Palestine during World War I and was exiled by the Ottomans for engaging in anti-Turkish activities. In 1918 he joined Britain's Jewish Legion (the Thirty-ninth Battalion). By 1930 he was leader of Mapai; from 1935 to 1948 he served as chairman of the Jewish Agency Executive, where he directed all Zionist affairs of the Jewish Agency together with Chaim Weizmann. Ben-Gurion was responsible for all military activity during the War of Independence. He disbanded the Haganah, ordered the destruction of the *Altalena*, and in May 1948, ordered the establishment of the Israel Defense Forces. Ben-Gurion's decision to declare independence immediately after the expiration of the British Mandate was actively opposed by the U.S. government and numerous Zionist leaders. He declared Jerusalem Israel's capital in December 1949, began the Israel Bond Drive in 1951, and pushed for accepting war reparations from West Germany. In 1954, claiming to be "unable to bear any longer the psychological strain," Ben-Gurion resigned the premiership. In 1955, prompted by the threat of war emanating from the Arab states, Mapai begged for Ben-Gurion's return. He was appointed defense minister and eventually replaced Moshe Sharett as prime minister. Ben-Gurion resigned again in June 1963 and returned to Kibbutz Sde Boker. In later years he would form the Rafi and State List parties, both meeting with only modest success. His final departure from politics occurred in 1970 when he resigned from the Knesset. Ben-Gurion's numerous books include *The Jews in Their Land* and *Rebirth and Destiny of Israel*.

224. Moshe Sharett (1894–1965)   Israel's second prime minister was born Moshe Shertok in the Ukraine. His parents brought him to Palestine in 1906 and settled in an Arab village. He served as a Turkish military officer in World War I, after which he returned to Palestine and served as editor of *Davar* in 1925. In 1931, he became secretary of the Jewish Agency's political department. After the assassination of Chaim Arlosoroff in 1933, Sharett became chairman of the political department, a post he held until 1948. In 1947, the British held Sharett in Latrun prison for four months. Shertok changed his name to Sharett upon becoming Israel's first foreign minister. When Ben-Gurion resigned the premiership, Sharett filled the post. In November 1955, Sharett became the second prime minister to resign, making room for Ben-Gurion's return as premier. He resumed the post of foreign minister, resigning in 1956 over differences with Ben-Gurion. Sharett helped form Israel's Foreign Service.

225. Levi Eshkol (1895–1969)   The third prime minister of Israel, Levi Eshkol was born to a Hasidic family, left Russia for Palestine in 1914, and began working in a kibbutz. He served in the Jewish Legion in 1920 and helped found the Mekorot Water Company, where he served as the first director. Eshkol oversaw the establishment of 371 Jewish settlements in his capacity as head of the Jewish Agency's Land Settlement Department. In the 1940s, Eshkol ran the Haganah's financial department; in 1949 he became treasurer of the Jewish Agency. In 1951 he was elected to the Knesset as a Mapai representative. Eshkol became Israel's prime minister and defense minister in 1963, filling the office vacated by Ben-Gurion's resignation. In 1964, when Syria began construction intended to divert the Jordan River's headwaters away from Israel, Eshkol approved air attacks against Syrian artillery positions and the water construction project. At President Lyndon B. Johnson's invitation, Eshkol became the first Israeli prime minister to visit the White House. When Egypt and Syria began threatening Israel in 1967, Eshkol established a Government of National Unity, relinquishing the defense portfolio to Moshe Dayan and bringing Menachem Begin of Herut into the cabinet. He led the country to its victory in the Six-Day War. He died in office on February 26, 1969, of a heart attack.

226. Golda Meir (1898–1978)   The fourth prime minister of Israel, Golda Mabovitch was born in Kiev, Russia, and raised in Milwaukee, Wisconsin. In 1917, she married Morris Meyerson and, in 1921, settled in Palestine's Kibbutz Merhavia. Meir worked her way up in local politics until June 1946, when, as a result of Britain's jailing of the entire Jewish leadership on Black Sabbath, she was assigned to lead the political department of the Jewish

Agency. In 1947 and 1948, Golda Meir held numerous secret meetings with Jordan's King Abdullah in an effort to negotiate peace. A lifelong member of Mapai, she served as Israel's first ambassador to the Soviet Union, minister of labor (1949–1956), and minister of foreign affairs (1956–1966). When she became foreign minister, she Hebraized her name to Meir. Upon Levi Eshkol's death, Meir became prime minister at age 71. Meir resigned in 1974 as a result of mounting criticism over her government's handling of the Yom Kippur War. Her autobiography, *My Life*, was a best-seller.

227. Yitzhak Rabin (1922–1995)   Israel's fifth prime minister, Yitzhak Rabin was the first native-born Israeli leader. Born in Jerusalem in 1922, he became active early on in the Jewish paramilitary forces and was a Palmach officer during the War of Independence. In 1953, Rabin was promoted to general and served as commander of the northern front between 1956 and 1959. As chief of staff of the IDF, a post he held from 1964 to 1968, he oversaw Israel's stunning victory in the Six-Day War. His foray into politics began with his appointment as ambassador to Washington in 1968. After a brief stint representing Mapai in the Knesset, Rabin was chosen to succeed Golda Meir as prime minister because of his record in the Six-Day War and his lack of connections to the government's ill-fated decisions prior to the Yom Kippur War. In April 1977, *Ha'aretz* revealed that Prime Minister Yitzhak Rabin's wife, Leah, had a secret bank account in the United States while he was stationed there as ambassador and that she illegally kept the account after they had returned to Israel. Rabin took responsibility for violating Israeli law and resigned. The scandal contributed to Labor's first-ever electoral defeat in 1977. Rabin returned as party leader in 1991 and led Labor to electoral victory in the elections the following year. His second term as prime minister was marked by the signing of the Oslo Accords by Israel and the Palestinians and a peace agreement signed between Israel and Jordan. On November 4, 1995, as he was leaving a peace rally in Tel Aviv, Rabin was assassinated by Yigal Amir.

228. Menachem Begin (1913–1993)   Israel's sixth prime minister and first non-Mapai leader, Menachem Begin was born in Brest-Litovsk, Poland. He joined the Betar movement as a teenager and in 1938 became leader of the movement in Poland. His Zionist activities resulted in a brief stay in a Russian prison camp in Siberia. He arrived in Palestine in 1942 as a member of the Polish army. In 1943, after being released from the service, he became commander of the Irgun Zvai Leumi, an underground military group following in the tradition of the Revisionist movement. With the Irgun, in 1944, he declared "armed warfare" against the British Mandate. The British offered a 10,000-pound bounty for his capture. In 1948, after the Irgun merged into the IDF, Begin led Herut, the political arm of the former Irgun, into the "loyal opposition." He led the protest against acceptance of German reparations in 1952.

Shortly before the Six–Day War he was named minister without portfolio in a national unity government. Begin led the Likud party to electoral victory in 1977, breaking the left-wing Labor Party's twenty-nine year grip on power. By signing the historic Camp David Peace Accords with Egypt, Menachem Begin became the first Premier to make peace with an Arab neighbor. Begin also ordered the air strike that destroyed Iraq's nuclear reactor in 1981 and began rescue operations to bring Ethiopia's Jews to Israel in the early 1980s. He resigned as prime minister and left the public scene completely in 1983 as a result of his despair over the course of the Lebanon War and the death of his wife. Menachem Begin recounted his exploits during Israel's struggle for independence in his book *The Revolt*.

229. Yitzhak Shamir (1915–)   Israel's seventh prime minister was born Yitzhak Jazernicki in Ruzinoy, Poland. He arrived in Palestine in 1935 and joined the Irgun. In 1940 he left the Irgun for the Lohami Herut Israel (Lehi), a more radical group. From 1955 to 1965, Shamir worked in the Mossad, Israel's intelligence agency. He was elected to the Knesset in 1973 as a member of the Herut party and served in various posts, including foreign minister in 1980. In 1983, Shamir succeeded Begin as leader of the Likud and prime minister of Israel. As a result of the 1984 elections, he alternated posts with Shimon Peres of the Labor Party under a National Unity Government, serving as foreign minister (1984–1986) and prime minister (1986–1988). After the 1988 elections, his Likud Party formed a coalition that returned Shamir to the premiership. After Labor's victory in the 1992 election, Shamir served in the Knesset and resigned as party leader of the Likud.

230. Shimon Peres (1923–)   The eighth prime minister of Israel, Shimon Peres was born in Poland. He emigrated to Palestine in 1934 and was chosen to head Mapai's youth wing at age twenty. Peres was involved with Haganah weapons procurement in 1947. He served as director general of the Defense Ministry from 1953 to 1959 and was elected to the Knesset in 1959 representing Mapai. Peres was instrumental in establishing Israel's nuclear program and forging military and political ties with France in the 1950s and 1960s. After a brief stint with the Rafi Party, Peres returned to Labor and over the next decade served as minister of absorption, transportation, communication, and defense. After Rabin's resignation in 1977, Peres led Labor in the opposition. By agreement with Likud as part of a National Unity Government, Peres served as prime minister while Shamir served as foreign minister from 1984 to 1986; they swapped roles from 1986 to 1988. Because of a string of electoral defeats, in 1991 Shimon Peres lost a party leadership battle to Rabin, who subsequently was elected prime minister. Upon Rabin's election as prime minister, Peres was appointed foreign minister. As foreign minister, he conducted secret negotiations with the PLO, ultimately leading to the Oslo Accords. For his efforts, he was awarded the Nobel Peace Prize simultaneously with Yitzhak Rabin and Yasser Arafat. When Rabin was assassinated, Shimon Peres became prime minister, only to lead Labor to another electoral defeat in the next election. In 2001, Shimon Peres served as foreign minister under a coalition government led by Likud Prime Minister Ariel Sharon. In 2005 he was appointed deputy prime minister in a new coalition led by Sharon.

231. Benjamin Netanyahu (1949–) Israel's ninth prime minister, Benjamin "Bibi" Netanyahu was born in Jerusalem. Netanyahu lived in the United States during his high school years and returned to Israel in 1967 to join the Israeli army. In the army he served in an elite antiterror commando unit and took part in the rescue of the hijacked Sabena Airlines hostages at Ben-Gurion Airport, during which he was wounded. Netanyahu returned to the United States after completing his military service and received degrees in architecture and management from MIT. Netanyahu worked for private industry for a number of years. His first foray into politics occurred in 1979 when he organized an international conference through the Jonathan Institute, an institute named after his brother Jonathan, who died rescuing Jewish hostages being held in Entebbe. In 1982, Netanyahu was appointed deputy chief of mission at the Israeli Embassy in Washington, and soon after was appointed Israel's ambassador to the United Nations. Returning to Israel in 1988, Netanyahu was elected to the twelfth Knesset as a Likud member and was appointed deputy foreign minister. During the Gulf War, he was Israel's most visible spokesman. In 1993, Netanyahu was elected Likud Party chairman and then prime minister in 1996, a post he held until losing reelection in 1999 to Ehud Barak, his former military commander. After losing the election, Netanyahu resigned from the Knesset, only to return to politics and become foreign minister in 2002. In 2003, he was appointed as finance minister. Benjamin Netanyahu has authored a number of books, including *A Durable Peace: Israel and Its Place among the Nations*, *Fighting Terrorism: How Democracies Can Defeat Domestic and International Terrorism*, *A Place among the Nations*, and *Terrorism: How the West Can Win*.

232. Ehud Barak (1942–) Israel's tenth prime minister, Ehud Barak, was born in Kibbutz Mishmar Hasharon. The most decorated soldier in Israeli history, he served in an elite antiterrorist unit and worked his way through the ranks of the IDF as tank brigade commander, armored division commander and head of the IDF Intelligence Branch. During his military career he fought in the Six-Day War, the Yom Kippur War, and the Lebanon war. In April 1991, he was promoted to the rank of lieutenant general and became chief of the General Staff of the IDF. Barak helped forge the 1994 peace agreement with Jordan. Barak holds a BS in physics and mathematics from the Hebrew University in Jerusalem (1976) and a MS in economic-engineering systems from Stanford University, California (1978). In July 1995, after resigning as chief of staff of the IDF, he was appointed minister of the interior. He served as minister of foreign affairs from November 1995 until June 1996. He subsequently served as chairman of the Labor Party and a member of Knesset. In May 1999, Barak defeated incumbent Prime Minister Benjamin Netanyahu and became prime minister. He resigned as prime minister and called for new elections, only to lose to Likud opponent Ariel Sharon in 2001.

233. Ariel Sharon (1928–)   Israel's eleventh prime minister was born Ariel Sheinerman in Kfar Malal, Israel. Ariel Sharon joined the Haganah and commanded an infantry company during the War of Independence. In 1953, he established an antiterrorist commando unit within the IDF. Sharon served as a paratroop commander in the Sinai Campaign and in 1957 attended the Camberely Staff College in Great Britain. While in the military, Sharon received a law degree from Tel Aviv University. In the Six-Day War, Sharon commanded an armored division. Subsequently, he served as commander of the IDF armored brigades, head of Northern Command Staff, and head of Southern Command Staff. In the Yom Kippur War, Sharon commanded an armored division. In a daring maneuver that was in violation of his standing orders, he led his troops across the Suez Canal, encircling and capturing Egypt's Third Army. That same year, Sharon helped establish the Likud Party and won a seat in the Knesset. He soon resigned his seat to become Prime Minister Yitzhak Rabin's special security adviser. Reelected to the Knesset in 1977, he was appointed minister of agriculture. Sharon served as minister of defense from 1981 to 1983 and was the chief architect of the 1982 Israeli invasion of Lebanon. He resigned after a government commission found him indirectly responsible for the September 1982 massacre of Palestinians at the hands of Lebanese Christians in the Sabra and Shatila refugee camps. Sharon remained in the government, serving in various ministerial positions until he became chairman of the Likud following the resignation of Benjamin Netanyahu. In a special election for prime minister on February 6, 2001, Sharon defeated incumbent Ehud Barak by winning 62.5 percent of the vote. He was reelected prime minister by a margin of 15 percent over the opposition candidate as a result of the 2003 Knesset elections.

Presidents

234. Chaim Weizmann (1874–1952)   Israel's first president was born in Motol, Russia. He studied biochemistry in Switzerland and Germany, and as a young man he was very active in the Zionist movement. When he moved to England in 1905 he was elected to the General Zionist Council. During World War I Weizmann played a key role in England's war effort by inventing a method of producing acetone, a substance required in the production of artillery shells. This discovery helped Weizmann forge strong relationships with British leaders. Weizmann used these relationships to influence British policy toward Palestine, and he played a pivotal role in the issuance of the Balfour Declaration. In 1918, Weizmann met with Emir Faisal (the leader of Arab nationalism) and also laid the first stones of Hebrew University. In 1920, Weizmann became president of the Zionist Organization. His failure to be reelected in 1930 was not the end of his political career. Weizmann influenced the Peel Commission recommendation to establish a Jewish state. Nevertheless, his position in the Jewish world began to wane due in part to his refusal to take a hard line against British policy in Palestine. While Weizmann believed the British to be allies of the Zionist cause, Jews in Palestine began seeing Britain as an obstacle to the creation of a Jewish state. Still, Weizmann addressed the United Nations General Assembly during the debate on partition in 1947 and influenced President Truman to recognize Israel immediately. In the 1930s, Weizmann laid the foundations of the Daniel Sieff Research Institute in Rehovot, which later became the Weizmann Institute. Weizmann became president of Israel in 1949 and died in office. Upon becoming president, he moved into a mansion on the grounds of the Weizmann Institute in Rehovot. Because of his figurehead role in the governance of the state, British politician Richard Crossman referred to him as the "prisoner of Rehovot."

235. Izhak Ben-Zvi (1884–1963)   Israel's second president was born in the Ukraine. He was active in the Jewish defense organizations formed to defend against the frequent pogroms that marked the period. In 1907 he moved to Palestine and was deported by the Turks in 1910. He returned to Palestine after World War I, where he became active in the Haganah and represented Palestine in negotiations with the British. A leader of Zionist socialism, he was elected to the first Knesset as a member of the Mapai Party and acceded to the presidency in 1952, a post he held until his death. Ben-Zvi published numerous scholarly works that explored far-flung Jewish sects and communities. He was the longest-serving president in Israel's history, having just begun his third five-year term when he died at the age of 79.

236. Zalman Shazar (1889–1974)   Israel's third president was born Shneur Zalman Rubashov to Hasidic parents in Russia, studied in *heder*, spent two months in a Russian jail due to his Zionist activities, and attended university in Germany. After making aliyah in 1924, Shazar served on *Davar*'s editorial staff and the Histadrut's executive committee. Shazar eventually became editor in chief of the paper. He was a member of the Jewish Agency's delegation to the United Nations in November 1947 and was elected to the first Knesset as a member of Mapai. On May 21, 1963, at the age of 74, Shazar was elected president, a position he retained until 1973.

237. Efraim Katzir (1916–)   The fourth president of Israel, Efraim Katzir was born in Kiev. When his family moved to Palestine, Katzir was just six years old. He received a doctorate from Hebrew University in 1941 and, at the invitation of Chaim Weizmann, joined the Weizmann Institute in 1948, where he headed the institute's biophysics department. Katzir worked in the field of polyamino acids and developed a synthetic fiber used to make stitches for surgery that dissolve in the body. As a result of his work, Katzir was the first Israeli to become a member of the U.S. National Academy of Sciences. Efraim Katzir's older brother Aharon was killed by a Japanese terrorist during the 1972 Lod airport terrorist attack. Katzir's only foray into politics was his election as president from 1973 to 1978.

238. Yitzhak Navon (1921–)   Israel's fifth president was the first Sephardi and first *sabra* (native-born Israeli) to hold the post. Born in Jerusalem, Navon worked at Hebrew University on Islamic culture, which helped secure his position as head of the Haganah's Arab section from 1946 to 1948. As an aide to Ben-Gurion for more than a decade, he helped form the Rafi Party. He was elected to the Knesset in 1965, representing first Rafi and later Labor. He served as president from 1978 to 1983 and, in October 1980, visited Egypt—the first official visit by an Israeli president to an Arab state. After his term, Navon returned to the Knesset, serving as minister of education and culture.

239. Chaim Herzog (1918–1997)   Israel's sixth president was born in Ireland to Chief Rabbi Isaac Herzog. He served as a British soldier and intelligence officer during World War II and fought in Israel's War of Independence as head of Israel Military Intelligence and chief of staff of Southern Command. Upon retiring from the military in 1962, Herzog served as a commentator on Israeli Radio and wrote *Israel's Finest Hour*. He was appointed Israeli ambassador to the United Nations and elected to the Knesset representing Rafi and Labor. He was elected president in 1983 and reelected in 1988.

240. Ezer Weizman (1924–2005)   Israel's seventh president was born in Tel Aviv in 1924 and is the nephew of Israel's first President, Chaim Weizmann. Ezer Weizman served as a fighter pilot with the Royal Air Force during World War II. Weizman helped establish what would become the Israel Air Force. He served as a fighter pilot during the War of Independence and was named head of operations of the Air Force in 1950. He became commander in chief of the Israel Air Force in 1958. He authored the strategy utilized during the Six-Day War to smash Arab air forces within hours. He retired from the army in 1969 and was elected chairman of the Herut Party in 1971. Originally an adherent of right-wing ideology, Weizman became a devout dove as a result of the Egypt-Israel peace agreement. Weizman was elected president in 1993 and reelected in 1998. In 2000, Weizman resigned as president under pressure due to the public revelation that he failed to declare a substantial sum of money that he received from a friend while serving as an elected official.

241. Moshe Katsav (1945–)   Israel's eighth president was born in Iran and moved to Israel as a young child. He grew up in Kiryat Malachi, an absorption camp for immigrants. He studied agriculture before joining the military. After being discharged from the army, Katsav returned to Kiryat Malachi and was elected mayor of the town when he was twenty-four. Katsav earned a degree in economics and history from the Hebrew University and wrote for *Yediot Aharonot*. He was elected to the Knesset in 1977. Katsav held the posts of deputy minister of housing and construction (1981–1984), minister of labor and social affairs (1984–1988), minister of transport (1988–1992), chairman of the Likud's Knesset faction (1992–1996), minister of tourism and deputy prime minister (1996–1999). On August 1, 2000, Katsav was sworn in as the newest president of Israel.

Religious Figures

242. Rav Avraham Isaac Kook (1865–1935)   The first Ashkenazi Chief Rabbi of modern Israel, Kook was born in Latvia and moved to Palestine in 1904 where he became Chief Rabbi of Jaffa. Kook's early fervent support of the Zionist movement was a break from traditional Orthodox Jewish thinking and helped establish modern Religious Zionism. He was appointed Chief Rabbi of Jerusalem after World War I and Chief Rabbi of Palestine (Ashkenaz) in 1921. Kook was a great rabbinic scholar, Kabbalist, and political leader who believed that the Messianic Era was at hand. In 1924, Kook established a yeshiva in Jerusalem that uniquely synthesized religious philosophy and positivist Zionism. Today, the yeshiva is known as Merkaz ha-Rav Kook.

243. Rabbi Jacob Meir (1856–1939)   Israel's first Sephardic Chief Rabbi was born in Jerusalem. He was appointed Chief Rabbi of Jerusalem in 1911 and in 1921 he was installed as the first Chief Rabbi of Palestine, holding the title Rishon Le-Zion (First to Zion). Rabbi Meir received honors and decorations from governments around the world, including from Britain, Greece, France (where he received the French Legion of Honor), and Turkey, and from King Hussein of Hejaz. Meir dedicated much of his career to making Hebrew a spoken language.

244. Rabbi Isaac Herzog (1888–1959)   Israel's second Chief Rabbi of Israel (Ashkenaz) established the Mizrachi Federation of Great Britain and Ireland and served as Chief Rabbi of Ireland. He assumed the post of Chief Rabbi in 1937.

245. Rabbi Ben-Zion Meir Hai Ouziel (1880–1953)   Israel's second Chief Rabbi (Sephardic Rishon le-Zion) was born in Jerusalem. Ouziel moved to Jaffa and worked closely with the Chief Ashkenazic Rabbi of the city, Rav Kook. He was temporarily exiled by the Turks for his efforts supporting the Jewish community. He became Chief Rabbi of Tel Aviv in 1923 and Chief Rabbi of Israel in 1939. Ouziel was present at the meeting that established the Jewish Agency, was a member of the Va'ad Leumi, and founded the Sha'ar Zion Yeshiva in Jerusalem.

246. Rabbi Shlomo Goren (1917–1994)   Born in Poland, Goren studied in a Jerusalem yeshiva and quickly became a prodigy, publishing his first commentary when he was only seventeen. In 1936, Goren joined the Haganah; during the War of Independence he was appointed by the Chief Rabbis as Chief Chaplain of the army. Famed for his bravery, Goren became a paratrooper in the Israel Defense Forces and attained the rank of brigadier general. During the Six-Day War, Goren led the troops who liberated the Western Wall in prayer and blew a shofar to mark the occasion. Also during the Six-Day War, believing that the IDF had already captured Hebron, Goren drove into the city. White sheets were flying throughout the city, and he met no resistance. However, the IDF had not yet entered the Hebron, thus making Goren and his driver the "force" that captured Hebron during the war. He was elected Chief Rabbi of Israel (Ashkenaz) in 1972.

247. Rabbi Ovadiah Yosef (1920–)   Born in Baghdad, Yosef moved to Israel as a young child. He became a rabbi at the age of twenty. In 1947 he returned to Egypt where he assumed the post of Deputy Chief Rabbi of Egypt. His refusal at the time to condemn the State of Israel ran counter to the sentiments of many in the Orthodox community. He returned to Israel in 1950, where he became Chief Rabbi of Tel Aviv-Jaffa (Sephardic). He became Sephardi Chief Rabbi of Israel in 1973. Yosef is the spiritual leader of the Shas political party.

248. Rabbi Israel Meir Lau (1937–) Born in Pyotrekov, Poland, Lau immigrated to Israel in 1946 after being liberated from the Buchenwald concentration camp. He arrived in Israel as an orphan whose parents were killed in the Holocaust. His uncle raised him and sent him to study at various yeshivas, including Ponovitz in Bnei Brak. Rabbi Lau was elected Chief Rabbi of Netanya, Chief Rabbi and President of the Rabbinical Court of Tel Aviv-Yafo, and, in 1993, Ashkenazi Chief Rabbi of Israel. An expert on medical ethics, he has published two volumes on medicine, ethics, and Jewish customs.

249. The Chazon Ish (1878–1953)   Avraham Yishayahu Karelitz, known as the Chazon Ish, was born in Poland. He was one of the outstanding Talmudic scholars of his generation who believed in studying science and math to better understand Judaism. He wrote commentaries on the *Shulchan Aruch* under the pen name Chazon Ish (visionary). When he moved to Palestine in 1933, Karelitz became a worldwide authority on cultivation during the sabbatical year and on different issues dealing with biblical commandments relating to the land of Israel. Politically, he opposed the Zionist movement.

250. Rabbi Eliezer Menachem Shach (1898–2001)   Shach was born in Lithuania and learned Talmud in yeshivas there. He immigrated to Palestine in 1941 and settled in Jerusalem, teaching in various yeshivas and eventually being chosen to head Ponevich Yeshiva in Bnei Brak. He was instrumental in creating the Shas party. In 1988, Shach broke away from Shas and formed an Ashkenazi ultra-religious party, Degel Hatorah. Shach opposed Zionism.

251. Rabbi Jacob Herzog (1920–1972)   An ordained Orthodox Rabbi, lawyer, and doctor of international law, Herzog was a member of Haganah intelligence during the British Mandate. Herzog held a number of government posts, including ambassador to Canada, assistant director general of the Foreign Ministry, and director-general of the Prime Minister's Office.

252. Rabbi Yehuda Amital (1925–)   Born in Transylvania, Amital lost his family at Auschwitz, while he worked in a labor camp. Amital immigrated to Palestine after the war and studied in a Jerusalem yeshiva. During the War of Independence, Amital joined the Haganah. He was instrumental in creating the first *yeshivat hesder* at Yeshivat HaDarom, where students combined serving in the military with studying Torah. Amital continued expanding the *yeshivat hesder* concept, establishing Yeshivat Har Etzion near Gush Etzion in 1968. Amital holds the rank of captain (reserves) in the army and remains one of the leading figures in the *yeshivat hesder* movement. In 1993 he founded the centrist religious party Meimad and from 1995 to 1996 served as a minister without portfolio.

Cultural Icons

253. Hayyim Nahman Bialik (1873–1934)   Born in Radi, Russia, to an Orthodox family, Bialik studied at Yeshivat Volozhin in Lithuania. Bialik left traditional Judaism and embraced the ideals of the Enlightenment. In 1898 he wrote his first poem, "HaMatmid" ("The Talmud Student"), which explored his drift away from Torah Judaism. Bialik turned his attention to Zionism, the topic of his first published poem, "El Ha-Tzipor" ("To the Bird"). In 1901, he published a collection of poems. Bialik continued writing and supplemented his income with teaching and various business ventures. In 1921 he started a publishing house in Berlin, moving the operation to Tel Aviv in 1924. In Palestine, Bialik met with much literary success, and in 1927 he became head of the Hebrew Writers Union. Bialik became known in Palestine as the national poet, but his works reached a wider audience, having been translated into a number of languages. His works remain popular in Israel.

254. Shmuel Yosef (Shai) Agnon (1888–1970)   A famed Hebrew author who wrote about the waning of traditional and spiritual Judaism, Agnon was born in Buczacz, Galicia. He moved to Israel in 1907 and went to Germany in 1913, where he heavily influenced the Zionist Youth Movement. He returned to Israel in 1924 and settled in Jerusalem. Agnon twice received the Israel Prize and, in 1966, became the first Hebrew writer to receive the Nobel Prize for literature. *The Day Before Yesterday* (1945), considered one of his greatest novels, relates to issues confronting Westernized Jews who immigrate to Israel. His other works include *The Bridal Canopy* (1919) and *A Guest for the Night* (1938).

255. Eliezer L. Sukenik (1889–1953)   Born in Poland, Sukenik moved to Palestine in 1912 and became an important Israeli archaeologist. Sukenik was appointed field archaeologist of the Hebrew University and was involved in the unearthing of the remains of the Jerusalem third wall. In 1938 he was appointed to direct the University Museum of Jewish Antiquities. In 1947, Sukenik played an instrumental role in securing the Dead Sea Scrolls. He dedicated the rest of his life to their study. Sukenik is the father of Yigal Yadin.

256. Yigal Yadin (1917–1984)   Born in Jerusalem to famed archaeologist Eliezer L. Sukenik, Yadin joined the Haganah in 1933 and quickly rose through the ranks. In 1947, as operations and planning officer, he was charged with planning and executing the military strategy employed during the War of Independence. In 1949, Yadin assumed the post of chief of staff of the IDF, where he oversaw the establishment of the reserves and the draft. In 1952, he retired from military service. By 1955, Yadin received a doctorate from Hebrew University for his work on the Dead Sea Scrolls and won the Israel Prize. He oversaw archaeological projects throughout Israel, including Masada and Megiddo, and initiated the construction of the Shrine of the Book at the Israel Museum. His works on archaeology were published in numerous languages and in a wide array of publications. He served as head of Hebrew University's Institute of Archaeology and on the Agranat Commission, exploring the Israeli response during the Yom Kippur War. In 1976, Yadin entered politics and was elected to the Knesset representing his newly established Democratic Party for Change (Dash). He assumed the post of deputy prime minister in 1977 and, when the party split, headed the faction named Shinui. He left politics in 1981.

257. Yehuda Amichai (1924–2000)   A leading Hebrew poet who helped create modern Israeli poetry, Amichai was born in Germany to a religious family. Amichai's parents brought him to Israel in 1935. He fought with the Jewish Brigade of the British Army and joined the Palmach after World War II. After the War of Independence, Amichai studied biblical texts and Hebrew literature at Hebrew University. His poetic work, *Achshav Uve-Yamim*

HaAharim (Now and in Other Days), was published in 1955. Amichai's works are marked by a unique use of contemporary imagery and a bold use of Hebrew. Amichai, known as the "poet who plays with words," authored idioms and slang expressions that entered the Hebrew language. He was awarded the Israel Prize in 1982. In addition to his numerous volumes of poetry, he authored short stories, novels, radio programs, and children's books.

258. Amos Oz (1939–)   One of Israel's most famous writers, Oz was born in Jerusalem and educated at Hebrew University and Oxford. He was a visiting fellow at Oxford and named Officer of Arts and Letters of France. *Newsweek* referred to him as "a kind of Zionist Orwell." His works explore the darker side of humanity that is found beneath the calm of daily existence. His best-known works, *My Michael* (1968) and *Black Box* (1987), consider the conflicts of everyday life in Israel. His other works include *Where the Jackals Howl and Other Stories* (1965).

259. Moshe Safdi (1938–)   A world-renowned and award-winning Israeli architect, Safdi's designs include the Habitat for the World's Fair in Montreal and Mamilah, a complex of apartments, fountains, and water pools located just outside the wall of the Old City of Jerusalem. Safdi also designed the reconstructed Jewish quarter in the Old City of Jerusalem. More recently, he designed the new library in Salt Lake City with rooftop gardens, shops, and private businesses in 2003, and a new $3 billion terminal at Toronto's Pearson International Airport in 2004.

260. Itzhak Perlman (1945–)   Born in Tel Aviv, Perlman is a musical genius who made his U.S. television debut at thirteen despite being crippled due to a bout of polio that struck him when he was four years old. He honed his skills as a violinist at New York's Julliard School. He emerged as a world-renowned musician and his career as orchestral soloist and chamber-music player includes numerous scores and recordings. He has appeared on television (including repeat appearances on *Rehov Sumsum*, the Israeli version of *Sesame Street*), plays jazz and klezmer music, and is active in training young musicians.

261. Daniel Barenboim (1942–)   Born in Buenos Aires, Argentina, Barenboim moved to Israel with his family in 1952. He studied music with his father, Enrique, who taught at the Vienna Music Academy. Barenboim gave his first recital at age seven and, by the time he was a teenager, had become an accomplished soloist. He subsequently began conducting and was named conductor of Orchestre de Paris in 1974. He has served as the musical adviser to the Israel Festival, music director of the Chicago Symphony Orchestra, and general music director of the Deutsche Staatsoper Berlin. In 1999, Barenboim held a piano recital at the Palestinian Birzeit University.

262. Shlomo Artzi (1949–)   Artzi began his career in the army, where he served as a soloist in the navy choral troupe. Continuing his musical career after leaving the army, he took first place in the Israel Folk Festivals in 1970 for *Pitom Hayom, Pitom Achshav* (Suddenly Today, Suddenly Right Now); in 1973 for *Shir Baboker Baboker* (Early Morning Song); and in 1974 for *Haballada al Baruch Jemili* (The Ballad for Baruch Jemili). In 1978, Artzi released the album *Gever Holech Leibud* (A Man Losing His Way). This and subsequent releases have made him one of the most popular Israeli singers in history; he has sold more albums than any other Israeli entertainer.

263. Miki Berkovitch (1954–)   Born in Kfar Saba, Berkovitch is one of the most famous Israeli basketball players. He led his high school team in international competitions and was the key to Israel's junior all-star team's fourth place finish in the 1972 European Games. Berkovitch played most of his professional career with Maccabi Tel Aviv, leading the most storied team in Israeli sports to twice winning the European Championships. Maccabi Tel Aviv never lost a national championship when Berkovitch was playing on the team. Berkovitch wrote an autobiography entitled *Born to Win*.

264. Yaacov Agam (1928–)   Born Jacob Gipstein, this son of a Russian rabbi grew up in Rishon Le-Zion and became the leading exponent of optical and kinetic art. When first introduced, his works broke from the idea that art is a fixed image. His work has influenced trends in art, architecture, and public sculptures. As one critic put it, he has "sought a unique form of expression that reflects the reality of Judaism as something removed from the art rooted in other civilizations." He is best known for his three-dimensional paintings and sculptures, including the water fountain on Dizengoff Street in the heart of Tel Aviv. The 1999 Eurovision first-place trophy was a sculpture by Agam shaped like a harp (in honor of the harp played by King David) and a seven-branch *menorah* like the one that was found in the Temple. His works have appeared in the Metropolitan Museum of Art (New York), Museum Jan van der Togt (Netherlands), and the Hirshhorn Museum and Sculpture Garden (Washington, D.C.)

Miscellaneous

265. Abie Nathan (1927–)   Born in Iran and later educated by Jesuit priests in India, Nathan fought in World War II as a fighter pilot with the Royal Air Force. After the war he immigrated to Israel where he joined the Israeli Air Force. Leaving the military in 1951, Nathan embarked on a successful career as a restaurateur. On February 28, 1966, Nathan flew his private airplane to Cairo on a self-proclaimed peace mission. Neither the Israeli nor Egyptian governments were informed of the flight until after Nathan landed in Egypt and presented the Egyptian soldier he met with a petition with 100,000 signatures. He was sent back to Israel. Nathan pulled a similar stunt on June 28,

1967, when he again flew to Egypt. Nathan created the "Voice of Peace," a pirate radio station that broadcast for twenty years from a ship "somewhere in the Mediterranean." The station became popular with young people because it broadcast in English and played Top 40 music. In 1977, Nathan met with Anwar Sadat and later engaged in talks with Yasser Arafat and other PLO officials. In 1993, mounting financial losses led Nathan to close the radio station and scuttle his ship.

266. Israel's Billy the Kid   Roni Leibowitz created a cult following when he robbed 22 banks in seven months. Leibowitz would drive up to a bank on a motorcycle, display a gun, rob the bank, and flee before the police arrived. His exploits made headlines around the country. Caught on September 18, 1990, Leibowitz was sentenced to 20 years in jail.

267. Meyer Lansky (1902–1983)   The reputed financial mastermind of organized crime, Lansky spent years attempting to become an Israeli citizen. Israel repeatedly refused his request. In November 1972, he was expelled from Israel.

268. Dr. Albert Bruce Sabin (1906–1993)   Sabin was born in Bialystok, Poland. His family settled in New Jersey in 1921. Sabin received his medical degree from New York University in 1931. During World War II, he served in the U.S. Army Medical Corps, where he was involved with the development of a vaccine against dengue fever and the successful vaccination of 65,000 military personnel against the Japanese type of polio. After the war, Sabin continued his research on polio. While Jonas Salk developed a vaccine using dead virus, Sabin devised one that used live virus. He later produced a pill vaccine and, in 1955, conducted experiments with prisoners who had volunteered. From 1957 to 1959, the Soviet Union and the other Eastern Bloc nations administered Sabin's pill, with its advantages of oral administration and long-term immunity. It was subsequently accepted in the United States. Sabin moved to Rehovot in 1970 and assumed the post of president of the Weizmann Institute of Science until 1972. He returned to the United States for the remainder of his career.

269. Dylan Returns   In 1978, Robert Allen Zimmerman, better known as Bob Dylan, converted to Christianity from Judaism. In the summer of 1982, he went to Israel for the bar mitzvah of his son (who was already 15) and subsequently became interested in Judaism.

POLITICS AND GOVERNMENT

270. "Israel"   The name "Israel" is first found in the Bible after Jacob struggles with an angel and God declares, "Your name shall be called no more

Jacob but Israel, for you have striven with God and with men and prevailed" (Genesis 32:28–29). Jacob's children became known as "the children of Israel" (Exodus 1:1). The State of Israel received its name on May 14, 1948, with the issuance of the Declaration of Independence, which states, "Accordingly, we, the members of the National Council, representing the Jewish people in Palestine and the Zionist movement of the world, met together in solemn assembly today, the day of the termination of the British mandate for Palestine, by virtue of the natural and historic right of the Jewish people and of the Resolution of the General Assembly of the United Nations, hereby proclaim the establishment of the Jewish State in Palestine, to be called ISRAEL."

271. The Flag of Israel   Composed of two blue horizontal lines and a centered blue Star of David (Magen David), placed on a white background. The two stripes symbolize a *Tallit*, the Jewish prayer shawl, and the Star of David represents Jews and Zionism.

272. "Hatikvah" (The Hope)   Israel's national anthem was written as a poem in the late 1800s by Naphtali Imber and set to music by Samuel Cohen. "Hatikvah" served as the anthem of the Zionist movement. The first Zionist Congress ended in a ceremonial signing of the "Hatikvah" by convention delegates. "Hatikvah" was sung at the opening ceremony marking the signing of the Declaration of Independence, with accompaniment by the Palestine Symphony Orchestra.

273. *Menorah* (candelabrum)   The official symbol of Israel is modeled after the *menorah* found on the Arch of Titus in Rome. The arch, commissioned in celebration of the Roman conquest of Jerusalem in 70 C.E., depicts the carrying of the Temple's seven-branched *menorah* and other Jewish articles to Rome. The *menorah* is also found in the Chagall windows in Hadassah Hospital, and a large bronze *menorah*, forged by Benno Elkan, is located near the Knesset.

274. Yom Ha'atzmaut (Day of Independence)   Israel's Independence Day is celebrated each year on the fifth of Iyar on the Hebrew calendar (roughly the first week in May). The holiday, established by law in 1949, begins at the conclusion of Yom Hazikaron, Israel's memorial day. The celebration begins in the evening at Mt. Herzl when the speaker of the Knesset lights twelve torches, symbolizing the twelve tribes of Israel. The day is marked by fireworks, bands playing and people dancing in the streets, military displays, and official ceremonies. Jews around the world recite special prayers and hold celebrations to mark the historic occasion of the establishment of a Jewish state in Israel.

275. Recognition of Israel   On May 14, 1948, the United States, under President Harry Truman, became the first country to give de facto recognition to the State of Israel. The Soviet Union was the second state to extend recognition. The United States extended de jure recognition to Israel on January 31, 1949, after Israel held its first election. Britain was the last world power to recognize the State of Israel—on April 28, 1950.

276. Yom Hazikaron (Day of the Remembrance)   Israel's Memorial Day was established to commemorate those Jews who fell in battle during the War of Independence. The national holiday begins at sunset when air raid sirens are sounded nationwide. All flags are flown at half-mast, and memorial candles are lit at schools, military bases, and synagogues. Places of entertainment are closed by law for the duration of the holiday. Israelis visit the grave sites of fallen soldiers, particularly those located at Mt. Herzl, where the prime minister delivers an address to the nation. During the day, a national two-minute moment of silence coincides with a second sounding of air raid sirens. The moment of silence is marked by Israelis halting what they are doing for the duration. Even on the roads, many people silently step out of their cars to honor the memories of Israeli soldiers. The name Yom Hazikaron is also another name for *Rosh Hashana*, the Jewish New Year and the day when Jews are supposed to reflect upon their lives and their loved ones.

277. First Debate   In May 1977, the candidates for prime minister, Menachem Begin and Shimon Peres, engaged in the first U.S.-style political debate held in Israel.

278. Direct Election   The first direct election for prime minister was held in 1996 with Benjamin Netanyahu defeating Shimon Peres by a mere 30,000 votes, a margin of less than 1 percent of the total vote. However, on March 7, 2001, the Knesset passed an amendment returning elections for prime minister to the pre-1996 system. Under this amendment, which took effect in 2003, the Israeli electorate votes for political parties running for the Knesset; the Knesset, in turn, chooses the prime minister.

279. The Presidency (*Nasi*)   Israel's president bears the ancient title of the head of the *Sanhedrin,* the supreme legislative and judicial body of the Jewish people in the Land of Israel in ancient times. The president is the head of the state, with the presidency symbolizing the nation's unity, above the fray of party politics. The president is elected by a simple majority of the Knesset from among candidates nominated on the basis of their personal stature and lifelong contribution to the state. Until recently, a president was able to serve up to two consecutive five-year terms. Now, a president may serve only one seven-year term. Presidential duties, which are mostly ceremonial and formal, are defined by law and include opening the first session of a new Knesset; accepting the credentials of foreign envoys; signing treaties and laws adopted by the Knesset; appointing, on recommendation of appropriate bodies, the heads of Israel's diplomatic missions abroad, judges, and the governor of the Bank of Israel; and pardoning prisoners, on advice of the minister of justice. In addition, the president performs public functions and informal tasks such as hearing citizens' appeals, lending prestige to community organizations, and strengthening campaigns to improve the quality of life in the society at large.

280. Knesset (Assembly)   Israel's parliament derives its name and number of seats (120) from the Jewish assembly (*Knesset ha-Gedolah*) that presided over Israel during the era of the Second Temple. Knesset members are elected every four years through a proportional representation system. The parliament may dissolve itself and hold new national elections at any time. Because of the multiplicity of parties, governing coalitions are stitched together; no single party has ever held an outright majority. Seated in Jerusalem, the Knesset does not hold plenary sessions on Friday, Saturday, or Sunday in consideration of Muslim, Jewish, and Christian members.

281. Political Instability   The Knesset is highly fragmented and politically unstable. Since 1948, there have been thirty separate ruling government coalitions in Israel. Only once, under Golda Meir (1969–1974), did a coalition government complete a four-year term. Two other governing coalitions led by Golda Meir lasted less than six months. In the 2003 elections, twenty-seven different parties ran for the Knesset, and thirteen of those won seats.

282. Knesset Building   Located in Jerusalem, the Knesset's home was inaugurated on August 30, 1966. In celebration, torches were lit on mountaintops throughout the nation. The Rothschild family subsidized construction of the building.

283. Political Parties   Israeli politics is marked by a large number of political parties. Many parties have had a short life span. Thirty-six parties were created and disbanded within one Knesset term; thirty-seven parties were elected to serve in the Knesset but ceased to remain independent parties before the end of the Knesset term. No Knesset term has had less than fourteen individual parties (or unaffiliated Members of Knesset). In the 1996 elections, thirty-one parties received votes; fifteen slates won seats in the Knesset in 1999.

284. Ahdut Ha'avodah (Unity of Labor)   Founded in 1919 to succeed Po'alei Zion, Ahdut merged with HaPo'el HaTzair in 1930 to form Mapai. In 1944, Siah Bet, a faction that split from Mapai, used Ahdut's name and formed a new political party with *HaKibbutz HaMeuhad* (United Kibbutz Movement). In 1954, Ahdut Ha'avodah reemerged when some members left Mapam and joined with members of *HaKibbutz HaMeuhad*. In 1968, Ahdut aligned itself with Mapai and was then absorbed by the Labor Party.

285. Mapai (*Mifleget Po'alei Eretz Israel*—Land of Israel Worker's Party)   Established in 1930 as a Zionist-socialist party, Mapai dominated politics in the Zionist movement before Israel was established and during the early years of the state. From 1948 until 1968, Mapai led every governing coalition and had a monopoly on the premiership. Mapai joined the Labor alignment in 1968.

286. Mapam (United Workers' Party)   Mapam was the second largest political party and shared a Zionist-socialist outlook with Mapai. Mapam joined with Mapai to form the backbone of the Labor alignment from 1969 to 1984. The Mapam faction ran independently in 1988 and returned to Labor in 1992.

287. Rafi (Israel Labor List)   In 1965, David Ben-Gurion broke away from Mapai over the Lavon affair and led a slate of candidates in the newly established Rafi Party. Rafi won ten seats in the elections. Shimon Peres, the party's secretary general, negotiated a return of Rafi into the Labor Party in 1968.

288. Labor Party (*Mifleget ha-Avodah ha-Yisraelit/Maarach*)   Established in 1968 with the joining of Mapai, Ahdut Ha'avodah, and Rafi, Labor is the dominant left-of-center party in Israel. Until Menachem Begin's victory in 1977, every Israeli prime minister came from Labor or one of its founding parties. Since 1977, Labor leaders Yitzhak Rabin, Shimon Peres, and Ehud Barak have served as prime ministers. Seven of Israel's prime ministers have come from the Labor Party, more than any other political party in Israel.

289. Citizens' Rights Movement (CRM, also known as *Ratz*)   Established in 1973 by Shulamit Aloni, a former Labor Party Knesset member, CRM favors strengthening civil rights in Israel, reducing religious political influence, and negotiating a compromise in the Israeli-Palestinian conflict. Its main constituents are the Ashkenazi urban middle class and the intelligentsia. CRM won three seats in the 1973 elections and briefly joined the coalition. It was part of the Labor alignment in the 1977 and 1981 elections but broke away in 1984. In 1984 it won three Knesset seats, and another five mandates in the 1988 elections. CRM joined Mapam and Shinui to form Meretz/Democratic Israel during the 1992 elections.

290. Shinui (Change)   Shinui was established in 1974 as "the political and social revival movement" as a result of the government's failed handling of the Yom Kippur War. In 1977 the party joined with The Democratic Movement and won fifteen seats under its new name "Dash—The Democratic Movement for Change." Shinui left Dash when it chose to join a right-wing coalition government. In 1992, Shinui, along with Ratz and Mapam, established the Meretz alignment. In 1999 Shinui again ran independently and won six Knesset seats. In 2003, the party became the largest political party in Israel, winning fifteen Knesset seats. Shinui joined a Likud coalition as a senior partner. In December 2004, Prime Minister Ariel Sharon dismissed Shinui from the coalition, in favor of Labor. Shinui is a liberal political party that is best known for its demands for a separation between religion and state.

291. Democratic Movement for Change (Dash—DMC)   Yigal Yadin and several other groups, including Shinui, founded Dash in 1976 partly as a response to the government's handling of the Yom Kippur War. After winning fifteen seats in the 1977 elections, Dash broke apart when Shinui disagreed with other member groups about staying in a coalition with the Likud government.

292. Meretz/Yahad   The left-wing party was founded by Shulamit Aloni in 1992 by a union of CRM, Mapam, and Shinui. In the 1992 Knesset elections, Meretz won twelve seats, making it the third largest party, and joined the coalition led by Yitzhak Rabin. Yossi Sarid led Meretz during the 1996 elections when it obtained nine seats and joined the opposition. It won ten seats in the 1999 elections and six seats in 2003. Meretz merged with SHAHAR and The Democratic Choice to form a new party called *Yahad* (together).

293. One Nation (Am Echad)   Splitting from the Labor Party in 1999, former Histadrut Chairman and Labor MK Amir Peretz created a party for Israel's working class. Am Echad won two seats in the fifteenth Knesset and three seats in the sixteenth Knesset. The party merged into Labor in 2004.

294. The Third Way (*Derech Hashlishit*)   A centrist movement that split from the Labor Party for the 1996 elections. The Third Way expressed concern over returning the Golan Heights to Syria and returning to the Oslo process with the Palestinians. The party was led by Avigdor Kahalani, a hero of the 1973 war, and was formed in response to concessions made in peace talks by the Rabin-Peres governments. The party failed to win any seats in 1999.

295. National Religious Party (NRP-Mafdal)   Established in 1956 when Mizrachi, Ha'Poel Mizrachi, and other religious Zionist groups merged, the NRP is a modern Orthodox religious party that strives to influence Israeli law to adhere more closely to *halachic* positions. The NRP is closely aligned with the *hesder* movement and is largely responsible for the fact that parents can choose to send their children to state-funded religious schools, the establishment of religious courts endowed with legal authority over issues of personal jurisdiction in the Jewish community, and the exclusive use of kosher food in the army and at government functions. The NRP consistently polled roughly 10 percent of the popular vote until 1981, when it lost voters to other right-wing and nationalist parties. The NRP has served in most of Israel's coalition governments and until recently was viewed as a centrist party. Today, the party is aligned with a nationalist ideology.

296. Meimad (Dimensions   Movements of the Religious Center) Established as a movement in 1988 by Rabbi Yehuda Amital as a religious Zionist alternative to the National Religious Party (NRP), Meimad became a political party to advocate the inclusion of religious practice into Israeli life without enacting coercive legislation. Meimad maintained that peace between

Israelis and Arabs is possible and that Israel can negotiate land for peace because of the concept of *pikuach nefesh*, which states that saving a life is more important than holding territory. In 1999, Meimad joined with Labor. Meimad has run in the Knesset jointly with other parties, but has never successfully run independently.

297. *Aguddat Israel* (Association of Israel)   Established in 1912 by Orthodox German Jews, the party represents ultra-religious Jews and often opposes new ideas that are not perceived as of the Torah and has adopted an anti-Zionist orientation. According to the *Aguddat*, national redemption can only be realized through the will of God and therefore it opposes the establishment of a nonreligious state. *Aguddat Israel* seeks to influence the Israeli government to fund religious institutions and adhere to strict religious rules. Because the party is not as concerned with Israel's foreign policy, it has been able to serve in coalitions with Likud and Labor. In 1992 *Aguddat Israel* joined with *Degel Hatorah* to form the United Torah Judaism party.

298. Shas (*Shomrei Torah Sephardim*—Sephardi Torah Guardians)   An ultra-religious, non-Zionist, Sephardi party established in 1984 to represent the Sephardic sector of the *Aguddat Israel*. The party's founding spiritual leaders are ex-Sephardi Chief Rabbi Ovadia Yosef and Lithuanian Rabbi Eliezer Shach. Members adopt policies according to the will of their rabbis. The leaders of Shas are centrist on foreign affairs and security issues, though the rank and file tend to be more hawkish. Because of its centrist positions, Shas won an unexpected seventeen Knesset seats in the 1999 elections and, for the first time in Israeli history, posed a threat to Likud and Labor, the two leading political parties. In 2003, Shas won only eleven seats and lost its position as the third-largest political party.

299. *Degel Hatorah* (Flag of the Torah)   In Israel, the Lithuanian yeshiva world remained affiliated with the *Aguddat Israel*. In the 1980s, the Lithuanian community, led by Rabbi Eliezer Shach, split off to become *Degel Hatorah,* a distinct political party devoted to the promotion of its own interests (especially its schools) and continued hostility toward secular Zionism. The party joined with *Aguddat Israel* in 1992 to form the United Torah Judaism party.

300. United Torah Judaism (*Yahdut Hatorah*—UTJ)   Formed in 1992 by the merger of two ultra-Orthodox parties, *Aguddat Israel* and *Degel Hatorah.* The party won four Knesset seats in 1992 and five seats in 1999 and 2003. UTJ is right wing on security and foreign policy issues and opposes negotiations with the Palestinians and the formation of a Palestinian state, and it wants to maintain a status quo relationship in regard to religion and state issues. UTJ also supports increasing settlements throughout Israel for economic, social, and security reasons.

301. Yisrael Ba'Aliya (Israel in Immigration)   Established in 1996, this moderate right-wing party mainly serves Israel's immigrant population from the former Soviet Union. Led by Natan Sharansky, the party advocates Zionism, perpetuating the Law of Return, and increasing funding for immigrant absorption. *Yisrael Ba'Aliya* supports Palestinian autonomy but not a Palestinian state. In 1996, *Yisrael Ba'Aliya* won seven Knesset seats, and in 1999, it won six seats. It merged into the Likud after winning just two seats in 2003.

302. Yisrael Beitenu (Israel Is Our Home)   Founded before the 1999 elections by Avigdor Lieberman, the former director-general for Prime Minister Benjamin Netanyahu, *Yisrael Beitenu* won four seats in the fifteenth Knesset. *Yisrael Beitenu* vied with *Yisrael Ba'Aliya* for political representation of the Russian-speaking immigrant population. The party merged into the National Union Party prior to the 2003 elections.

303. Center Party (*Hamercaz*)   Established in 1999 by Yitzhak Mordechai, Amnon Lipkin-Shahak, Roni Milo, and Dan Meridor, the Center Party tried to carve out a centrist position between Labor and Likud in the 1999 elections. Yitzhak Mordechai was the party's candidate for prime minister but dropped out at the last minute when it became clear he had no chance for victory. The Center Party advocated improving the economy, investing in education, negotiating with Syria and the Palestinians, and uprooting political corruption. The Center Party disbanded in 2001.

304. General Zionists/Liberal Party   The General Zionists were the most influential faction during the early Zionist Congresses until Palestine's labor movement organized under the leadership of David Ben-Gurion. After Israel declared independence, the General Zionists formed a political party that was represented in the first five Knessets. In 1965, the party merged into Gahal, the forerunner of the Likud party.

305. Gahal (*Gush Herut-Liberalim*—Freedom-Liberal Block)   Formed in 1965 by the merger of Herut and the Liberal Party (formerly the General Zionists). Gahal joined a unity government in 1967 before the onset of the Six-Day War. Gahal joined the State List and Free Center to form the Likud in 1973.

306. Herut (*Tnuat HaHerut*—Freedom Movement)   After the establishment of the State of Israel, the Irgun formed a political party named Herut, which was led by Menachem Begin. Herut represented the Revisionist movement and was the largest faction in Gahal and Likud. Attempting to reestablish a Revisionist political party to challenge Likud, Benny Begin, the son of Menachem Begin, established *Herut Hadasha* (The New Herut) in 1998. The party merged with Moledet and Tekuma to form the National Union Party. In February 2000, Herut left the National Union Party and failed to win a single seat in the 2001 elections.

307. Likud (Union)   Likud is Israel's right-wing party and has dominated Israeli politics since first coming to power in 1977. The party was established in 1973 by the merger of the Free Center, Laam, and Gahal. All of
Likud's leaders—Menachem Begin, Yitzhak Shamir, Benjamin Netanyahu, and
Ariel Sharon—have served as prime minister. In the 1984 election, Likud
joined with Labor to form a national unity government; both Shamir and Shimon Peres served as prime minister.

308. Kach   Rabbi Meir Kahane formed the Kach Party in 1971 and
ran in the 1980 Knesset election. Kach, a Zionist party, called for the transfer
of Israel's Arab population to other Arab lands. In 1984, Rabbi Kahane won
his first Knesset seat; however, he was banned from running for office in 1988,
and Kach was outlawed because of its racist and antidemocratic platform.

309. *Tehiya* (Revival or Renaissance)   *Tehiya* was established in 1981 by
a faction that seceded from the National Religious Party to create a right-wing
religious-nationalist movement. The party called for the forcible transfer of
Palestinian Arabs to neighboring Arab countries. *Tehiya* won three seats in the
tenth Knesset, five seats in the eleventh Knesset as part of a joint list with
Tzomet, and three seats in the twelfth Knesset, when it ran again as an independent party. *Tehiya* failed to win any seats in the thirteenth Knesset elections
of 1992.

310. *Tzomet* (Movement for Renewed Zionism)   This right-wing
party was established in 1983 and first ran for the Knesset as part of a joint list
with *Tehiya* in 1984. The party ran independently in 1988 and was most successful in 1992, when it captured eight seats. *Tzomet* ran on a joint list with
Likud and Gesher in 1996. In 1999, the party ran independently and failed to
win a single seat in the Knesset.

311. *Moledet* (Homeland)   Formed in 1988 by former General Rehavam Ze'evi, *Moledet* won two seats in the Knesset and joined a Likud coalition, only to leave the coalition in 1990. The party won three seats in both the
1992 and 1996 Knesset elections and joined the National Unity Party in 1999.
After the 1992 election, opponents of the party tried and failed to disqualify
Moledet from participating in the Knesset on the grounds that its platform
called for transferring Arabs out of the West Bank and Gaza Strip. Rehavam
Ze'evi advocated the transfer of Arabs from Israel. Rehavam Ze'evi was serving as minister of tourism when he was assassinated by a Palestinian militant in
2001.

312. National Union Party (*Haichud HaLeumi*)   Created in 1999 by the
joining of *Herut*, *Moledet*, and *Tekuma*, National Union is a right-wing party that
won four seats in 1999 and seven seats in 2003. *Yisrael Beitenu* joined the National Union shortly after the 1999 elections. The party adheres to a nationalist
ideology and believes in maintaining control over the West Bank and Gaza Strip.

313. *Hadash-Ta'al*   This Arab party was formed by the merger of *Hadash* (the Democratic Front for Peace and Equality) and *Ta'al* (the Arab Movement for Renewal). It won three seats in the sixteenth Knesset.

314. National Democratic Assembly (BALAD)   This Arab party debuted in the fourteenth Knesset in a joint list with *Hadash*; its faction won two seats. In the fifteenth Knesset BALAD ran independently, winning two seats. In the sixteenth Knesset elections BALAD won three seats.

315. United Arab List   Joining with the Arab Democratic Party for the fourteenth Knesset, this Arab party ran independently in the fifteenth Knesset, capturing five seats, and in the sixteenth Knesset, capturing two seats.

316. Voting Age   Every Israeli citizen is eligible to vote at age eighteen.

317. First Knesset (1949)   Approximately 427,000 votes were cast (87 percent of the voting population) and the Knesset was split as follows: Mapai (46 seats), Mapam (19), the religious parties (16), Herut (14), General Zionist (7), Independent Liberals (5), Communists (4), *Sephardim* list (4), Arab Nazareth Democratic List (2), and others (3). David Ben-Gurion became prime minister. The first national election, held on January 25, was declared a national holiday.

318. Second Knesset (1951)   Election results: Mapai (45), Mapam (15), General Zionists (20), Herut (8), National Religious Party (10), Aguddat parties (5), Arab parties (1), Independent Liberals (4), Communists (5), others (7). Ben-Gurion remained prime minister.

319. Third Knesset (1955)   Election results: Mapai (40), Ahdut Ha'avodah (10), Mapam (9), General Zionists (13), Herut (15), NRP (11), Aguddat parties (6), Arab lists (4), Independent Liberals (5), Communists (6), others (1). After having resigned in 1954, Ben-Gurion returned to political life and once again became prime minister.

320. Fourth Knesset (1959)   Election results: Mapai (47), Ahdut Ha'avodah (7), Mapam (9), Liberals—formerly General Zionists (8), Herut (17), NRP (12), Aguddah parties (6), Arab lists (5), Independent Liberals (6), Communists (3). David Ben-Gurion retained the premiership.

321. Fifth Knesset (1961)   Election results: Mapai (42), Ahdut Ha'avodah (8), Mapam (9), Liberals (17), Herut (17), NRP (12), Aguddah parties (6), Arab lists (4), Communists (5). For the last time, Ben-Gurion headed the Mapai ticket and was elected prime minister.

322. Sixth Knesset (1965)   Election results: Mapai/Ahdut Ha'avodah joint list (45), Rafi (10), Mapam (8), Gahal—merger of Herut and Liberals (26), NRP (11), Aguddah parties (6), Arab lists (4), Independent Liberals (5), Communists (4), others (1). Levi Eshkol assumed the premiership.

323. Seventh Knesset (1969)   Election results: Labor Alignment merge of Mapai, Ahdut Ha'avodah, Rafi, and Mapam (56), Gahal (26), NRP

(12), Aguddah parties (6), Arab lists (4), Independent Liberals (4), Communists (4), State List (4), others (4). Golda Meir served as prime minister.

324. Eight Knesset (1973)   Election results: Labor (51), Likud—merge of Gahal, State List, and Free Center (39), NRP (10), Aguddah parties (5), Arab lists (3), Independent Liberals (4), Communists (5), others (3). Golda Meir was elected premier.

325. Ninth Knesset (1977)   Election results: Labor (32), Likud (43), NRP (12), Aguddah parties (5), Arab lists (1), Democratic Movement for Change (15), Independent Liberals (1), Communists (5), Citizens' Rights Movement (1), others (5). Menachem Begin became prime minister.

326. Tenth Knesset (1981)   Election results: Labor (47), Likud (48), NRP (6), Aguddah (4), Communist (4), Tehiya (3), Shinui (2), CRM (1), others (5). Menachem Begin's coalition remained in power.

327. Eleventh Knesset (1984)   Election results: Labor (44), Likud (41), NRP (4), Shas religious party (4), Aguddah parties (4), Arab lists (2), Communists (4), Tehiya (5), Shinui (3), CRM (3), Kach (1), others (5). A National Unity Government between Likud and Labor resulted in a midterm switch of control of the prime minister and foreign minister posts by the Likud's Yitzhak Shamir and Labor's Shimon Peres.

328. Twelfth Knesset (1988)   Election results: Labor (39), Mapam (3), Likud (40), NRP (5), Shas (6), Aguddah (5), Degel Hatorah (2), Arab lists (2), Communists (4), CRM (5), Tehiya (3), Tzomet (2), Moledet (2), Shinui (2). A National Unity government was formed by Likud and Labor with Likud receiving the premiership (Yitzhak Shamir) and foreign ministry, and Labor holding the finance and defense ministries.

329. Thirteenth Knesset (1992)   Election results: Labor (44), Likud (32), Meretz (12), Tsomet (8), NRP (6), Shas (6), Yahadut Hatorah (4), Hadash (3), Moledet (3), Arab Democratic Party (2). prime minister Yitzhak Rabin resumed the post of premier after resigning as prime minister fifteen years earlier.

330. Fourteenth Knesset (1996)   Election results: Labor (34), Likud-Gesher-Tsomet (32), Shas (10), National Religious Party (9), Meretz (9), Yisrael Ba'Aliya (7), Hadash (5), Yahadut Hatorah (4), The Third Way (4), United Arab List (4), Moledet (2). Likud Leader Benjamin Netanyahu was elected prime minister in the first direct election of a prime minister.

331. Fifteenth Knesset (1999)   Election results: One Israel—joint list of Labor, Gesher, Meimad (26), Likud (19), Shas (17), Meretz/Democratic Israel (10), Yisrael Ba'Aliya (6), Shinui (6), Center Party (6), NRP (5), United Torah Judaism (4), United Arab List (5), National Unity (4), Yisrael Beitenu (4), Hadash (3), National Democratic Alliance (2), One Nation (2). Ehud Barak of the One Israel Party was elected prime minister.

332. Sixteenth Knesset (2003)   In the lowest voter turnout (68.5 percent) and the worst election showing for Labor in Israel's history, the election results were: Likud (38), Labor (19), Shinui (15), Shas (11), National Union (7), National Religious Party (6), Meretz (6), United Torah Judaism (5), One Nation (3), Hadash (3), Balad (3), United Arab List (2), Yisrael Ba'Aliya (2). Ariel Sharon was reelected prime minister (he was first elected in 2001 in a direct election for prime minister).

333. Basic Laws   When Israel declared its independence, the intention was that the First Knesset would draft a constitution. This was never done, however, because of differences of opinion between the secular and religious parties. In place of a constitution, the Knesset legislated a series of basic laws which were expected to help form a constitution in the future. Basic Laws were enacted to codify the fundamental underpinnings and operations of the State of Israel. Eleven Basic Laws were passed in the following categories: The Army; Freedom of Occupation; The Government; Human Dignity and Liberty; Israel Lands; Jerusalem, Capital of Israel; The Judicature; The Knesset; The President of the State; The State Comptroller; and The State Economy. In Israel, a Basic Law can be enacted, and most can be amended, with an ordinary majority of those present. Only the Freedom of Occupation and the Government Basic Laws require the assent of sixty-one members of Knesset to amend the law. In an effort to strengthen the importance of the Basic Laws, the Supreme Court has ruled that a Basic Law can only be amended by another Basic Law.

334. Peace Now (*Shalom Akhshav*)   Established in July 1978 by 34,800 IDF reserve officers who sent a letter to then Prime Minister Menachem Begin requesting that he return the West Bank and Gaza Strip to the Arabs. Under the slogan "Better peace than the wholeness of the Land of Israel," the group is independent of any political party. It held its first mass demonstration, over 20,000 strong, in Tel Aviv on April 1, 1978. Peace Now remains an active and influential advocate of the peace process.

335. *Gush Emunim* (Bloc of the Faithful)   A religious/political movement intent upon establishing Jewish control over all the territories captured by Israel in the Six-Day War, though it is active primarily in the West Bank. *Gush Emunim* was established in 1974. Its spiritual leader was Rabbi Zvi Judah Kook, son of Rabbi Abraham Isaac Kook, Israel's first Chief Rabbi (Ashkenaz).

336. Elon Moreh   The first of many confrontations to come between the government and Jewish settlers was provoked when a settler group established a settlement without government permission on the hilltop of Elon Moreh in November 1975. A month later, the settlers agreed to a compromise and evacuated the area, moving to a nearby army base.

337. Israel's FBI (Shin Bet—*Sherut Habitachon Haklali*)   Israel's internal security, counterespionage, and counterterrorist agency is usually referred to as the Shin Bet. It is also known as the Israel Security Service and, in Israel, by its acronym Shabak. It is responsible for the security and protection of Israel's prime minister and other governmental leaders as well as of defense industries, sensitive economic locations, and Israeli government installations abroad. The Shin Bet, which is sometimes compared to the U.S. Federal Bureau of Investigation (FBI), also handles overall security for Israel's national airline, EL AL.

338. Supreme Court   Israel's highest court of appeals has jurisdiction over civil and criminal cases heard in the District Courts and special jurisdiction in other situations, including Knesset elections and administrative detentions. Cases are heard in panels of three or more judges. Judges are chosen by a panel made up of two ministers (one must be the justice minister), two Knesset members (one from the coalition and one from the opposition), two members of Israel's Bar Association, and three members of the Supreme Court itself. The number of justices on the Court is fixed by Knesset statute, and in 2004 the Court had seventeen members. By tradition, the oldest member of the Court serves as its chief justice. Israeli Supreme Court justices are subject to a mandatory retirement age of seventy years that is applicable to all judges in Israel's secular courts.

339. First Arab Justice   In March 1999, Abdel Rahman Zuabi became the first Israeli Arab to sit on the Supreme Court.

340. Juries   Israel's judicial system does not use juries.

341. Death Penalty   Israel has the death penalty on its books for crimes against the Jewish people and humanity, but it has been applied only once, in the case of Adolf Eichmann, who was hanged for his role in implementing the Final Solution during the Holocaust.

SOCIETY AND CULTURE

342. First Census   The British conducted the first census in Palestine in 1922 and found a total population of 757,200: 83,800 Jews and 673,400 Arabs.

343. First State Census   On September 8, 1948, a nationwide curfew was imposed in Israel from 5:00 p.m. to midnight during which 15,000 census takers fanned out across the country and counted 872,000 people—716,700 Jews and 156,000 non-Jews.

344. One Million Jews   In November 1949, the Jewish population of Israel hit one million.

345. Population   On Israel's fifty-sixth birthday in May 2004, the population stood at 6.8 million. Roughly 81 percent of the population is Jewish and 19 percent Arab. More than 75 percent of the Arab population is Muslim; the remaining are Christian (113,000) or Druze (106,000). More than 13 percent of the Israeli population arrived as immigrants over the past fifteen years.

346. Youthful Population   The median age of the Israeli population is 29.2.

347. Melting Pot   About one-third of the current Israeli population emigrated from over seventy different countries.

348. Sabras   Native-born Israelis. The word comes from the name of a cactus plant that is prickly and tough on the outside and soft on the inside. The Israeli character is often said to resemble this fruit. In 2004, 66 percent of Israel's Jewish population was born in Israel, compared to just 35 percent in 1948.

349. *Ashkenazim/Sephardim*   *Ashkenazim* are Jews who arrived in Israel from Europe, Russia, and the Americas; *Sephardim* are Jews who trace their ancestry to the Jewish communities in Spain or Portugal before the expulsion of 1492. In Israel, the term *Sephardim* is generally applied to Jews who originated in Asia, Africa, and the Middle East. The Israeli population was roughly evenly split between *Ashkenazim* and *Sephardim* until the influx of Russian Jews in the 1990s created an Ashkenazic majority.

350. Russians   Now the largest ethnic bloc in Israel, 1.2 million Israelis were either born in the former Soviet Union or to a father who was born in there.

351. Moroccans   The second largest ethnic group in Israel, Moroccans number some 500,000 residents.

352. Ethiopians   More than 80,000 Ethiopian Jews live in Israel today.

353. Israeli Arabs   Arabs who live in the State of Israel's borders are vested with the full rights that flow from citizenship. They can vote, serve in the Knesset, and become members of the *Histadrut*. Not all Israeli Arabs share the anti-Zionist views of their Arab brethren. Their community is exempted from the draft so as not to require Israeli Arabs to face Arab armies in combat. Arabs residing inside Jerusalem after the 1967 war have a unique status, and special rules are placed upon them. Though given the option of becoming citizens, few accepted. Though technically equal citizens, Israeli Arabs do suffer hardships in a number of areas. Many jobs in Israel are related to military service and this makes it difficult, if not impossible, for Arabs to get those positions. In addition, government funding for predominantly Arab municipalities has long lagged significantly behind that given to Jewish communities.

354. Bedouins   Arabic-speaking nomadic people who live in Middle Eastern deserts, including those located in Israel. Over 170,000 Bedouins belonging to some thirty different tribes reside in Israel. The Bedouin population has increased tenfold since the establishment of the state (1948), due to a high natural increase—about 5 percent—which is unparalleled in Israel or elsewhere in the Middle East. Most are animal herders who move from the desert to arable land during the growing season. As a community, Bedouins are transitioning into a more settled, less nomadic societal structure and are integrating into the Israeli workforce. Though not drafted by the Israeli army, they volunteer in significant numbers and are noted for their ability to serve as trackers.

355. Druze   A distinct Arab sect numbering about one million and possessing a unique religion. Druze live primarily in parts of Syria, Lebanon, and northern Israel. Even though they speak Arabic and are part of the Arab culture, the Druze prohibit marriage outside of their own community, do not admit converts or discuss their religion with outsiders, and have a long history of armed conflicts with intolerant Arab rulers and rival tribes. Their religious roots are found in Islam. Their religion is monotheistic, and they believe that the deity operates in the world through a series of five cosmic principles. The Druze pay homage to Yitro, the father-in-law of Moses. Approximately 106,000 Druze live in Israel, mostly in the upper Galilee. Although Israeli law exempts Druze from the military draft, much of the community has self-imposed a draft, requiring their young men to volunteer for the army. The Druze community located in Israel is generally supportive of the state. Since 1957, Israel has recognized the Druze as a separate religious community. The Golan's 18,000 Druze residents are permitted to maintain their previous citizenship, but were given the option of becoming full Israeli citizens. For various reasons, few have done so.

356. Circassians   Sunni Muslims who fled Russian subjugation of Cherkessia in 1864. Located in the villages of Kafr Kama and al-Rihaniyya in northern Israel's Galilee region, the Circassian community numbers approximately 3,000 and its members voluntarily serve in the IDF.

357. Black Hebrews   "The Original African Hebrew Israelite Nation of Jerusalem" is a sect primarily located in Chicago and Dimona. About 2,500 members live in Israel. The Black Hebrews believe that they are descended from the ten lost tribes of Israel. The community lives by its own code of conduct that includes permitting polygamy, forbidding birth control, and prohibiting the consumption of meat, dairy products, eggs, and sugar. Upon joining the sect, members adopt Hebraic names. The first Black Hebrews began arriving in Israel in 1969. Because the Chief Rabbinate of Israel declared that the Black Hebrews were not Jews, members are not extended Israeli citizenship under the Law of Return. The Black Hebrews acquired legal status in an agreement reached with the Israel Ministry of the Interior in May 1990 and became legal residents after a solidarity trip to the region by singer Whitney Houston in 2003. Members of the community started voluntarily serving in the IDF in 2004.

358. *Kibbutz* Originally, settlements that adhered to a Marxist/socialist form of government. Historically, members of the collective possess no private wealth; the community meets all personal needs, including communal meals, education, housing, and toiletries. Until recently, most *kibbutzim* housed children in group quarters. In the early days of Jewish settlement in Palestine and statehood, *kibbutzim* revolved around an agricultural economy; today, industry, tourism, and technology serve as major sources of income. Because of the extreme difficulty in establishing agricultural settlements in regions dominated by deserts and swamps, coupled with the relative poverty of many early immigrants to Palestine, the *kibbutz's* collective mentality was vital to the successful settlement and defense of the land. Different *kibbutzim* banded together in federations in accordance to ideological belief. Fewer and fewer *kibbutzim* now follow the strict socialist formula of their founders and, rather than striving for total equality, most seek to minimize inequality. In the 1980s, triple-digit inflation and exorbitant interest rates caused near economic ruin for many *kibbutzim*, and the impact of that period is still being felt. The first *kibbutz*, Degania, was created by pioneers near the southern end of the Sea of Galilee in 1909. In 1948, roughly 6.5 percent of Israelis lived in a *kibbutz*. Today, approximately 268 *kibbutzim* remain in Israel with a population of approximately 120,000 (roughly 2 percent of the population).

359. *Ha-kibbutz Ha-Dati* (The Religious Kibbutz) Whereas other kibbutz federations were founded upon varying theories of socialism and kibbutz organization, *Ha-Kibbutz Ha-Dati* adheres to an ideology fusing religious adherence and labor (*Torah va-Avodah*) into a religious socialism. The movement is allied with the Bnei Akiva youth movement and the National Religious Party.

360. *Moshav* (Workers Settlement) A worker's agricultural cooperative combining the philosophy of private ownership and communal living. The first *moshavim*, Nahalal and Kefar Yehezkel, were established in 1921. By 1948, 58 *moshavim* could be found in Israel; by 1970, some 75,000 Israelis resided in 212 *moshavim*. The *Te'nuat Moshavim* organization represents the *moshav* movement.

361. *Mo'ezet Ha-Po'alot* (Council of Women Workers) Organization founded in 1922 as part of the Histadrut. The early years were geared to securing equal rights and recognition for women workers and pioneers. Having achieved its early goals, the organization now concentrates on social issues and unique challenges of working women.

362. Shimron Commission A government investigation in 1978 confirmed that organized crime exists in Israel.

363. Crime Trend In 1999, the Israeli crime rate declined for the first time in 20 years.

364. Smoke Free?   The Restriction on Smoking in Public Places Law of 1983 imposed restrictions on smoking in places such as cinemas, theaters, concert halls, hospitals, libraries, elevators, taxis, and buses; nevertheless, about the only place one is likely to go in Israel where people will not be smoking is on an airplane.

Writing, Publishing, and Radio

365. People of the Book   Israelis buy more books per capita than any other people.

366. Published in Israel   The first publishing house in Israel was established by Eliezer ben Isaac Ashkenazi in Safed in 1577 as a Hebrew press. In 1605, the press was sold to a printer from Damascus.

367. *Ha-levanon* (The Lebanon)   The first Hebrew newspaper established in Israel hit the stands in March 1863. The paper ceased publication in 1882.

368. *Yediot Aharonot* (Latest News)   Boasting a circulation that includes some two-thirds of all newspaper readers in Israel, *Yediot* is a daily newspaper that debuted in 1939.

369. *Ma'ariv* (Evening)   Established as an afternoon paper in 1948 by former editors of *Yediot Aharonot*. It is now second in circulation to that paper.

370. *Ha'aretz* (The Land)   Israel's oldest surviving daily newspaper ran its presses for the first time on June 18, 1919, under the name *Hadashot Haaretz*. An English edition is now available on the Internet.

371. *Jerusalem Post*   Israel's first English daily newspaper was incorporated in 1932 as the *Palestine Post*. Initially, only 1,200 copies were printed. The *Post* maintained a rocky relationship with the British authorities because of the paper's outspoken criticism of the Mandatory government. In retaliation for Jewish terrorism, the *Post*'s offices were destroyed on February 1, 1948, by a bomb planted by a joint British-Arab venture. Renamed the *Jerusalem Post* in 1950, the newspaper began a weekly overseas edition in 1959, and now boasts the fourth-largest daily circulation in the state of Israel, as well as an online edition.

372. Pub to Pol   The editor of the *Jerusalem Post*, Gershon Agron, was elected mayor of Jerusalem in 1955.

373. Party Papers   Once flourishing, papers published by political parties are now disappearing in Israel. Only three such papers remain, all intended for religious readers—*Hatsofeh*, *Hamodia*, and *Yated Ne'eman*.

374. *Davar* (Word)   The first daily newspaper for Israel's entire labor movement. Established in 1925, the paper historically supported the Histadrut. Zalman Shazar and Moshe Sharett worked for the paper. It ceased publication in the 1990s.

375. First Radio Station   The first radio station in Palestine, Radio Tel Aviv, went on the air on April 7, 1932, broadcasting a speech by Tel Aviv Mayor Meir Dizengoff. The station ceased programming in April 1935.

376. Kol Israel (The Voice of Israel)   This underground radio station was created by the Haganah in March 1940. On May 14, 1948, the station became an Israeli government-funded station called Kol Israel. Today, In addition to networks that broadcast exclusively in Hebrew and in Arabic, Kol Israel offers programming for immigrants and overseas communities in various languages including Russian, Amharic, English, French, Spanish, Yiddish, Hungarian, Romanian, Moghrabi, Ladino, Persian, and Bukharian.

377. Academy of the Hebrew Language   Established by the Knesset in 1953, the academy serves as the official body charged with the "development of Hebrew" and addressing linguistic problems, including spelling, pronunciation, and transliteration. The academy supplanted the Hebrew Language Committee, established in 1890. The committee transformed Hebrew from a dead to a living language, inventing new words for modern use.

378. Nobel Prize for Literature   In 1966, Shmuel Yosef Agnon won the Nobel Prize for Literature, becoming the first Israeli and Hebrew writer to win the award. He was cited "for his profoundly characteristic narrative art with motifs from the life of the Jewish people." In September 1959, the street outside of Shmuel Yosef Agnon's Jerusalem residence was closed to traffic between the hours of 10:00 p.m. and 7:00 a.m. because the noise interfered with his ability to concentrate.

379. Greatest Jewish Library   The Jewish National and University Library of the Hebrew University of Jerusalem houses the largest collection of books, manuscripts, documents, and microfilms of works written by or pertaining to Jews. There are some 3,000,000 volumes of books and periodicals, as well as thousands of items in special collections, such as manuscripts and archives, maps, and music recordings.

380. Beep Beep   Charles Glidden of Boston drove the first automobile in Palestine in 1908.

381. Largest Jewish Video Library   The Steven Spielberg Jewish Family Archive at the Hebrew University of Jerusalem contains the world's largest and most complete collection of films and videotapes on Jewish topics.

382. Movie Time   The first movie house, the Olympia, opened in Jerusalem in 1908.

383. First Hebrew Movies   The first Hebrew language films were *Return to Zion* (1920) and *Oded the Nomad* (1932)

384. Golden Globe I   *Salah Shabbati*, a film directed by Ephraim Kishon, won a Golden Globe in 1965 in the category of Best Foreign Film.

385. Golden Globe II   Efraim Kishon's 1972 film, *Azulai the Police-man*, won a Golden Globe.

386. *Star Wars* Star   Natalie Portman, the actress who portrayed Queen Padme Amidala Naberrie in the *Star Wars* movies, was born in Jerusalem on June 9, 1981, and speaks Hebrew fluently.

387. *Rambo III*   Parts of the third installment of Sylvester Stallone's hit action series were filmed in Eilat and the caves of Beit Guvrin.

388. *Jesus Christ Superstar*   Segments of the film were shot in the Nabatean cities of Avdat and Mamshit.

Music and Dance

389. Israel Philharmonic Orchestra   Deemed one of the top orchestras in the world, the Palestine Symphony Orchestra was established in 1936 by Polish violinist Bronislaw Huberman and 75 other Jewish musicians from top European orchestras fleeing anti–Semitism. The orchestra was originally called the Palestine Orchestra. Its first conductor was Arturo Toscanini. On October 3, 1948, the symphony, with Leonard Bernstein as conductor and soloist, held its first concert under its new name, the Israel Philharmonic Orchestra. Some of the world's greatest musical talents have performed with the orchestra. In 1968, Zubin Mehta was appointed music adviser (later music director). Leonard Bernstein was named laureate conductor in 1988. In 1992, Kurt Maser became the honorary guest conductor.

390. Ban on Wagner   Richard Wagner, who lived decades before the birth of Nazism, influenced the National Socialist movement and Adolf Hitler. He was an anti-Semite whose music held a singular importance in the Nazi psyche. Thus, for Jewish survivors of the Nazi horrors, Wagner's music represents a vivid reminder of that regime. In 1981, the Israel Philharmonic Orchestra prepared to play Wagner's *Tristan und Isolde* as an encore. Conductor Zubin Mehta said that Israel was a democracy in which all music should be played and said listeners who might be offended were free to leave. (Two orchestra members had, at their request, been excused from playing the encore.) Some older members of the audience quietly got up and went home. A few continued for a while to protest noisily, even running threateningly onto the stage, but the piece was played to the end. In August 1995, Wagner's opera *The Flying Dutchman* was broadcast on Israel radio for the first time since being unofficially banned in Israel after Kristallnacht in 1938.

391. "Jerusalem of Gold"   ("Yerushalayim Shel Zahav") Naomi Shemer's moving song was performed for the first time on Independence Day, May 15, 1967, and became the city's unofficial anthem.

392. "Abanibi"   Israel's entry in the 1978 Eurovision Song Contest was the winner, the first victory for Israel in the event.

393. "Hallelujah"   Israel won the 1979 Eurovision Song Contest for the second consecutive year with this entry.

394. Israel Rocks   Many of the world's leading rock and pop acts have toured Israel, including Michael Jackson, Madonna, Brian Wilson, Bob Dylan, and the Boys Choir of Harlem.

395. Israeli Kiss   Gene Simmons, the cofounder of the rock band Kiss, noted for his makeup and tongue-wagging, was born Chaim Witz in Haifa, August 25, 1949.

396. *Habimah* (The Stage)   The first professional Hebrew theater was established in Russia in 1917. The company relocated to Palestine in 1931. In 1958, *Habimah* became the National Theater of Israel.

Museums and Art

397. Museum of the Jewish Diaspora (*Beit Hatefutsoth*)   Opened in Tel Aviv on Israel's thirtieth birthday, May 15, 1978. *Beit Hatefutsoth* is dedicated to the history of Jewish Diaspora from the time of the exile over 2,500 years ago to modern times. The permanent exhibit is divided into six sections: Family, Community, Faith, Culture, Among the Nations, and Return to Israel. The museum also hosts numerous temporary exhibits.

398. The Israel Museum   Housed near the Knesset and Supreme Court building with nearly 50,000 square feet of exhibit space, the museum contains some 500,000 objects. Founded by Jerusalem Mayor Teddy Kollek, the museum's director is currently James Snyder, a Harvard graduate and the former deputy director of the Museum of Modern Art (MOMA) in New York City. More than 950,000 people visit the museum annually. Museum exhibits include world culture from prehistoric to modern times, a six-acre art garden, the world's most comprehensive collection of Judaica, and exhibits on the State of Israel and the history of the Jewish people. One of the most famous museum exhibits is the Dead Sea Scrolls, housed in a special building of the Israel Museum known as the Shrine of the Book. The distinctive white, domed-shaped ceiling of the building is modeled after the clay jars in which the scrolls were found. The Israel Museum started in the home of the Dizengoff family in 1932 and formally became the Israel Museum in 1965.

399. Yad Vashem   Established by Israeli law in 1953 to commemorate the six million Jews and their communities wiped out in the Holocaust. The museum's name is taken from the sentence in Isaiah that reads: "And to them will I give in my house and within my walls a memorial and a name (*yad vashem*) that shall not be cut off" (Isaiah 56:5). Located in Jerusalem on Mount of Remembrance (next to Mount Herzl), Yad Vashem's sixty-two million documents, over 267,500 pictures, and 90,000 books are the largest and most comprehensive archive and information repository on the Holocaust. The Historical and Art Museums, as well as the Hall of Remembrance, Valley of the Communities, Children's Memorial, and other monuments attest to the tragic events that befell the Jewish people and instruct visitors to Yad Vashem on the uniqueness of the Holocaust and its universal lessons. The Hall of Names is part of an effort to collect the names of every Jewish man, woman, and child murdered in the Shoah. To date, more than 3.2 million names of Holocaust victims have been compiled. Yad Vashem also houses the International Institute for Holocaust Studies, which teaches over 100,000 students and 50,000 soldiers, as well as thousands of educators from around the world. Yad Vashem also pays tribute to the courageous non-Jews, such as Oskar Schindler and Raoul Wallenberg, who risked their lives to save Jews from certain death. These rescuers are awarded the title of "Righteous among Nations" and have their names enshrined in the Avenue and Garden of the Righteous among Nations.

400. Righteous among Nations (*Hasidei Ummot Ha-olam*)   The official term of the State of Israel, codified in the Martyrs' and Heroes' Remembrance Law (1953), that is applied to non-Jews who risked their lives to save Jews from Nazi persecution. Israel established a commission to investigate the authenticity of every name submitted to qualify for this category. Those who are recognized are given a certificate and a medal with the Talmudic inscription "Whoever saves a single soul, it is as if he has saved the entire world." Two thousand trees have been planted on the Avenue of the Righteous, each marked by a plaque bearing the name and nationality of the Righteous Person. An additional 18,000 have their names engraved in the walls by the Garden of the Righteous.

401. Chagall Windows   "The Twelve Tribes of Israel," stained-glass windows created by Marc Chagall, are on display in the synagogue at Hadassah Hospital in Jerusalem. Chagall's inspiration for the motifs on the windows was the Bible. It took two years for Chagall and his assistant to complete all the windows. The windows were dedicated on February 6, 1962, and they were exhibited in New York and Paris before being installed in the hospital's synagogue. Chagall refused to accept a fee when he was commissioned to design the windows. During the 1967 war, several windows were damaged and Chagall repaired them, leaving a small bullet hole in one as a reminder of the conflict.

Sports

402. Israel's First Olympic Team   Israel was represented in the Olympic Games for the first time at the Helsinki Summer Games in 1952.

403. **1980 Olympic Boycott**   Israel joined the United States and some sixty other nations in boycotting the 1980 Summer Olympics in Moscow to protest the Russian invasion of Afghanistan.

404. **Olympic Medal I**   Yael Arad became the first Israeli to capture an Olympic medal when she won a silver medal in judo at the 1992 games in Barcelona.

405. **Olympic Medal II**   Two days after Yael Arad won Israel's first Olympic medal, Oren Smadja took a bronze medal in judo at the 1992 Olympics at Barcelona.

406. **Olympic Medal III**   Israeli windsurfer Gal Friedman won a bronze medal at the 1996 Summer Games in Atlanta.

407. **Olympic Medal IV**   After the influx of Russian immigrants, many of whom were outstanding athletes, Israel had high hopes for collecting several medals at the 2000 Summer Olympics in Sydney. In the end, only one Israeli won a medal, Michael Kalganov, the bronze medalist in kayaking. Still, this was the third consecutive summer Olympics in which Israel collected a medal.

408. **Olympic Medal V**   Arik Ze'evi won a bronze medal in judo at the 2004 Summer Games in Athens.

409. **Olympic Medal VI—Striking Gold**   In 2004 Israel won its first Olympic gold medal when Gal Friedman won the windsurfing event. He dedicated the medal to the Israeli Olympians who were killed during the 1972 Munich Games.

410. **Winter Olympics**   Figure skater Misha Shmerkin, an immigrant from Russia, became the first athlete to represent Israel at the Winter Olympics when he competed in figure skating in Nagano, Japan, in 1998. In Nagano, Galit Chait and Sergei Sakanovsky represented Israel in the ice dancing competition.

411. **World Title**   Israel's first world title in any sport came in 1969 when Zefania Carmel and Lydia Lazarov captured a yachting title in the Team 420 Non-Olympic Sailing Class at Sandham, Sweden. Carmel also won the championship in the individual event.

412. **Israel Excluded from Playing**   Israel was banned from participating in the Fourth Asian Games in Jakarta in 1962. In 1976, Israel was expelled from the Asian Games Federation. Israel has been barred from participating in the Mediterranean Games since they began in 1951 as well as from the Arab Games since 1974. Additionally, many athletes from the Islamic world refuse to compete against Israeli athletes. As recently as the 2004 Summer Olympic Games, Iranian world champion judoka Arash Mir-Esmaeili withdrew from the Olympics instead of facing his Israeli opponent Ehud.

413. **Flawless Basketball**   In Israel's professional basketball league, one team remains the team to beat. In 2004, Maccabi Tel Aviv won its 44th basketball championship. They are the only team to represent Israel in the European Basketball Championships.

414. European Basketball Championship I   Maccabi Tel Aviv, an Israeli basketball team, captured first place in the European basketball competition in 1977.

415. European Basketball Championship II   Maccabi Tel Aviv recaptured the European title in basketball in 1981.

416. European Basketball Championship III, IV, V, and VI   Maccabi Tel Aviv won four European basketball titles in a span of six years, winning the competition in 2000, 2001, 2004, and 2005.

417. Kayaking Champ   Michael Kalganov became the first Israeli to receive a gold medal in the world kayak championships in June 1998.

418. Top Pole Vaulter   Israeli pole vaulter Alexander Averbukh won the gold medal in the 2000 European indoor pole vaulting championship in Belgium. Averbukh cleared nearly nineteen feet on his first try. He had immigrated to Israel from Russia more than a year before. In August 2002, Averbukh was killed by Palestinian violence in the Intifada.

419. Judo Triple   Arik Ze'evi won the title in the European Judo Championships in the under-100-kilo category in 2001, 2003, and 2004. During the 2004 competition Yoel Rozbozov won a silver medal in the under-73-kilo category.

420. Windsurfing Winner   Gal Friedman won windsurfing's Mistral World Championship in Thailand in 2002, becoming the first Israeli to win the event.

421. Woman Winner   In September 2003, nineteen-year-old Lee Korsitz won the gold medal in the women's mistral event at the World Sailing Championship in Cadiz, Spain, becoming the first female Israeli athlete to win a world championship in any sport.

422. Israeli in the NHL   Max Birbraer, an immigrant to Israel from Kazakhstan, was picked in the third round of the 2001 National Hockey League draft by the New Jersey Devils, becoming the first Israeli in the professional hockey league.

423. It's All Downhill   Mount Hermon in the Golan Heights is home to Israel's sole ski resort.

424. Maccabiah Games   Held in Israel every four years, the Maccabiah Games are named for Jewish warrior Judah Maccabee who led the revolt against the ancient Greeks. Many notable athletes have competed in the Maccabiah, including swimmer Mark Spitz, swimmer Lenny Krayzelburg, gymnast Mitch Gaylord, golfer Corey Pavin, basketball players Ernie Grunfeld and Danny Shayes, basketball coach Herb Brown, and tennis player Dick Savitt. The Maccabiah Games are the third-largest sporting event in the world. Only the Olympics and the Commonwealth Games attract more athletes.

425. Maccabiah I (1932)   The first Maccabiah Games was nicknamed the "White Horse Olympics" because Tel Aviv Mayor Dizengoff led a parade honoring the games through the city streets while riding a white horse. The opening ceremony witnessed the release of 120 carrier pigeons, ten pigeons for each of the twelve tribes of Israel, whose mission was to send to the world news of the opening of the first Maccabiah games. Approximately 390 athletes from fourteen countries participated in the competition.

426. Maccabiah II (1935)   These games were held despite official opposition by the British Mandatory government. A German delegation of 134 Jews flouted Nazi Germany's order not to attend the games, and the delegation refused to fly the German flag during the opening ceremonies. The games became known as the "Aliyah Olympics" because many of the athletes from the various countries chose to remain and settle in Israel. With few exceptions, the Bulgarian delegation stayed in Israel, sending home their sports equipment and musical instruments. A total of twenty-eight countries were represented by 1,350 athletes.

427. Maccabiah III (1950)   Originally scheduled for 1938, the event was postponed because of the international political situation and British fears of an upsurge in illegal immigration. The first games to be held after the Holocaust and the establishment of the State of Israel were attended by 800 athletes representing nineteen countries.

428. Maccabiah IV (1953)   This Maccabiah initiated the tradition of bringing from Modi'in, Judah Maccabee's birthplace, the torch used to light the flame at the opening ceremony. A total of 890 athletes from twenty-one countries participated.

429. Maccabiah V (1957)   Some Eastern European countries did not send delegations to protest the Sinai Campaign. Competitors included American weight-lifter and Olympic gold medalist Isaac Berger and Australian national tennis champion Eva Dulding. Hungarian Agnes Kleti, who won ten Olympic medals (five gold) over three Olympic games, performed in two exhibitions. The policy of playing the Maccabiah every four years was established.

430. Maccabiah VI (1961)   The International Olympic Committee endowed the Maccabi World Union with Olympic standing and declared the Maccabiah a "Regional Sports Event." American Dick Savitt won two gold medals. Exhibitions were performed by two American Olympic medalists, Rafer Johnson (decathlon) and John Thomas (high jump). The event had 1,000 competitors from 27 nations.

431. Maccabiah VII (1965)   Several well-known athletes won medals, including swimmer Mark Spitz (winner of seven gold medals in the

Munich Olympics), swimmer Marilyn Ramenofsky (then USA record holder and silver medalist in the Rome Olympics in the 400-meter freestyle) and international tennis player Tom Okker (Holland). This Maccabiah was the first international competition in which fifteen-year-old Mark Spitz participated.

432. Maccabiah VIII (1969)   Wimbledon winner Julie Heldman participated in the eighth Maccabiah. Some 1,500 participants from 27 countries competed in the games.

433. Maccabiah IX (1973)   This event was dedicated to the eleven Israeli Olympians murdered by terrorists during the 1972 Munich Olympics.

434. Maccabiah X (1977)   "The Jubilee Maccabiah" marked twenty-five years of Maccabiah competition. More than 2,700 competitors from thirty-three countries participated.

435. Maccabiah XI (1981)   The games honored the memory of Maccabiah World Union President and International Maccabiah Games Committee President Pierre Gildesgame, who died in a car accident. Thirty countries sent 3,450 competitors to play in the games. Dan Shayes, the future Denver Nugget, played for the American basketball squad.

436. Maccabiah XII (1985)   Olympic legend Mark Spitz opened the games by lighting a torch with the help of three children of Israeli Olympians murdered at the Munich Olympics. Four thousand athletes from forty countries attended the games. The Junior Maccabiah was established.

437. Maccabiah XIII (1989)   The opening torch was carried by former world swimming champion Hanoch Budin, an IDF disabled veteran. The event brought together 4,500 athletes from forty-five countries.

438. Maccabiah XIV (1993)   Mor than 5,000 athletes from 48 nations competed in these games.

439. Maccabiah XV (1997)   Former Montreal Canadien coach Jacques Demers led a Canadian hockey squad consisting of numerous NHL players, and Canadian tennis player Debbie Schwartz participated and medaled in the games. The event was marred when a pedestrian bridge used by the athletes during the opening ceremonies collapsed; four Australian athletes were killed and more than sixty people were injured. More than 5,000 participants from fifty-three countries competed in the games.

440. Maccabiah XVI (2001)   Due to a stepped-up terrorism campaign by Palestinians that included suicide bombings and shootings, several countries and athletes pulled out of the Maccabiah games weeks before the opening ceremonies. The U.S. team almost canceled as well, and many urged world organizers to postpone the games until 2002. Israel pleaded for participants not to give in to terrorism. Larry Shyatt, Clemson University's basketball coach, withdrew as coach of the American men's basketball team, and most players followed his lead. NBA Hall of Famer Dolph Schayes and newly appointed head coach Herb Brown convinced the players to participate in the games. At the opening ceremonies, Olympic swimmer and triple gold medal winner Lenny Krayzelburg carried the American flag.

Miscellaneous

441. Israel Prize   Established in 1953, the prize is awarded for outstanding work and achievement in Jewish studies, humanities, social sciences, exact sciences, science, and the arts. In 1972, an additional Special Prize was established for contributions to the advancement and development of society and the state. Winners of the prize include Lipman Halpern (medicine), Golda Meir (Special Prize), Yigal Yadin (Jewish studies), S. Y. Agnon (Hebrew literature), and Yuval Ne'eman (exact science). The prize is awarded when deemed appropriate by the governing committee: some years no awards are bestowed; other years witness multiple winners.

442. Wolf Prize   Established in 1978 by German-born Ricardo Wolf and his wife Francisca Subirana-Wolf. Dr. Wolf, an inventor, diplomat, and philanthropist, lived in Cuba and served as Fidel Castro's ambassador to Israel from 1961 to 1973. When Cuba severed ties with Israel in 1973, Dr. Wolf decided to remain in Israel. The Israel-based Wolf Prize is awarded to outstanding scientists and artists, "for achievement in the interest of mankind and friendly relations among peoples." The annual prizes of $100,000 are given in four out of five scientific fields in rotation: Agriculture, Chemistry, Mathematics, Medicine, and Physics. In the arts, the prize rotates among Architecture, Music, Painting, and Sculpture.

443. The Malcha Mall   The Jerusalem Mall in Malcha, built in 1992, is the largest mall in the Middle East.

444. McDonald's   The first McDonald's in Israel opened in Ramat Gan on October 14, 1993.

445. Miss Universe   Israeli Rina Mor-Messinger won the crown in 1976, the first Israeli woman to do so.

446. Russian Miss Israel   A new immigrant from Russia, 20-year-old Yana Hodriker was named Miss Israel in 1993.

447. Miss Europe   Israeli Lilakh Ben-Simon was named Miss Europe in 1994.

448. Miss World   Linor Abargil, an 18-year-old Israeli student, was crowned Miss World in November 1998.

449. Arab Miss Israel   In 1999, 21-year-old Rana Raslan became the first Arab woman to be named Miss Israel.

450. Mrs. World I   Sima Bakhar was crowned Mrs. World in February 2005.

RELIGION

451. Freedom of Religion   Israel's Declaration of Independence states that Israel "will guarantee freedom of religion and conscience, of language, education, and culture. It will safeguard the Holy Places of all religions." The Supreme Court ruled that even though the Declaration of Independence is not law, this excerpt "expresses the nation's vision and its credo" and should be taken into consideration "when we attempt to interpret or clarify the laws of the State." Compliance with these principles has also been assured through criminal law.

452. Religious Communities   There are fifteen distinct religious communities recognized by the Israeli government: Muslim, Jewish, Eastern Orthodox, Latin (Catholic), Gregorian Armenian, Armenian (Catholic), Syrian (Catholic), Chaldean (Uniate), Greek (Catholic), Melkite, Maronite, Syrian Orthodox, Druze, Episcopal-Evangelical (since 1970), and Bahai (since 1971). All of the religious communities (with the exception of the Episcopal and Bahai) have religious courts endowed with legal jurisdiction over matters of personal status. Priests of the various communities are responsible for celebrating marriages and notifying the authorities of any changes in registration status.

453. Religious Courts   Each recognized religious community has legal authority over its members in matters of marriage, divorce, maintenance, guardianship, and adoption. Secular courts have primacy over questions of inheritance, but parties, by mutual agreement, may bring cases to religious courts. Jewish and Druze families may ask for some family status matters, such as alimony and child custody in divorces, to be adjudicated in civil courts as an alternative to religious courts. Christians may ask that child custody and child support be adjudicated in civil courts as an alternative to religious courts. Muslims have not had recourse to civil courts in family-status matters.

454. The Holy City   Jerusalem is the only city in the world holy to three major religions—Judaism, Christianity, and Islam.

455. Belief in God   According to surveys, roughly 90 percent of Americans believe in God, while only 30 percent of Israelis do.

Judaism

456. *Mishpat Ivri*   Term referring to those laws in Judaism that pertain to relations between people (to the exclusion of rules governing the human-God relationship). *Mishpat Ivri* has been quoted in Israeli Supreme Court decisions and has contributed to the formation of the laws of the State of Israel. In matters of personal jurisdiction, rabbinical court decisions are endowed with legal authority.

457. Rabbinical Courts   During the British Mandate, Jewish law was endowed with legal authority over all issues of personal status in the Jewish community (e.g., marriage, divorce, adoption). This situation continued after the establishment of Israel and was codified by the Knesset in 1953, granting the rabbinical courts exclusive jurisdiction over marriage and divorce, and concurrent jurisdiction in adoption, succession, and conversion.

458. Chief Rabbinate   This religious institution was given legal authority by the British in 1920. It consists of two Chief Rabbis, representing the Ashkenazic and Sephardic communities. The first Chief Rabbis of Israel were Rabbi Abraham Isaac Kook (Ashkenazic) and Rabbi Jacob Meir (Sephardic). The current Chief Rabbis are Ashkenazi Rabbi Yonah Metzger and Sephardi Rabbi Shlomo Amar.

459. Hechal Shlomo   Located in Jerusalem, this complex includes rabbinical courts, a library, and a museum of religious items. It is the Chief Rabbinate of Israel's official seat. Named by Sir Isaac Wolfson, who contributed most of the construction cost in memory of his father, Hechal Shlomo, the complex opened in 1958.

460. Prayer for Israel   A Prayer for the Welfare of the State was written by the Chief Rabbinate in 1948. The prayer is recited in synagogues around the world on the Sabbath and Jewish holidays.

461. Institute for Science and Halacha   Established as a nonpolitical joint venture by four Orthodox organizations (Machon Harry Fischel, the Organization of Orthodox Scientists, the Organization of Orthodox Engineers, and Yad Harav Herzog), the institute is dedicated to applying technology to solve halachic problems in the modern era—for example, soldiers performing tasks on the Sabbath.

462. The Western Wall (*Kotel*)   A remnant of the supporting wall of the Temple Mount, this wall is the only intact structure remaining from the second Temple period (70 C.E.). The Western Wall plaza serves as a gathering place for Jews to pray because it is the location closest to where the Temple stood. The mourning and crying over the destruction of the Temple at this location is the source of the moniker the Wailing Wall, a term not used by Jews. The stones that make up the wall average 3.5 feet in height (1 meter) and ten feet in length (3.3 meters). The largest stone in the Western Wall is twelve yards long and four yards wide and weighs 300 tons. Between 1949 and 1967, in violation of the armistice agreement, Jordan denied Jews access to the Wall.

463. The Wall Reopens   After its capture, the Western Wall was first opened to the Israeli public on June 14, 1967, marking the Jewish holiday of Shavuot. Approximately 200,000 Jews prayed at the Wall that day.

464. Scrolls of the Wall   During the Yom Kippur War, when the tide of battle did not favor Israel, the rabbis in the army removed the Torah scrolls kept at the Western Wall and brought them to the battlefront, reminiscent of ancient times when the ark containing the Ten Commandments would be brought with the Jewish army into battle.

465. Oldest Synagogue   The Zealot's Synagogue on Masada, believed to have been built during 66–73 B.C.E., is considered the oldest synagogue in Israel.

466. The Abouhav Miracle and Curse   According to legend, the sixteenth-century Abouhav synagogue in Safed was destroyed in the great earthquake of 1837, but, miraculously, the wall containing the Holy Ark survived. Today, the rebuilt synagogue has two arks, one that is opened only on the High Holy Days and Shavuot, and another for other occasions. Locals believe that anyone who fails to observe this custom is cursed. As proof, they say the Torah scrolls had to be temporarily removed from the special ark because of a renovation project. Within a year, all twelve men who shared the task died.

467. Bnei Akiva   The world's largest religious Zionist youth organization was established in Jerusalem in 1924. With a motto of *"Torah va-Avodah"* (Torah and labor), the organization believes in an ideal that combines Torah adherence and pioneering the land of Israel.

468. Naturei Karta (Guardians of the City)   A small, extreme, ultrareligious sect who view the establishment of Israel as a sin. A 1935 splinter from Aguddat Israel, the group is concentrated in Jerusalem. Some members do not recognize the authority of the government, refusing to vote, hold identity cards, or recognize the competency of courts.

469. Who Is a Jew?   On June 24, 1958, the National Religious Party pulled out of the governing coalition and forced new elections because the government passed a law establishing that a person can be registered as a Jew in Israel if both parents claim the child is Jewish. Traditional Jewish law requires a child's mother to be Jewish for the child to be considered a Jew.

470. Autopsy Demonstration   On April 18, 1967, more than 10,000 Haredi Jews rallied against the autopsy performed on Rebbetzin Rachel Nardel without the family's consent and in violation of Jewish law.

471. Shabbat Protest   In one of the periodic protests against automobile travel on the Sabbath, 12,000 Hasidim turned out on July 14, 1977, to demonstrate in Bnei Brak.

472. Bones of Contention   In August 1981, ultra-Orthodox Jews staged the first of many protests against archaeologists they believed were digging in ancient Jewish cemeteries. In this case the protest was over a dig in the City of David. The controversy went all the way to the Supreme Court, which ultimately ruled the dig could continue.

473. The Seven Species of Israel Listed in the Bible   The Seven Species listed in the Bible were the staple foods consumed by the Jewish people in the Land of Israel during biblical times. They were: olives, grapes, wheat, barley, figs, pomegranates, and dates.

Christianity

474. Church of the Holy Sepulcher   Christians revere the church as the site of the death, burial, and resurrection of Jesus Christ. In the fourth century, Helena, the mother of Emperor Constantine and a convert to Christianity, traveled to Palestine and identified the location of the crucifixion in Jerusalem; her son then built a magnificent church. The church was destroyed and rebuilt several times over the centuries. The building standing today dates from the twelfth century.

475. Keys to the Church   Control of the Church of the Holy Sepulcher is zealously guarded by different denominations. The Greek Orthodox, Roman Catholics, Armenians, and Copts are among those that oversee different parts of the church. In the twelfth century, fighting among different denominations over who should keep the key to the church led the Arab conqueror Saladin to entrust the key to the Muslim Nuseibeh and Joudeh families. Today, eight centuries later, the ten-inch metal key is still safeguarded in the house of the Joudeh family. Every morning at dawn, Wajeeh Nuseibeh, who took over the job of doorkeeper from his father more than twenty years ago, picks up the key and opens the massive wooden church doors. Every night at 8:00 p.m. he returns to shut and lock them. Recently, a second door to the church not controlled by the Nuseibeh family was built for safety reasons.

476. Via Dolorosa   The "Way of Suffering" is the route Christians believe Jesus traveled carrying the cross from his trial to the place of his crucifixion and burial. Fourteen stations along the route commemorate incidents that occurred along the way. The first seven stations wind through the Muslim Quarter and the next two are placed in the Christian Quarter. The last five are inside the Church of the Holy Sepulcher. The tradition of following the Via Dolorosa dates to the Byzantine period. The stations commemorate where Pontius Pilate sentenced Jesus to death; Jesus was given the cross he had to carry; Jesus first fell while carrying the cross; Mary saw her son; Simon the Cyrene began to help Jesus carry the cross; Veronica wiped the face of Jesus; Jesus fell a second time; Jesus comforted the women of Jerusalem; Jesus fell a third time; Jesus' clothes were removed; Jesus was nailed to the cross; Jesus died; Jesus was taken down from the cross; and the burial place of Jesus.

477. The Mount of Beatitudes   Overlooking the Sea of Galilee, this is where Jesus is believed to have preached the Sermon on the Mount. Today, an Italian convent sits on this hill. It was built in 1937 under the auspices of Mussolini.

478. The Jerusalem YMCA   The American Association of the YMCA sent director Archibald Harte to Jerusalem. He promptly fell in love with the city and wanted to build a center in which the three monotheistic religions would find expression. Arthur Louis Harmon, the man who designed the Empire State Building, was hired for the job. He infused construction of the building with religious symbolism: the forty columns in the forecourt arcades represent the Jews' years of wandering in the desert and Jesus' days of temptation; the twelve windows in the dome of the auditorium represent the tribes of Israel, the disciples of Jesus, and the followers of Muhammad; and the four corners of a section of the tower that houses the carillon have symbols of the four Evangelists. Contributions from American and British YMCAs and the Jewish community of Manchester enabled the purchase of the site for the YMCA from the Greek Patriarchate. On April 18, 1933, the Jerusalem YMCA, located opposite the King David Hotel, was opened by Field Marshall Lord Allenby. From the top of the 50-meter tower one has a panoramic view of Jerusalem and its environs. The YMCA has 35 carillon bells, a library of 50,000 volumes in five languages, and a Jewish–Arab kindergarten where some 130 youngsters learn to live and play together.

479. Papal Delicacy   The olives of the oldest olive tree in Jerusalem's Garden of Gethsemane (derived from the Aramaic for "oil press"), where Jesus was arrested by the Romans, were flown to the Vatican especially for Pope John Paul II.

480. Vatican Recognition of Israel   The Vatican refused to recognize the State of Israel until the signing of the Fundamental Agreement between the Church and the State of Israel on December 30, 1993.

481. Papal Visit I   On January 5, 1964, Pope Paul VI made an 11-hour visit to Israel during which he defended the actions during the Holocaust of Pope Pius XII, whom Jews accuse of remaining silent and failing to use his influence to save European Jews.

482. Papal Visit II   Pope John Paul II arrived in Israel on March 21, 2000, for a historic five-day visit, during which he visited the holy sites of the three major religions and met with Israel's political leaders and Chief Rabbis. Though ostensibly a trip focused on religion, the Pope also touched on political issues, blessing Israel, expressing support for a Palestinian homeland, and apologizing for sins committed by Christians against Jews.

483. Christmas Trees   Every year Jerusalem distributes about 1,200 free Christmas trees to local Christian leaders, foreign diplomats in Israel, foreign media, and others who celebrate Christmas.

Islam

484. Dome of the Rock   This shrine was built between 685 and 691 by Caliph Abd al Malik ibn Marwan as a shrine for Muslim pilgrims. It covers the rock where Muslims believe Mohammed ascended to heaven. Jews believe it is the place where Abraham prepared to sacrifice his son Isaac and where the

Holy of Holies of King Solomon's temple was located. The shrine (it is not a mosque) is located on the Temple Mount and is still used today. The building's magnificent gold dome overlooks the Western Wall and has become a symbolic image of Israel. In 1994, under the auspices of King Hussein of Jordan, the dome was completely reconstructed and regilded with 80 kilograms of 24-karat gold.

485. Well of Souls   Under the rock in the Dome of the Rock is a chamber known as the Well of the Souls. This is where Muslim tradition believes the souls of the dead congregate.

486. Mohammad's Hair   Inside the Dome of the Rock is a box containing two hairs that Muslim tradition holds belonged to Mohammad.

487. Al-Aksa Mosque   At the southern end of the Temple Mount is the gray-domed Al-Aksa mosque. The name means "the distant one" and refers to the fact that it was the most distant sanctuary visited by Mohammed. It is also the place where Mohammed experienced the "night journey," which is why it is considered the third holiest Islamic shrine after Mecca and Medina.

488. Al-Aksa Fire   In August 1969, a mentally ill Australian tourist, Michael Rohan, set fire to the Al-Aksa mosque. Israel was blamed by the Muslim world for the incident.

489. Mufti of Jerusalem   A Mufti is the person responsible for interpreting Muslim law and is held in high esteem by the population. The Mufti's opinion is expressed in a document called a *fatwa*. The Mufti of Jerusalem is one of the leading religious authorities. During the Mandate period, the Mufti of Jerusalem, Hajj Amin Husseini, was the most influential cleric and politician in the Palestine Arab community and an instigator of much of the violence in the country. Today, the Mufti has far less influence in both the political and religious realms.

490. Waqf   Under Ottoman rule, from 1517 to 1917, a religious foundation, or Waqf, administered the Islamic holy places in Jerusalem, including the Temple Mount. Under British Mandatory rule, a Supreme Muslim Council administered the Muslim holy places. Since 1948, the Waqf has administered Muslim sites in West Jerusalem, and its authority was extended in 1967 to East Jerusalem as well. The Waqf has authority over the Temple Mount.

HEALTH AND MEDICINE

491. Doctors in Israel   Israel has the highest per capita number of physicians in the world.

492. Ethiopian Doctor   In November 1999, twenty-seven-year-old Avraham Yitzhak became the first Ethiopian immigrant to earn an MD degree.

Yitzhak graduated from Ben-Gurion University of the Negev's medical school in Beersheba. Yitzhak came to Israel in 1991 from Addis Ababa, three weeks before Operation Solomon brought 15,000 Ethiopian Jews in a mass airlift.

493. Life Expectancy   In 2004, the average life expectancy for men in Israel was 77.08 years; for women it was 81.37. In 2002, the United Nations ranked Israel's life expectancy of 79.1 eighth highest in the world, higher than that of the United States.

494. Infant Mortality   The infant mortality rate for Israel is 7.37 per 1,000 live births. By comparison, the figure for the United States is 6.75. Japan has the lowest rate, 3.30.

495. Oldest Jewish Hospital   The first Jewish hospital, Rothschild Hospital, was set up in 1854 in the Old City of Jerusalem.

496. Shaare Zedek Medical Center   In 1873, the Central Committee for the Construction of a Jewish Hospital in Jerusalem was established to build a hospital capable of serving Jerusalem's Jewish population of 8,000. The committee raised money from around the world. Years later, in 1902, the committee's efforts resulted in the opening of Shaare Zedek, the first Jewish hospital in Jerusalem outside of the Old City Walls. Dr. Moshe Wallach was appointed the first medical director of the hospital, which started with only twenty beds and an outpatient center. During the Six-Day War, Shaare Zedek Hospital, located near the battle lines, treated 450 wounded soldiers and performed 200 operations in a 70-hour span. Today, Shaare Zedek's 500-bed facility treats more than 200,000 patients annually.

497. Hadassah Hospital   Located on Mount Scopus, Hadassah Hospital opened its doors in 1938. The hospital was the idea of Hadassah, the Zionist women's organization in the United States. The American Jewish Physicians Committee, formed by Albert Einstein, Chaim Weizmann, and the 82,000 members of Hadassah, raised funds for the project. The 200-bed hospital was completed in 1938 at a cost of $1 million. Patients from many lands, including neighboring countries, were treated in the hospital when it opened. On April 13, 1948, an armed group of Arabs ambushed a convoy of doctors and nurses on their way to the hospital, killing seventy-eight. The hospital stopped functioning and was cut off from the Jewish population of Jerusalem. An alternate site was chosen in Ein Karem, at the other end of the city, and Jerusalem's second Hadassah Hospital was built there. In 1978, the Hadassah Hospital on Mount Scopus was reopened. Today the institution boasts over 850 doctors, some 2,000 nurses, 1,000 beds, and 31 operating areas. Approximately one million people are treated at the hospital annually.

498. Magen David Adom (Red Shield of David)   Originally established in 1930 as the medical unit of the Haganah, the organization now acts as Israel's emergency medical services, operating under a Knesset law passed in

1950. In 1948, the organization requested membership in the League of Red Cross Societies, consisting of the Red Cross, Red Crescent (Muslim), and the Red Lion and Sun (Iran). The request was denied, ostensibly because the Star of David was not an acceptable symbol, making the Magen David Adom the only national first-aid society not recognized as an official member. The International Red Cross has yet to admit the Magen David Adom. The organization runs first-aid stations and blood donor programs and has some 6,000 volunteers working throughout Israel.

499. Yad Sarah   A volunteer organization with a budget of over $12 million that helps some 380,000 people annually by lending medical equipment on a short-term basis for anyone in need. Yad Sarah has a stock of approximately 300,000 items and 300 types of medical rehabilitative equipment, including crutches, wheelchairs, beds, and oxygen pumps. Founded in 1976, Yad Sarah's over 6,000 volunteers and 103 branches throughout the country make it Israel's largest volunteer organization. Yad Sarah also makes over 34,000 home visits a year and provides meals-on-wheels, transportation and day care centers, dental clinics, laundry, and other services for the elderly or handicapped. In June 2003, Yad Sarah signed an agreement with the government of Uzbekistan to advise on building an organization in Uzbekistan that caters to 10,000 children of special needs. In November 2004, a delegation from South Korea visited Yad Sarah to explore setting up a similar organization in their country.

500. Jerusalem Syndrome   Documented mental illness in which people who visit Jerusalem believe they are the messiah or some other biblical figure.

501. Road Rage   More Israelis have died in traffic accidents than in all the wars and terrorist attacks combined.

502. Handicapped Space   Israel was the first country to grant handicapped drivers permanently assigned parking spaces in front of their homes.

503. Biggest Sperm Bank   The sperm bank at Tel Aviv's Ichilov Hospital is reported to be one of the world's largest, with 50,000 frozen doses.

504. Paternity Leave   Fathers of newborns in Israel are given paid leave. They also are given time off for the day of the *bris* (circumcision), if the child is a boy.

505. Multiple Births   In 1999, 60 women from Jerusalem gave birth to their seventeenth child. Approximately 2,600 Jerusalem women give birth to their seventh child each year.

506. Medical Innovations   Israel is at the forefront of technological innovations in medicine, including developing 80 percent of the world's biotechnology; the first ingestible video camera; the first fully computerized diagnostic for breast cancer; pioneering technology for CAT scans; and cutting-edge ER management techniques.

EDUCATION

507. Hebrew University   The stones for Israel's first university were laid on July 24, 1918. The land upon which the university stands (Mount Scopus) was acquired by Isaac Goldberg. The first lecture was given in 1923 by Albert Einstein, two years before the formal opening of the institution. After the War of Independence, Mount Scopus was an Israeli stronghold completely surrounded by Arab-held territory. Resupply convoys supported the hilltop. Since studies could not take place at the besieged university, a second campus was constructed in Israeli-controlled West Jerusalem. In 1967, the original facility was reopened. Today, 24,000 students from all over the world study at Hebrew University in such diverse disciplines as science, business, agriculture, history, and philosophy. Since its inception, the institution has granted more than 120,000 bachelor's, master's, and doctoral degrees. Hebrew University owns the rights to Einstein's likeness.

508. Bar-Ilan University   Established in 1955 and named in honor of Rabbi Meir Bar-Ilan (Berlin), a spiritual leader who led traditional Judaism from the ashes of Europe to rebirth and renaissance in the Land of Israel. Its mission is to blend Jewish tradition with modern technologies and scholarship. Bar-Ilan endeavors to teach the ethics of Jewish heritage while providing a first-rate academic education and to bridge the gap between religious and secular Israelis. The first president was its founder, Pinkhos Churgin (1955–1957). The seventy-acre campus is located east of Ramat Gan, outside of Tel Aviv. Today, Bar-Ilan boasts libraries containing over one million volumes and a student body of more than 32,000.

509. Tel Aviv University (TAU)   Established in 1956 with the merger of three schools, Tel Aviv University is the largest university in Israel and the biggest Jewish university in the world. Sitting on approximately 220 acres in the Ramat Gan neighborhood of Tel Aviv, the university boasts 28,000 students, 2,200 faculty members, over 100 departments, and ninety research institutes, including the Jaffee Center for Strategic Studies. TAU offers numerous undergraduate, graduate, and doctoral programs, including medicine, law, business administration, education, the arts, and humanities.

510. Ben-Gurion University of the Negev   Built in 1964, the university of the Negev was renamed in 1973 to commemorate the recent death of Prime Minister David Ben-Gurion who often espoused the dream of developing the Negev. Located in Beerheba, the university has approximately 17,000 students and offers degrees in engineering sciences, humanities and social sciences, health sciences, and management. Ben-Gurion University is spearheading the development of the Negev and has an expertise in desert research. Other areas of development research include immigrant absorption, urban renewal, environmental issues, biotechnology applications to industry, and solar energy use.

511. The University of Haifa   Located on Mount Carmel, the only liberal arts university in northern Israel has a student body of some 13,000 students. The university offers graduate and undergraduate degrees in humanities, social sciences, law, science and science education, and business. The University of Haifa is also home to one of the few IBM research centers found outside of the United States.

512. Weizmann Institute of Science   A leading multidisciplinary research center boasting a staff of 2,500 scientists, technicians, and research students. The Weizmann Institute grew out of the Daniel Sieff Research Institute, which was founded in 1934 with just ten scientists and ten technicians, by Israel and Rebecca Sieff in memory of their son. The driving force behind its establishment was the Institute's first president, Dr. Chaim Weizmann, a noted chemist who later became the first president of Israel. On November 2, 1949, with the agreement of the Sieff family, the Institute was renamed and formally dedicated as the Weizmann Institute of Science.

513. Technion Israel Institute of Technology   Israel's first engineering university was founded in 1912 but didn't open until 1924 because of the onset of World War I and an internal dispute over whether the school should teach in German, the native language of many of the scientists, or in newly revived Hebrew, the language ultimately chosen. The school's graduates represent over half of all Israeli-educated scientists and engineers and more than 70 percent of all domestic founders and managers of high-tech industries. Technion has over 13,000 undergraduate, master's, and doctoral students. The Technion faculty boasts two Nobel Prize laureates and is where genetic evidence was discovered that proves Jews who are *Cohanim* (of the priestly blood line) can trace their lineage directly to Aaron, the High Priest named in the Bible.

514. Bezalel School   Israel's school for the arts is named after the biblical Bezalel, whom Moses asked to build the Tabernacle. It was founded in Jerusalem in 1906 by Boris Schatz.

515. Yeshiva University   The New York City institution has been a longtime hotbed of Zionist activity. Two Yeshiva University students died in the 1929 Hebron riots. The first American to die during the War of Independence was Moshe Pearlstein, a Yeshiva University graduate. During every war, Yeshiva University students flocked to Israel to serve as doctors and soldiers, and in any other capacity needed. More than 2,000 alumni from Yeshiva University live in Israel, and more than 500 students study in Israel every year through Yeshiva University's study abroad program.

516. Ulpan   An institution established by the Israeli government in September 1949 to teach Hebrew to adult immigrants.

517. Gadna (*Gedudai Noar*—Youth Battalions) Established in 1948, Gadna is a government-sponsored organization responsible for training teens in self-defense, swimming, shooting, and Israeli geography. Members are also given the opportunity to participate in numerous projects, including building settlements, assisting in immigrant absorption, and assisting archeological excavations.

518. Literacy Rate The adult literacy rate of Israeli Jews is 97 percent. The rate for Israeli Arabs is 90 percent. Israel's overall literacy rate of 95 percent is the highest in the region. By comparison, the rate for Iran is 79 percent, Saudi Arabia 79 percent, Syria 77 percent, Egypt 58 percent, and Iraq 40 percent.

519. Schools There are four types of schools in Israel: state schools, state religious schools (emphasizing Jewish studies), Arab and Druze schools, and independent schools (affiliated with various Orthodox sects). Education in Israel is compulsory for 11 years, from age five to fifteen.

520. First Hebrew High School The world's first Hebrew high school, the Gymnasia Herzliya, opened in Jaffa in 1905.

Science and Technology

521. Going Nuclear In June 1960, Israel's first nuclear reactor went online at Nahal Sorek.

522. Quirks and Quarks In 1975, Weizmann Institute physicist Haim Harari was the first to suggest that there should be six types of quarks, the most elementary particles, rather than the four that scientists already knew about at that time. He called these the bottom and top quarks. The former was found in 1977, but the latter's existence was not confirmed until 1994.

523. Ofek 1 On September 19, 1988, Israel became the first Middle Eastern country to launch a satellite.

524. Turig Prize In 1996, Weizmann Institute mathematician Amir Pru-eli won the Turing Prize, the computer science equivalent of the Nobel Prize, for his work on verifying the correctness and reliability of computer systems.

525. First Israeli Astronaut Ilan Ramon became Israel's first astronaut when he joined the crew of the Space Shuttle Columbia that was launched on January 16, 2003. Ramon, along with his six crewmates, died on February 1, 2003, when the Columbia broke apart during reentry into the atmosphere. He trained for the space flight at NASA's Johnson Space Center in Houston. Ilan Ramon was a colonel in the IAF and was one of the pilots who destroyed Iraq's nuclear reactor in 1980.

526. Nobel Prize in Economics In 2002, Daniel Kahneman won a Nobel Prize in economics for "having integrated insights for psychological research into economic science, especially concerning human judgment and decision-making under uncertainty." He was born in Tel Aviv, holds dual Israeli and American citizenship, teaches at Princeton, and is a fellow at the Hebrew University.

527. Nobel Prize in Chemistry   In 2004, two Israelis, Aaron Ciechanover and Avram Hershko, shared the Nobel Prize for chemistry with American Irwin Rose for their research in explaining how the immune system attacks faulty proteins to protect against such diseases as cancer. Both Israelis are affiliated with the Technion.

528. Technology Innovation   Israel has been at the forefront of technological innovation, including serving as the site of the development of: the cell phone by Motorola, Intel's Centrino processor and Intel's Pentium MMX chip, Instant Messenger, much of Windows NT, voice mail, and the first PC antivirus.

529. Most Engineers   Israel has the world's highest per capita number of engineers.

Business and Economy

530. Pound for Pound   The Palestine pound was the legal tender in Israel until September 15, 1948, when it was replaced by the new Israel pound, the lira.

531. Newly Minted Coins   In August 1948, the Israeli Treasury minted its first coins, in part because of a shortage of coins in Israel that had led to the illegal issuing of tokens. The first coin minted was 25 mils, made of aluminum, and had a picture of a cluster of grapes modeled after a coin from the Bar-Kokhba war against the Romans. This set a precedent followed to this day of using designs from ancient Jewish coins for new Israeli ones. Coins are dated according to the Jewish calendar year.

532. Commemorative Coin   The first Israeli commemorative coin was issued in 1958 in honor of the state's tenth anniversary.

533. The Shekel   Israel's currency unit is mentioned in the Bible as a weight measurement used for gold and silver currency (e.g., Genesis 24:22, Genesis 23:16). The Jews used the shekel upon their Exodus from Egypt. The shekel reappeared in modern times at the First Zionist Congress as the moniker of the fee for Zionist membership (originally set at 1 frank—the equivalent of 50 cents). The shekel replaced the lira as Israel's monetary unit in 1970.

534. EL AL   Israel's national airline was founded in 1948 as a means of transportation for incoming Jewish immigrants. Its maiden flight brought the president of the provisional government, Chaim Weizmann, from Geneva to Israel on November 15, 1948. EL AL's first fleet consisted of DC-4 and C-46 planes. By 1949, EL AL was flying scheduled routes between Israel, Rome, and Paris. In 1950, regularly scheduled flights also flew to Athens, Vienna, Zurich,

London, Nairobi, Johannesburg, and New York. Today, EL AL carries nearly three million passengers on her twenty-eight Boeing jets. EL AL has one of the best safety records in the industry and has developed a reputation for tight and effective security.

535. Zim (Israel Navigation Company, Ltd.)   Established in June 1945 by the Histadrut, the Jewish Agency, and the Palestine Maritime League to create a domestic fleet capable of weaning Israel off of her dependency on foreign shipping. Zim is the term used in the Bible to refer to ships (Num. 24:24). In 1965, the first Israeli-constructed ship, the *Esther*, was built in Haifa and delivered to Zim. Today Zim is the tenth-largest container shipping company in the world. It operates more than eighty vessels and has become the dominant force in Israeli shipping.

536. Israel Bonds   Established on September 3, 1950, when David Ben-Gurion, Israel's first prime minister, met with a group of 50 American and Israeli leaders in Jerusalem's King David Hotel and decided to bring the idea of Israel Bonds to the American public. In October 1950, Golda Meir met with American Jewish leaders in Washington, D.C., to plan the launch of Israel's first bond issue in the United States. The Development Corporation for Israel (originally founded as the American Finance and Development Corporation for Israel) was created in February 1951 to offer the securities in the United States. The Knesset adopted a law authorizing the flotation of Israel's first bond issue, known as the Israel Independence Issue, representing the first time Israel asked for a public loan instead of a philanthropic gift. In May 1951, Ben-Gurion officially launched the Israel Bond Organization at a rally in Madison Square Garden. A coast-to-coast tour to build support followed and generated $52.6 million in bond sales for Israel. When Golda Meir was asked what collateral she could offer, she said the only collateral she had was the children and future of the State of Israel. Israel bonds are backed by the full faith and credit of the Government of Israel, which has maintained a perfect record of repayment of interest and principal since the first bond was issued more than 50 years ago. Israel Bonds are rated "investment grade" by both Moody's and Standard & Poor's. Through 1999, Israel Bonds have raised more than $25 billion on behalf of the State of Israel.

537. Highest Inflation Rate   Inflation grew at a rate of 444.9 percent during 1984, the highest inflation rate in Israeli history.

538. Economic Stabilization Plan   The combination of shouldering the enormous defense burden imposed by Arab hostility, dependence on imported raw materials and fuel, and the high cost of absorbing waves of destitute immigrants and providing them with a full range of social services led to extensive borrowing and a huge foreign debt. The cumulative impact of these expenditures over the years triggered a crisis in 1984–1985. Foreign reserves plummeted, unemployment reached an eighteen-year high, and inflation raged at nearly 450 percent. Israel requested economic assistance from the United States, but Secretary of State George Shultz insisted that Israel first undertake economic reforms that included budget cuts, tighter control of the money supply, and devaluation of the shekel. When Israel took these and other steps, President Reagan approved a $1.5 billion emergency aid program, which helped save the Israeli economy from collapse, stimulated the recovery that reduced inflation from triple digits to the low double digits (dropping to zero in 2000), and laid the groundwork for Israel to have one of the world's fastest growth rates just a decade later.

539. Israel's Budget   For the year 2004, Israel passed an austere budget of approximately $51 billion.

540. GNP Growth   Israel's national product grew at the average rate of 10 percent annually from 1948 to 1973, one of the highest rates in the world.

541. GDP   In 2004, the Israeli gross domestic product was estimated at $120.9 billion. Israel's per capita GDP was approximately $19,800 in 2004, up from $5,800 in 1950. Internationally, Israel ranks as the thirty-fifth-richest country based on per capita income.

542. Histadrut   (*Ha-Histadrut Ha-Kelalit Shel Ha-ovdim Be Eretz Yisrael*—General Association of the Workers in the Land of Israel)   Founded as a Jewish trade union in December 1920, the Histadrut adhered to the principles of the Russian-Jewish socialist movement. The Histadrut actively participated in Jewish cultural activities, the settlement of Palestine, and the revival of the Hebrew language. In the early days of the Zionist movement and the State of Israel, the Histadrut was one of the most powerful and influential institutions of the country. In the 1920s, roughly 75 percent of the Jewish workers in Palestine belonged to the Histadrut. The Histadrut not only dominated the economic landscape but was closely tied with the Labor political parties that monopolized political power until 1977. Today, Arab workers receive full membership and accompanying rights if they join the Histadrut. The union itself ultimately became the largest employer in Israel. The Histadrut, strongly associated with the left-leaning Labor Party, conducts extensive economic programs, mutual aid, and cultural activities. The organization owns leading banking, industrial, export, insurance, and building companies, and its health system, *Kuppat Holim*, is the largest in the country.

543. Trade Bridge   Israel is the only country with free trade agreements with both the United States and the European community, which enables Israel to act as a bridge for international trade between America and Europe.

544. EU Trade Deal   On November 20, 1995, Israel and the European Union signed a trade agreement to provide a framework for political dialogue and to strengthen economic relations between the EU and Israel. The "Treaty of Association" established an association between Israel and the EU based upon the principle of reciprocity, giving expression to the special relations prevailing between Israel and the EU. Israel can participate in the EU's research and development committees (without voting privileges). Israel is one of only two countries, the other being Switzerland, that are not EU members but have the right to take part in EU R&D projects. With regard to industrial products, the agreement forbids customs duties from being imposed on imports and exports between Israel and the EU. In 2000, Israel became an associate member of the EU.

545. Natural Resources   Israel's principal natural resources are copper, phosphate, bromide, potash, clay, sand, sulfur, bitumen, and manganese.

546. Agricultural Products   Israel's main agricultural products are citrus and other fruits, vegetables, beef, dairy, flowers, and poultry.

547. Fruitarians   Israelis are the biggest per capita consumers of fruits and vegetables in the world.

548. Got Milk   A cow from an Israeli kibbutz was cited as Israel's top milk producer after it produced an average of some 16,000 quarts per year. The statistic was released ahead of the Shavuot holiday, when dairy foods are traditionally eaten.

549. Big Citron   In 1999, a huge *etrog* (citron)—about 10.5 x 8 inches, weighing 8.6 pounds—was found in Neot Kedumim during the Sukkot holiday. The Guinness Book of World Records certified it as the world's largest.

550. Major Industry   Israel's major industries are food processing, diamond cutting and polishing, textiles and apparel, chemicals, metal products, military equipment, transport equipment, electrical equipment, potash mining, high-technology electronics, and tourism.

551. Imports   Israel imported over $32 billion worth of goods in 2004. Israel's principal imports are military equipment, rough diamonds, oil, chemicals, machinery, iron and steel, textiles, vehicles, ships, and aircraft. Roughly 20 percent of Israel's imports come from the United States.

552. Exports   Israel exported some $30 billion worth of goods in 2004. The United States is Israel's biggest international market, buying almost 40 percent of all exports. Principal exports are machinery and equipment, cut diamonds, chemicals, textiles and apparel, agricultural products, and metals.

553. Military Exports   Israel exported some $4.1 billion worth of military equipment in 2002, and $3 billion in 2003 and 2004. In 2003 *Defense News* ranked Israel the third-largest exporter of military equipment, behind only the United States and Russia. It is estimated that Israel has captured more that 10 percent of the worldwide military export market.

554. Trade Partners   Israel's main trading partners are the United States, European Union, India, Hong Kong, Japan, and South Korea.

555. Work Force   In 2004, Israel had a labor force of approximately 2.6 million, with unemployment hovering above 10 percent. In 1996, workers were employed in the following industries: public services, 31.2 percent; manufacturing, 20.2 percent; finance and business, 13.1 percent; commerce, 12.8 percent; construction, 7.5 percent; personal and other services, 6.4 percent; transport, storage, and communications, 6.2 percent; agriculture, forestry, and fishing, 2.6 percent.

556. High-Tech   Israel has the world's highest density of high-tech start-ups, nearly 4,000 in a country of six million. *Wired* magazine ranked Israel as the fourth most influential high-tech hub in the world in July 2000. The top three were Silicon Valley, California; Boston, Massachusetts; and Stockholm, Sweden.

557. Israeli Stocks on Wall Street   More than 120 Israeli companies are listed on Wall Street exchanges. Only Canada has more non-U.S. listings. These companies' presence on the American Stock Exchange, NASDAQ, and New York Stock Exchange is a tangible testament to Israel's growing importance in global trade and business.

558. R&D Leader   Israel is a leader in technology and ranks first in the world in the percent of its gross domestic product it invests in research and development.

559. Computer Crazy   Approximately 70 percent of Israelis have computers at home, the highest per capita percentage in the world.

560. Heavy Web Users   Some 50 percent of Israeli household have high-speed Internet access. This compares to just 22 percent of households in the United States and some 10 percent throughout Europe.

561. Heavy Cell Phone Users   Israel has one of the highest percentages of cellular phones per capita in the world. The penetration rate of mobile phone subscription is 95 percent.

562. Transit for the Masses   Israel is one of the only countries where every town has bus service. In 1948, Israel had a total of 965 buses and the cost of a ticket was less than one cent. Today, Israel has approximately 5,800 buses.

THE LAND OF ISRAEL

Archaeology

563. The Rockefeller Museum   Increased archaeological activity in the Holy Land in the first decades of the twentieth century prompted the need for a dignified venue to store and exhibit the finds. American philanthropist John D. Rockefeller donated $2 million for building, equipping, and maintaining a museum, and the British Mandatory government also provided a subsidy. Rockefeller stipulated that the museum, originally called the Palestine Archeological Museum, be an archaeological, not a natural science museum, and that the museum's exhibits should shed light on the part played by the people of the Holy Land in world history. The building was to be located opposite the northeast corner of Jerusalem's Old City walls. After 1948, when the area came under Jordanian rule, the museum was administered briefly by an international council, but, recognizing its tremendous value, the Jordanian government soon nationalized it. In 1968, the management of the Rockefeller Museum was transferred to the Israel Museum.

564. The Dead Sea Scrolls   A Bedouin shepherd stumbled upon a cave full of clay jars in the Dead Sea region in 1947. Inside the jars were well-preserved scrolls. The shepherd sold three of the seven scrolls he found to an antiquities dealer in Bethlehem, who in turn sold them to archaeologist Eliezer Sukenik. The four remaining scrolls found their way to the United States and were purchased in 1954 by Professor Sukenik's son, Yigal Yadin, on behalf of the government of Israel. Over the years, thousands more fragments of parchment, some papyrus and some leather, were found and pieced together into eighty documents. Today, the majority of the Dead Sea Scrolls have been interpreted and published. Since 1965, a selection have been on display at the Israel Museum in the Shrine of the Book exhibit. The scrolls are significant because they contain the oldest known copy of the Old Testament. Fragments of all twenty-four books of the Hebrew Bible were found in the caves (the only exception being the Book of Esther). Many scholars believe the scrolls date back to 100 B.C.E.

565. The Tomb of the Kings   The largest tomb in Jerusalem is located north of the Old City. Named for its association with the kings of Judah, the Tomb of the Kings is actually the tomb of Queen Helena of Caucasus, who converted with her family to Judaism in the first century and built a palace in Jerusalem. According to Josephus Flavius, she died in Adiabene, but her remains and those of some family members were transferred for burial in the mausoleum she had built for her family in Jerusalem.

566. Tombs of the Unknowns   From the Mount of Olives can be seen the conical-roofed Absalom's Tomb and the pyramid-roofed Zechariah's Tomb. These are tombs of anonymous second-century citizens of Jerusalem and have nothing to do with their biblical namesakes. The names were given to the structures by Jewish pilgrims in the Middle Ages who got the idea from the biblical passage, "Absalom in his lifetime had set up for himself the pillar which is in the King's Valley—and it is called Absalom's monument to this day" (II Samuel 18).

567. The City of David   Excavations in the City of David, today the village of Silwan, just south of Jerusalem's Old City walls, show that the site has been continuously occupied for some 5,000 years. Jerusalem also appears in several ancient documents, apart from the Bible. The earliest known reference dates to 1900 B.C.E. in the so-called Execration Texts. The names of the enemies of the Egyptian ruler were inscribed on pottery, which was then smashed in the hope of bringing destruction upon them. Jerusalem at that time was apparently an enemy of Egypt, as indicated by letters written on clay tablets found in the ruins of Amarna, the palace of Pharaoh Akhnetan. In one tablet, dating to the fourteenth century B.C.E., Abdu-Heba, the king of Jerusalem, pledges his loyalty to the Egyptian ruler.

568. Not a Surviving Relic of Solomon's Temple   A thumb-sized ivory pomegranate, 43 millimeters high, was thought to be the only surviving artifact from the Temple. A partial inscription on the pomegranate reads: sacred donation for the priests of the house of [Yahwe]h. The item was purchased by the Israel Museum in the 1980s from an anonymous source by placing $550,000 into a secret Swiss bank account. The pomegranate was one of the prize pieces of the Israel Museum until December 2004, when the museum announced that it was a forgery.

569. The Western Wall Tunnel   A portion of the Western Wall has stood exposed above ground level for 2,000 years. Excavations began following the Six-Day War to expose additional portions of the Wall. Archaeologists found a medieval complex of subterranean vaulted spaces. This complex ends at Wilson's Arch, named after the explorer who discovered it in the middle of the nineteenth century. Debris and construction from later periods were removed to reveal the entire length of the Herodian Western Wall. One section was discovered in pristine condition, exactly as constructed by Herod.

570. Tunnel Affair   Many Muslims were upset by the excavation of the Western Wall tunnel, falsely claiming it was conducted under the Temple Mount and endangering their holy places. The sensitivity of the issue discouraged Israeli officials from opening an exit to the tunnel, which ended in the Muslim Quarter. On September 24, 1996, Prime Minister Netanyahu ordered the exit opened in the middle of the night, prompting Arab protests. Over the next several days, sixty-nine Palestinians and eleven Israeli soldiers died in clashes over the decision. The exit remains open.

571. The Cardo   A colonnaded street extending along the north-south axis of the Old City that was built by the Romans. The Cardo was roughly 74 feet wide, divided by two rows of stone columns into a broad street flanked on either side by five-meter-wide covered passageways. Shops lined the street along its southwestern part; more shops were located behind the arcade of arches. The Cardo linked the Holy Sepulcher and the Nea Church. A nearly

660-foot-long section of the original street, thirteen feet below present-day street level, has been excavated and transformed into a modern shopping area, reminiscent of the market of 1,500 years ago.

572. Arch of Titus   An arch erected in Rome to commemorate General Titus' victory over Judea, conquering of Jerusalem, and destruction of the Temple in 70 C.E. The Arch depicts the victorious general, the captive Jews, and the furnishings of the Temple and its sacred objects being carried to Rome. Traditional Judaism bars Jews from walking under the arch. A cast from the relief of the Arch is in Beit Hatefutsoth in Tel Aviv.

573. Treasure Chest   Archaeologists excavating a Byzantine synagogue near Ein Gedi found a cash box with about 5,000 coins.

574. Acre's Crusader History   According to legend, a bulldozer working on the street pavement chipped a corner off a Turkish building and sand poured out. Archaeologists arrived and, as tons and tons of sand were removed, a huge and magnificent Crusader hall with three massive columns in the center supporting a cross-vaulted ceiling was revealed.

575. Roman Aqueduct   The Romans built an aqueduct near Caesarea in the second century. It still stands today, stretching roughly six miles, though much of it is now buried under the sand.

576. Jesus' Boat   A 26-foot-long fishing boat discovered on the bottom of the Kinneret in 1986, was dated by carbon-14 testing to a period around 40 B.C.E. Because Jesus is believed to have preached in the area around 30 C.E., it became known as the "Jesus boat." Because of its age and condition, the boat would disintegrate if its waterlogged wood dried out, so the boat was placed in a chemical bath at the Yigal Allon Center on Kibbutz Ginossar for seven years before being exposed to air. In February 2000, the boat was put into a new enclosure that makes it more accessible to the public.

577. Belvoir Castle   A Crusader castle constructed by the Knights Hospitalers in 1140 was conquered by Saladin in 1189 and dismantled in 1218 to prevent a Crusader reoccupation.

578. Montfort Castle   Originally built by the French Crusaders, the castle was captured by Saladin's army in 1187. The Crusaders recaptured it in 1192. It was ultimately overrun in 1271 by Sultan Baybars.

579. Largest Old Synagogue   Capernaum, a site better known for its association with the life of Jesus, is the home of the largest of the ancient synagogues found in Israel. Its main hall measures about 75 feet by 57 feet. There is some debate as to whether it was built in the third or fourth century.

580. Megiddo   The city of Megiddo dates back more that 5,000 years. Archaeologists have identified twenty-five distinct towns built on top of each other. The city was continuously inhabited for more than 3,500 years. Megiddo was strategically located along the Via Maris, one of the ancient world's roads that connected Egypt, Syria, Canaan, and Mesopotamia. Megiddo is the setting for the first recorded battle in history—the 1479 B.C.E. invasion of Canaan by Egyptian Pharaoh Thutmose III. Megiddo is mentioned in the Bible in Joshua 12:21. The New Testament refers to the location as Armageddon, a derivation of the Hebrew for Mount Megiddo, *Har Megiddo*. According to the book of Revelation, Megiddo is the location for the battle that will be fought when the forces of good triumph over the forces of evil. The city was completely destroyed following the Persian invasion of Palestine some 2,300 years ago and is now an archaeological site.

581. Discovered Remains   The remains of soldiers uncovered by archaeologists are given a proper Jewish military burial even if they fell in battles centuries earlier.

582. Pet Cemetery   Archaeologists have unearthed a large cemetery for dogs in Ashkelon. About 700 skeletons were found. No one knows the significance of this cemetery or why dogs would have merited this treatment; however, the assumption is that dogs were considered sacred and played a role in local healing rituals. This is one of the few ancient dog cemeteries in the world.

ENVIRONMENT

583. Nature Reserves   Israel has more than 150 nature reserves protecting roughly 2,500 types of indigenous wild plants, 20 species of freshwater fish, 400 breeds of birds, and 70 varieties of mammals. The Israel Nature and National Parks Protection Authority manages the nature reserves and national parks. The authority is also reintroducing into the wild species that have become extinct from the region. About twenty reserves have been developed for public use with visitors' centers, roads, and hiking trails, which attract more than two million people every year.

584. Nature Symbol   The symbol of the The Israel Nature and National Parks Protection Authority and the Ein Gedi Reserve is the ibex, a mountain goat that resembles an antelope.

585. National Parks   The The Israel Nature and National Parks Protection Authority, established by the Knesset in 1963, runs over forty national parks, including unique archaeological sites such as those at Masada, Caesarea, and Acre.

586. Ramon Crater   Located south of Beersheba in the Central Negev, Mitzpe Ramon is usually referred to as a crater, but it is not an impact crater from a meteorite. It is actually a *maktesh*, a valley surrounded by steep walls and drained by a single *wadi* (riverbed). The world's largest *maktesh*, it is twenty-five miles long, up to five miles wide, and 1,300 feet deep. Ramon's 154 square miles exposes layers of the earth that date back over 200 million years. The crater was created by erosion. It was not discovered until after the 1948 war.

587. A Pillar of Salt   Visible from the road south of the Dead Sea, rising from an eleven-mile range of pure salt, is Mount Sodom. On top of the mount stands a block of salt tourists are told is Lot's wife, who was turned into a pillar of salt for ignoring God's admonition not to look back when he destroyed Sodom and Gomorrah.

588. Gateway for the Birds   Approximately one billion birds traverse the area between the Mediterranean coast and the Jordan mountains, making southern Israel the site of one of the greatest concentrations of migrating birds in the world. Israel also hosts approximately 85 percent of the world's stork population.

589. The Iranian Donkey   A rare species of donkey was flown from Iran to the Hai Bar Nature Reserve only hours before revolutionaries closed the airport in 1979.

590. Hot Spot   The highest temperature ever recorded in Israel was 131 degrees F in June 1942 at Tirat Zevi in the Beth Shean Valley.

591. Earthquakes   Two significant earthquakes have struck Israel in the last two centuries. The first occurred in Safed on January 1, 1837, killing roughly 5,000 people and virtually destroying Tiberias. Tremors were felt as far south as Jerusalem. The second earthquake struck on July 11, 1927. The epicenter was located near Jericho, but the effects were felt in Lebanon, Transjordan, and the Negev. The death toll was 350.

592. Environmental Innovation   Israel has been at the forefront of environment-related innovations, including development of systems for: drip irrigation, detecting toxins in water, detecting gas and chemical leaks, and detecting sulfur and phosphorus compounds in the atmosphere.

593. Environmental Education to the World   Israel shares its expertise in environmental science by teaching some 10,000 trainees from more than 100 countries. Topics include techniques for growing and cultivating tropical and subtropical fruit, breeding and genetic improvement of sheep and cattle, and fruit crops and marketing.

Water

594. Water Supply   Israel has three main water sources: the coastal and mountain aquifers and Lake Kinneret (Sea of Galilee). Each source supplies approximately 25 percent of the total water consumed. Roughly 20 percent is derived from smaller aquifers. The remaining 5 percent comes from the Shafdan project that recycles sewage in metropolitan Tel Aviv.

595. Rain   The rainy season in Israel falls between October and May. During the rest of the year, precipitation does not fall in Israel. During the rainy season, Jews around the world insert into their prayers a plea for rain in Israel.

596. Gihon Spring   In a land as dry as the Land of Israel, a central consideration in determining the location of a city or village is its proximity to a water source. The only permanent water source of ancient Jerusalem was the Gihon Spring. Its name is derived from the fact that it doesn't flow steadily but rather erupts in random spurts (*Giha* in Hebrew means eruption).

597. Hot Springs of Tiberias   The ancient town of Hammat, which is located just outside of Tiberias, boasts the hottest (140° F) mineral springs in Israel.

598. Johnston Mission   In 1953, President Eisenhower announced the appointment of Eric Johnston as his special representative to undertake discussions with Israel, Egypt, Jordan, Syria, and Lebanon on a comprehensive plan for the development of the Jordan Valley. The engineers and lawyers of all sides agreed that the division of the waters he proposed was fair and reasonable, and that the proposed project would benefit the countries concerned. Jordan likely stood to gain the most, as a considerable area of the lower reaches of the river in Jordan territory could have been irrigated and opened to settlement by Palestine refugees living in refugee camps. Two hundred thousand refugees, it was said, could be so settled. Johnston's plan was derailed, however, by the Syrians, who would not agree to anything that would benefit Israel, even if the Arab states would achieve even greater benefits.

GEOGRAPHY

599. Size of Israel   The area of the State of Israel is 7,850 square miles, roughly the size of New Jersey. The area of Judea and Samaria is approximately 2,200 square miles.

600. Israel vs. Arab states   The Arab League's 21 states consist of approximately 5,414,000 square miles.

601. Beachfront Property   Israel's coastline is about 170 miles long.

602. 1967 Border   Prior to the Six-Day War, Egypt controlled the Gaza Strip, Syria retained the Golan Heights, and Jordan held the West Bank and the Eastern section of Jerusalem. At its narrowest point, Israel's borders were within nine miles of the Israeli coast, eleven miles from Tel Aviv, ten from Beersheba, twenty-one from Haifa, and one foot from Western Jerusalem.

603. "Green Line"   This was the demarcation between the 1967 borders of Israel and the West Bank territories captured in the Six-Day War. The reference came about because someone used a green pen on the map of the armistice agreement with Jordan to draw the border.

604. Golan Heights   A mountainous region overlooking northern Israel and southeastern Syria that was separated from the Palestinian Mandate in the 1920s. From 1948 to 1967, the Golan Heights served as a base for Syrian sniper and artillery attacks against Israeli settlements, causing hundreds of casualties. In 1967, Israel captured the Golan Heights, and in 1981, the Golan Heights Law subjected the region to Israeli law. Only 15 miles wide (at its widest) and 45 miles long, the Golan Heights towers 3,000 feet above the Sea of Galilee and is where the headwaters of the Jordan River are located. The Heights' steep slopes serve as a natural defense against armored attack. In biblical times, the Golan Heights was referred to as "Bashan"; the word *Golan* apparently derives from the biblical city of "Golan in Bashan" (Deuteronomy 4:43, Joshua 21:27). More than half of the area's 34,000 residents are Druze.

605. Mount Hermon   The highest mountain "in Israel," Mount Hermon rises to 9,220 feet (2,810 meters) above sea level. Located in the Golan Heights on a mountain range that runs through Lebanon, the mountain has a peak visible from a distance of sixty miles. Today, the mountain serves as a critical early warning station for the Israeli army. It straddles Israel's border, and both the United States and Syria have stations on the mountain. The top elevation under Israeli control is *Mizpe Shelagim*, the "Snow Observatory," 7,300 feet (2,224 meters) above sea level.

606. Galilee (*Ha-Galil*)   The term for Israel's northernmost region that makes up over one-third of Israel's area. This mostly mountainous region is mentioned in the Old and New Testaments.

607. Valley of the Rift   A fault line runs from southern Turkey through Syria, extends southward through Israel, and ends around Lake Victoria in Malawi, Africa. The rift created the mountains and valleys of the Galilee and is the cause of earthquakes and volcanic eruptions that have occurred over the centuries.

608. Sea of Galilee (Lake Kinneret)   Located in northeastern Israel, 695 feet (212 meters) below sea level, the sea abuts the Golan Heights and is Israel's largest freshwater body and the lowest freshwater lake in the world. The sea, which is really a lake, is shaped like a harp, *kinnor* in Hebrew, but this is not the origin of the name. Actually, Kinneret was a city on the northwestern edge of the lake during the Canaanite and Israelite periods. The New Testament contains several references to the lake, which is known alternatively as the Sea of Galilee, Sea of Tiberias, and the Sea of Gennesaret. This is where Jesus calmed the stormy sea (Matthew 8) and walked on the water (Matthew 14). The lake's 64 square miles (166 square kilometers) have a maximum depth of

57 feet (48 meters). and it feeds Israel's National Water Carrier, providing fresh water to most parts of the country. Famous for its tasty St. Peters fish, the Kinneret is also a popular recreational area, providing tourists and Israelis the opportunity for fishing, swimming, waterskiing, and boating.

609. Jordan River   A 186-mile (300 kilometer) river marking the eastern border of Israel and the West Bank. The Jordan flows southward from northern Galilee, through the Kinneret, and spills into the Dead Sea.

610. Tiberias   Located on the shores of the Sea of Galilee, Tiberius was founded by Herod Antipas, son of Herod the Great, and named for the reigning Roman emperor. Tiberias sits on the shore of the Sea of Galilee near the hottest natural mineral springs in Israel (reaching a temperature of 140 degrees Fahrenheit). It has drawn tourists from around the Middle East for thousands of years. According to the Bible, the *Sanhedrin* (Jewish religious authority) presided in Tiberias. The *Mishna* was completed in the city in 200 C.E., and the Jerusalem *Talmud* was written there in 400 C.E. Rabbi Akiva, Maimonides, and Rabbi Yochanan ben Zakkai, three of Judaism's most famous religious authorities, are buried in Tiberias. The Crusaders captured the city and made it the capital of the Galilee. Saladin defeated the Crusaders in 1187. Tiberias declined until the Turks reestablished it as a thriving city. In 1837, an earthquake devastated the city. Israel's first *kibbutzim* were established near Tiberias in the early 1900s and helped fuel the rebirth of the city. Today, the population is over 30,000.

611. Deganyah   The first kibbutz established in Palestine was founded on October 10, 1910, on one of the first parcels of land purchased by the Jewish National Fund. Deganyah was established just south of the Kinneret by twelve Jewish immigrants. During the War of Independence, Deganyah successfully halted the Syrian advance into Israeli territory. A Syrian tank abandoned in Deganyah's perimeter remains as a monument to the hard-fought battle.

612. Safed   At an altitude of 3,200 feet (900 meters), Safed is Israel's highest town. The city was first settled in Roman times and became a prominent center of Jewish learning in the late fifteenth and early sixteenth centuries. The first printing press to publish a Hebrew book was established in Safed in 1577. Saladin wrested control of the city from the Crusaders in the late twelfth century. The Crusaders recaptured Safed a half-century later and erected the largest Christian fortress in the East. The Crusaders remained in Safed until the Mamelukes seized the city in 1266. The Jewish population of the city swelled as a result of an influx of refugees fleeing the Spanish Inquisition in 1492. The city is considered a center of Jewish mysticism and the location where the teachings of the *Kabbalah* flourished. For 430 years, the Jewish community thrived in the city until continued Arab attacks drove many Jews to flee. Today, some 20,000 residents live in predominantly Jewish Safed.

613. Haifa   Situated at the foot of Mount Carmel, about 60 miles north of Tel Aviv, Haifa is the third-largest city in Israel, with a population exceeding 270,000. Haifa is first mentioned in the Talmud as a large Jewish city. However, archaeological evidence indicates that Haifa had been inhabited as far back as the Stone Age and continually until the Ottoman period. In the Middle Ages Haifa was a thriving port city. In 1099, the Crusaders captured the city and killed the entire Jewish community. Haifa fell prey to various occupiers: the Mamelukes in 1265, the Bedouins in 1750, the Turks in 1775, and the British in 1918. Two brief occupiers of the city were the French, who under Napoleon seized Haifa in 1799, and the Egyptians, who held the city from 1831 to 1840. During British control of Palestine, Haifa was a main entrance point for illegal Jewish immigration. For some 100 years, Haifa had a mixed Jewish and Arab population that enjoyed friendly relations. These relations turned sour during the 1940s, and in 1948, when the Haganah seized Haifa, most of the Arab population fled. Today, Haifa is Israel's leading seaport, a major industrial region, and a terminal for an oil pipeline stretching south to Eilat. Haifa University was established in 1964, and the Israel Institute of Technology, the Technion, was established there in 1912. Haifa is the world headquarters of the Bahai sect, and its port is a favorite stop of the United States Navy.

614. Rishon Le-Zion (First in Zion)   The first Jewish settlement was established in 1882 by ten Russian Jews. The first Hebrew kindergarten and elementary school in modern times was also started in Rishon Le-Zion. Baron Edmond de Rothschild provided funding that helped establish a wine industry, and the town is now one of Israel's principal wine centers. Rishon Le-Zion's population has risen from 11,000 in 1948 to over 200,000 today, making it Israel's fourth-largest city

615. Tirat Zvi   The first religious kibbutz, Tirat Zvi, was established in the Bet She'an Valley in 1937.

616. Nazareth   Nazareth is the largest Arab city in Israel, with a population of approximately 60,000. For years the population was split evenly between Christians and Muslims, but recently the Muslims have become a majority. Approximately 20 percent of all Christians in Israel live in the city. Nazareth was never an important site in Jewish history; it is not mentioned in the Old Testament or rabbinic literature, though Jews certainly lived there in Jesus' time. The first reference to the city is found in the New Testament (John 1:45), and even there, the town is referred to in a negative way ("Can any good thing come out of Nazareth?" 1:46). Nazareth holds deep meaning for Christians as it is the city where Jesus spent much of his life. According to Christian tradition the place where the Church of the Ascension now stands is where Jesus ascended to heaven. As a result of the role Nazareth has played in Christianity, approximately half of all tourists who come to Israel visit Nazareth.

Jews, especially new immigrants from the former Soviet Union, have recently begun to settle in Nazareth Illit (Upper Nazareth).

617. Jaffa Port   Located in the old city of Jaffa, next to Tel Aviv, the port was closed in 1965 after 3,000 years of continuous use. The port is mentioned by Pharaoh Thutmosis IV in a manuscript dating back to 1468 B.C.E. In Greek mythology, Poseidon chained Andromeda to a rock off the Jaffa coast where she was supposed to be eaten by a sea monster. Instead, she was rescued by Perseus, who married her.

618. Tel Aviv   Ahuzat Bayit was established in 1909 by 60 families as a Jewish bedroom community of Jaffa. The neighborhood changed its named to Tel Aviv in 1910. The name Tel Aviv, which means "hill of spring," was taken from Ezekiel 3:15—"and I came to the exiles at Tel Aviv"—and from Herzl's novel *Altneuland*. During World War I the Turks expelled most of the Jews from Tel Aviv. Jews returned to the city when Britain captured Palestine from the Turks in World War I. The population of Tel Aviv grew as Jews left neighboring Arab Jaffa for the safety of an all-Jewish city. By 1948 Tel Aviv was the only city in Palestine with a population exceeding 100,000. Arab forces in Jaffa shelled Tel Aviv in 1948 prior to the beginning of the War of Independence. Jewish forces responded by capturing the city two days before declaring independence. The declaration was made in the home of the city's mayor, Meir Dizengoff, because East Jerusalem was occupied by Jordan, and Tel Aviv served as the temporary capital and home of the government offices of the State of Israel. Tel Aviv is still home to foreign diplomats from countries that do not recognize Jerusalem as Israel's capital (including the United States). Today, Tel Aviv is Israel's second-largest city, with a population over 360,000. The greater metropolitan area of Tel Aviv, which includes several smaller neighborhoods, has a population of some two million inhabitants. It is the country's business and cultural center and boasts three outstanding universities, Bar-Ilan University, Tel Aviv University, and the Weizmann Institute.

619. Israel's Empire State Building   Israel's first skyscraper, the Shalom Tower, was built in Tel Aviv in 1957 on the site of the abandoned Gymnasia Herzliya. In 2003, the Moshe Aviv Tower, Israel's tallest skyscraper, opened in Ramat Gan, Tel Aviv. With 69 stories and a height of 250 meters (820 feet), it is the second-tallest building in the Middle East, dwarfed only by the Bourj al Arab Hotel in Dubai.

620. Bnei Brak   Formerly an ancient Jewish city mentioned in Assyrian sources dated 701 B.C.E. and in the *Talmud* as the location where Rabbi Akiva lived, the town of Bnei Brak was reestablished in 1924 by a handful of Orthodox Polish families. The town is famous for the strict public religious observance of its population. Men and women visiting the town are expected to dress in accordance to the rules of modesty as interpreted by the local population. On the Sabbath and Jewish holidays, streets and stores are closed. More than 120,000 residents live in the town.

621. Jerusalem Israel's capital and most populous city, boasting 700,000 residents (464,000 Jews and 289,000 Arabs), is located in the heart of the country. One of the best-known cities in the world, Jerusalem is holy to Christians (Jesus walked the Via Dolorosa on his way to crucifixion), the third-holiest city to Muslims (it is where Muhammad is believed to have ascended to heaven), and the holiest site to Jews (the location of the Temple). Jerusalem was divided between East (under Jordanian control) and West (under Israeli control) from 1948 until 1967. In 1949, in response to a UN General Assembly vote calling for the internationalization of the city, the Israeli government declared Jerusalem the capital of Israel; the Knesset was thereafter moved to Jerusalem. Most countries, including the United States, do not recognize Jerusalem as Israel's capital and do not have their embassies there. Jews have constituted a majority of Jerusalem's population as far back as 1896 and a plurality since 1844. The history of Jerusalem can be traced back some 5,000 years, when it was a Canaanite city. King David captured the city around 1000 B.C.E. and established Jerusalem as the capital of his kingdom. His son, Solomon, built the first Temple in Jerusalem. In 586 B.C.E. the Babylonians captured Jerusalem and razed the Temple. The Persians took Jerusalem in 537 B.C.E. and remained in control of the region until the arrival of Alexander the Great in 333 B.C.E. Subsequent invasions brought Jerusalem under the control of the Egyptians (323 B.C.E.), Seleucids (198 B.C.E.), Romans (63 B.C.E.), Persians (614 C.E.), Romans again (628 C.E.), Muslims (638 C.E.), Crusaders (1099 C.E.), Muslims again (1187 C.E.), Ottomans (1517 C.E.), and the British (1917).

622. Name That City In the period from its capture by David until the destruction of the Second Temple, Jerusalem was known by 70 names in Jewish lore, all expressions of affection and esteem (Ag. Song 1:1), as well as by the Name of the Holy One Blessed Be He (*Baba Batra* 75b).

623. Enlightened Jerusalem When Teddy Kollek became mayor of Jerusalem in 1965, he wanted to light up the Israel Museum for a few hours each night. He discovered, however, that the city budget only had enough money to do this one night a week.

624. Jerusalem on Top Jerusalem ranks among the top 10 urban spaces to visit and the 50 "greatest places of a lifetime," according to a survey in *National Geographic Traveler* magazine.

625. East Jerusalem Before 1860, the entire population of Jerusalem lived inside walls of the Old City (what today would be considered part of the eastern part of the city). Eventually, the population expanded beyond the city walls and both Jews and Arabs began to build in new areas. By 1948, a thriving Jewish community was living in the eastern part of Jerusalem, an area that included the Jewish Quarter of the Old City. This area also contains many sites of importance to the Jewish religion, including the City of David, Mount of Olives, Temple Mount, and Western Wall. In addition, major institutions like Hebrew University and the original Hadassah Hospital are located on Mount Scopus in eastern Jerusalem. The only time that the eastern part of Jerusalem was exclusively Arab was between 1949–1967, when Jordan occupied the area and expelled all the Jews.

626. The City of David   The original City of David, the Jerusalem of ancient times, is not synonymous with the Old City. In fact, the City of David was south of the Old City of today. The area is thought to be the burial site of King David and is sacred to Christians because the "coenaculum," or room of the Last Supper, is located nearby. The City of David is strategically located near the Kidron Valley, home of the Gihon Spring, the city's water supply.

627. Christian Quarter   Located in the northwest corner of the Old City, the Christian Quarter surrounds the Church of the Holy Sepulcher.

628. Armenian Quarter   The smallest of the four quarters of the Old City, the Armenian Quarter is located in the southwest corner of the Old City.

629. Muslim Quarter   By far the largest of the Old City quarters, the Muslim Quarter is located in the center and northeast section.

630. Jewish Quarter   Located in the southeastern section of the Old City, the current Jewish Quarter dates to roughly 1400 C.E. The oldest synagogues in the quarter—the Elijah the Prophet and Yohanan Ben Zakkai—are roughly 400 years old. The Quarter was destroyed by the Jordanians during the War of Independence and rebuilt after the Six-Day War according to designs by architect Moshe Safdi.

631. The Old City Wall   Construction of the wall surrounding the Old City was initiated in 1537 by order of Sultan Suleiman I the Magnificent. The walls took some four years to complete and encompass one square kilometer. The two architects responsible for construction of the gate are believed to be buried inside the walls near the Jaffa Gate. According to legend, Suleiman ordered their deaths either because they failed to include Mount Zion within the Old City or to ensure that they did not build anything more striking than the walls themselves.

632. Lover's Lane   According to a survey published in *Yediot Achronot*, Jerusalem's Old City walls are the most romantic spot in Israel. The archaeological excavation at Caesarea came in second and the Judean desert third.

633. Number of Jerusalem Gates   The walls of the Old City have eleven gates, only seven of which are open (Jaffa, Zion, Dung, Lions', Herod's, Damascus, and New).

634. Herod's (Flowers) Gate   Named after Herod Antipas, son of Herod the Great, this entrance leads into the Muslim Quarter through the northern wall. The ornamental flowers on the stone facing has also led many to call the entrance the Gate of Flowers.

635. Damascus Gate   Located on the northern wall, it is the busiest and most magnificent of all Jerusalem's gates. It consists of one large center gate originally intended for use by persons of high station, and two smaller side entrances for commoners.

636. New Gate   So named because it was constructed relatively recently—in 1889—the New Gate was built with permission of Sultan Abdul Hamid II. The gate is located near the northwestern corner of the city and leads into the Christian Quarter.

637. Jaffa Gate   The main entrance to the Old City was built by Suleiman in 1538. The name in Arabic, *Bab el-Halil* or Hebron Gate, means "The Beloved," and refers to Abraham, the beloved of God who is buried in Hebron. This gate, located on the western side of the Old City, marked the end of the highway leading from the Jaffa coast and now leads into the Muslim and Armenian Quarters.

638. Hole in the Wall   A road allows cars to enter the Old City through a wide gap in the wall between Jaffa Gate and the Citadel. This passage was originally built in 1898 when Kaiser Wilhelm II of Germany visited Jerusalem. The ruling Ottoman Turks opened it so the German emperor would not have to dismount his carriage to enter the city.

639. Zion Gate   Located in the south, this gate was used by the Israel Defense Forces in 1967 to enter and capture the Old City. The stones surrounding the gate are still pockmarked by weapons fire. This entrance leads to the Jewish and Armenian Quarters.

640. Dung Gate   Found in the south wall, this gate is closest in proximity to the Temple Mount. Since the second century, refuse has been hauled out of the city through this gate, hence the name.

641. Lions' Gate   Located in the east wall, the entrance leads to the Via Dolorosa. Near the gate's crest are four figures of lions, two on the left and two on the right. Legend has it that Sultan Suleiman placed the figures there because he believed that if he did not construct a wall around Jerusalem he would be killed by lions. Israeli paratroops from the fifty-fifth Paratroop Brigade came through this gate during the Six-Day War and unfurled the Israeli flag above the Temple Mount.

642. Triple Gate   Dating back to the pre-Ottoman era, the three arches of this gate are located in the south wall and are sealed shut.

643. Double Gate   This entrance to the south wall is sealed shut and also dates back to pre-Ottoman times.

644. Single Gate   Constructed prior to the Ottoman period along the southern wall, the now-sealed gate led to the underground area of the Temple Mount known as Solomon's Stables.

645. Golden (Mercy) Gate   Facing the Mount of Olives on the eastern side of the Old City, this gate was constructed in the post-Byzantine period. According to Jewish tradition, the Messiah will enter Jerusalem through this gate. To prevent this, the Muslims sealed the gate during the rule of Suleiman.

646. Temple Mount   Location in the Old City of Jerusalem where the Temple stood. When the Christians controlled Jerusalem, before the Muslim conquest, the Mount was a garbage dump. Because of the holiness attached to the site, Jewish law does not permit Jews to enter the area, though most non-Orthodox Jews ignore the prohibition. The Israeli government granted the Waqf full control over the area, retaining the right of entry for security reasons only. The Dome of the Rock and Al-Aksa mosque are located on the mount.

647. The Citadel   The citadel of Jerusalem rises above the Old City Walls to the south of the Jaffa Gate. From its vantage point atop the highest hill in the southwest quadrant of the city, the Citadel was higher than any other point in the ancient city (including the Temple Mount) and served as a bulwark against attack from the southwest. Within the Citadel stands David's Tower, a tower that dates back to the sixteenth century. Today, the Citadel hosts a museum that explores the history of Jerusalem.

648. Mount of Olives   Overlooking the eastern wall of the Old City of Jerusalem, the Mount of Olives provides the name for a chain of mountains that has multiple peaks, including Mount of Olives, Mount Scopus, and Mount of Anointing. The Mount of Olives is the highest peak in the range, standing at 2,700 feet. It has been a Jewish burial site for centuries. Jewish tradition holds that this is where the Messiah will resurrect the dead. The cemetery was desecrated during Jordan's rule from 1948 to 1967, when many headstones were broken and used to pave roads and build latrines. According to Christian tradition, Jesus led his followers to the Mount of Olives on Palm Sunday and spent the following days teaching his disciples in the mountain's caves. It is also believed that following the Last Supper, Jesus went to an olive grove in Gethsemane, located on the Mount of Olives. The olive grove remains to this day and is contained by the walls of the Basilica of the Agony. The Mount of Olives is also the place where Christians believe Jesus ascended to heaven. The Bible first mentions the Mount of Olives as the location where King David hid during the rebellion led by Absalom (2 Samuel 15:30).

649. The Valley of Hell   Child sacrifices were once practiced by pagans in Jerusalem's Valley of Hinnom. The Hebrew name of the valley, *Gehinom*, became synonymous with Hell. Today, the area is frequently used for outdoor concerts and sound and light shows using the Old City walls for a backdrop.

650. Yemin Moshe   In 1860, Sir Moses Montefiore funded the construction of *Mishkenot Sha'ananim*, the first Jewish housing complex outside of the walls of the Old City of Jerusalem. The complex was situated on a hill overlooking the old city. *Mishkenot Sha'ananim* was expanded and joined by other building projects, eventually growing into the neighborhood of Yemin Moshe, which was named after its benefactor, Moses Montefiore. Near the entrance of Yemin Moshe stands a windmill that was built in 1857 to serve the new Jewish community. The windmill was never used because of a lack of wind. The architectural style of the buildings, marked by long blocks of joined dwellings, was employed to maximize defense of the settlement.

651. Mea Shearim　A Jerusalem community built in 1874 by ultra-Orthodox Jews who left the Old City for the purpose of separating themselves from secular Jewish influences. The town's name was chosen from a verse in the Bible which reads, "Then Isaac sowed in the land, and received in the same year *Mea Shearim*" (Genesis 26:12). The term Mea Shearim can mean "hundredfold," as used in the verse, or "100 gates," as intended by the founders of the community—the town was originally designed as a walled complex containing 100 residences.

652. King David Hotel　The King David Hotel, the most famous hotel in Israel, opened in 1932 on Julian's Way. Because of the role that the King David Hotel played in the history of the region, the street was renamed King David Street. The hotel has hosted exiled leaders such as King Alfonso VIII of Spain, Emperor Haile Selassie of Ethiopia, and King George II of Greece. Other famous visitors have been the dowager empress of Persia and King Abdallah I of Jordan. The British military established its military and administrative headquarters for the region in the hotel. In 1946, the Irgun blew up the wing of the hotel that served as British headquarters. The King David did not serve as a hotel again until 1967. The King David returned to its days of glory and continues to host dignitaries and diplomats from around the world.

653. American Colony Hotel　Originally a palace built around 1860, the American Colony Hotel was founded in 1902 by Christians from Chicago who agreed to let their residence serve as a hostel for Baron Ustinov. On December 9, 1917, the Turkish governor of Jerusalem took a white sheet from the hotel, then serving as a hospital, and used it to surrender to the advancing Allied armies. Today, this elegant hotel is a popular haunt for foreign journalists and a place to meet with leading Palestinians.

654. Orient House　Built in 1897 as a residence by the al-Husseini family, an influential Palestinian family, Orient House has hosted such visitors as Kaiser Wilhelm II of Germany in 1898, King Abdallah of Jordan in 1930, and the Negus of Ethiopia Haile Selassie in 1936. The building was lent by the al-Husseini family to the United Nations for use in 1949–1950. Shortly thereafter, the residence was turned into a hotel. In 1967, the hotel closed and the al-Husseini family again lived in the house. Orient House served as the PLO's unofficial representation in East Jerusalem, and many international diplomats and politicians, including European foreign ministers, have made it a point to visit Orient House when they were in Jerusalem. The building was closed by the Israeli government on several occasions, including from 1988 to 1992 by then Defense Minister Yitzhak Rabin and from 2001 to the present by Prime Minister Ariel Sharon.

655. Har Herzl   Israel's military cemetery is located in Jerusalem on the same mountain as the Holocaust memorial, Yad Vashem. Originally called *Har Hamenuchot* (Mount of Rest), the cemetery, named after Theodor Herzl, serves as a testimonial to the military and ideological history of Israel. Along with Herzl, other well-known Israelis and Zionists buried in the cemetery include Zev Jabotinsky and Hannah Szenes and former Prime Ministers Golda Meir, Levi Eshkol, and Yitzhak Rabin. On Yom Hazikaron, Israel's Memorial Day, it is customary for the prime minister to deliver an address to the nation from the military cemetery.

656. Ammunition Hill   In 1967, Jordan held this strategic area in Jerusalem near the foot of Mount Scopus. Israeli forces captured the hill in heavy fighting on their way to taking East Jerusalem on June 6, 1967. The Jordanian bunkers were left intact, and a museum was created to commemorate the battle in which thirty-six Israeli paratroopers were killed.

657. Lohammei HaGetaot (The Ghetto Fighters)   A kibbutz founded in 1949 by a small group of survivors of Jewish ghettos in Poland and Lithuania. The kibbutz, located just outside of Jerusalem, houses the Ghetto Fighters' House, a museum of the Holocaust and Jewish Resistance.

658. West Bank   The West Bank is the area located on the western bank of the Jordan River. The biblical name for the region is Judea and Samaria; however, the biblical name is now used primarily by people who do not believe Israel should withdraw from the territories. The West Bank consists of a mountainous region (the Judean hills) and a desert region (the Samarian desert) totaling roughly 2,200 square miles. The term West Bank was coined by King Abdullah in 1948 to supplant Jewish claims to the land and strengthen his grip on the region. The area was annexed by the Hashemite Kingdom of Jordan in 1950. Only Britain and Pakistan recognized Jordan's annexation. Israel captured the area in 1967. Today, over 2,310,000 people live in the West Bank, approximately 187,000 of which are Jewish and the remainder predominantly Arab. An additional 170,000 Jews live in East Jerusalem, which was under Jordanian control until 1967. Because Israel never annexed the rest of the West Bank, Palestinians there were never extended Israeli citizenship or its accompanying benefits, including the right to vote.

659. Settlements   The Jewish towns and villages built in the West Bank and Gaza Strip since the Six-Day War are usually referred to as "settlements." In many cases, flourishing Jewish communities lived in these same areas thousands of years ago. Strategic concerns led both Labor and Likud governments to establish settlements. The objective was to secure a Jewish majority in key strategic regions of the West Bank, such as the Tel Aviv-Jerusalem corridor, the scene of heavy fighting in several Arab-Israeli wars. The Likud governments also provided financial incentives for Jews to move to parts of Judea and Samaria that did not necessarily have any strategic value. Many Jews also moved to areas such as Hebron because of their historical and religious significance to the Jewish people. A third group of Jews moved to the West Bank primarily for economic reasons, that is, the government provided financial incentives to live there and the towns were close to their jobs. Today, roughly 244 settlements are in the West Bank and a handful in the Gaza Strip.

660. Jericho   Thought to be the oldest continuously inhabited town in the world, Jericho is believed to have been settled between 6,000 and 8,000 years ago. The Bible recounts how the Israelites, under Joshua, captured Jericho after God destroyed the city's walls. Jericho is a natural desert oasis located 4.5 miles west of the Jordan River. Many travelers have been attracted to the city because of its warm climate and sources of water. Largely because of a biblical prohibition against Jews settling in Jericho, the town never had a Jewish community. In the wake of the War of Independence, Arab refugee camps were set up in the region. In the Declaration of Principles signed by Israel and the PLO, Jericho was the first West Bank region handed over to the Palestinian Authority and serves as the de facto seat of the Palestinian Authority.

661. New Oasis   In September 1998, the Oasis Casino opened in Jericho. It was an Austrian-run casino catering to Israelis. It was the first large, for-profit international investment in Palestinian territory, a $50 million project intended to generate millions in tax revenues for the cash-strapped Palestinian Authority. As the only place in the region to allow gambling, it was a popular spot for Israelis otherwise reluctant to travel into the Palestinian Authority. Islam prohibits gambling, so Muslims did not use the casino. Due to the upsurge in terrorist attacks against Jews, Israelis ceased going to the casino and the Oasis closed.

662. Kefar Etzion   Established in 1943 in the Judean Hills, this was the first of four original settlements known collectively as the Etzion Bloc. Strategically located fourteen miles south of Jerusalem, the Bloc played a crucial role in Israel's War of Independence, protecting the capital's southern flank. The Bloc fell to Arab Legion forces on May 14, 1948, and the surrendering fighters were killed by an Arab mob. The settlements were razed and a Jordanian army barracks was erected in its stead. When Israel retook the area during the Six-Day War, children of the settlers who fell in defense of the Bloc reestablished the settlement. Today the Etzion Bloc consists of some fifteen communities and a population of over 20,000 Jews.

663. Hebron Hebron is the site of the Tomb of the Patriarchs (the second-holiest site in Judaism) and where King David began his rule prior to establishing Jerusalem as his capital. The city is located in the Judean Hills some nineteen miles south of Jerusalem. In 1929, immediately prior to the Hebron Massacre, 700 of the 18,000 residence were Jews. After the massacre, in which sixty-seven Jews were killed, the Jewish community began to rebuild itself. Because of the 1936 Arab disturbances, the British evacuated the entire Jewish community on the evening of April 23, 1936. In 1968, less than one year after Israel captured the city during the Six-Day War, religious settlers went to Hebron on the eve of the Passover holiday to reestablish a Jewish presence. The Israeli government barred the Jews from settling in the city center. Some 120,000 Arabs and 500 Jews live in Hebron, making the city the second largest in the West Bank.

664. Beit Hadassah First built in Hebron as a charity institute and clinic in 1893, the building took its name in 1911 when it was expanded by the Hadassah Organization, which opened a clinic to provide free medical care for Jews and Arabs. In 1929, Arabs attacked and killed Jews living near the building and destroyed the clinic. After the Arab rioting in 1936, the Jews were forcibly removed by the British, and an Arab school was opened at Beit Hadassah. After the 1967 war, Jews were barred from returning to Hebron by the Israeli government. In 1979, a group of fifty Jews (ten women and forty men) left Kiryat Arba in the middle of the night and entered Beit Hadassah by climbing through one of the building's windows. The Israeli government initially opposed allowing the Jews to stay in the heart of Hebron, but later renovated and expanded the building for its Jewish inhabitants. Today, the Jewish community in Hebron, living in Beit Hadassah and its neighboring buildings, numbers some 500 people.

665. Cave of Machpelah (Tomb of the Patriarchs) Located in Hebron, the cave is the burial place of the patriarchs Abraham, Isaac, and Jacob and matriarchs Sarah, Rebecca, and Leah. The Bible (Genesis 33:19) recounts how Abraham purchased the location to bury his wife, Sarah. The site, holy to Jews and Muslims, has been the setting for much friction between the two communities.

666. Kiryat Arba When Israel recaptured the West Bank in 1967, the government initially barred Jews from settling in Hebron. In 1971, a group of Jews erected 250 houses on the outskirts of the city and named the new town Kiryat Arba—the biblical name of Hebron. Today, Kiryat Arba is home to more than 7,000 Jews.

667. Bethlehem Bethlehem is first mentioned in the Bible as the place the matriarch Rachel is buried (Genesis 35:19) and where King David was anointed (I Sam. 16:1–13). Bethlehem is also one of the most cherished Christian cities in the world. It is the place where Jesus was born and where for hundreds of years Christian pilgrims have gone to celebrate Christmas in Manger Square. Near the square is the Church of the Nativity that was built by Helena, the mother of the Emperor Constantine, in the fourth century. Bethlehem has a population that is almost equally split between Muslims and Christians, with Muslims holding a slight majority. In Hebrew, the town is *Bet Lehem* (House of Bread), and in Arabic, it is *Bet Lahm* (House of Meat).

668. The Dead Sea   The lowest spot on earth, the Dead Sea is more than 1,373 feet below sea level (398 meters). Located in central Israel near the Masada fortress, the sea measures fifty miles long and eleven miles wide. The term *Dead Sea* was coined by the Romans because it is uninhabitable to marine life. The Hebrew name, *Yam Ha-melach* (Sea of Salt) is appropriate because the water possesses the world's highest concentration of salt and other minerals. The sea serves as a magnet for tourists who flock to the region to take advantage of the unique health benefits offered by the sea's mud and minerals.

669. Aravah   The Hebrew name for a dessert valley region that extends 112 miles south of the Dead Sea to the Gulf of Eilat. The Aravah gets less than one inch of rain a year and temperatures often exceed 100 degrees.

670. Ein Gedi   Located on the Dead Sea's western shore, Ein Gedi is a desert oasis with waterfalls, pools of water, and two large streams. Four springs, the highest starting from 656 feet above the Dead Sea, combine to provide some three million cubic meters of water annually. It is a hiker's paradise, with beautiful foliage, exotic birds, and a range of wildlife, including rabbits, deer, antelopes, ibex, fox, wolves, hyenas, and leopards. Ein Gedi is mentioned in the Bible as one of the cities conquered by Joshua (Joshua 15:61–62) and as the place where King David hid from King Saul (I Samuel 24:1–2). Ein Gedi continued to be a city until sometime in the sixth century. The Ein Gedi Nature Reserve was established in 1972 and covers an area of 6,750 acres.

671. Masada   Famed for being the site where 960 Jewish men, women, and children held out against a prolonged siege by the Roman Tenth Legion in 72 C.E. Sensing defeat, the entire community, save two women and five children, committed suicide rather than submit to Roman rule and slavery. The primary source for information about Masada is the writings of Josephus, who recorded the history of Israel during the time of the Roman conquest. Located on a Judean Desert mountaintop that overlooks the Dead Sea from a height of 440 feet, the fortress was constructed by Herod between 37 and 31 B.C.E. Today, Masada serves as a popular tourist site and is the place where members of Israel's Armored Corps are sworn into the military under the flaming banner "Masada shall not fall again."

672. Negev   The triangular southern half of Israel that consists of about half of Israel's land mass but is home to less than 10 percent of the population.

Literally translated to mean *south*, the Negev extends from Beersheba to the port of Eilat on the Gulf of Aqaba. The region covers 4,600 square miles, and its elevation ranges from a depth of 1,150 feet below sea level to 3,400 feet above sea level. Beersheba is considered the capital of the Negev, but Eilat is its most famous city.

673. Beersheba   The Bible explains that *Beersheba,* which means "The Well of the Oath," derives its name from the oath that Abraham made to Abimelech regarding wells that were in dispute (Genesis 21:27–31). Because of the water supply in the area, small towns did survive in Beersheba during the Roman and Byzantine control of the area. However, until the Turks built a small community in the early 1900s, Beersheba was where Bedouins would congregate to water their sheep and camels. Today, Beersheba is a modern city of 183,000 and home to the Ben-Gurion University.

674. Sinai Peninsula   A mostly desert land mass of 23,500 square miles (61,000 square kilometers) sandwiched between Israel and the Suez Canal waterway. The Sinai was Egyptian territory but as a result of the 1956 Sinai Campaign, Israel seized and, under heavy international political pressure, withdrew from the peninsula. Egypt concentrated her forces on Israel's border prior to the Six-Day War and again lost the territory in battle. In 1973, when Egyptian forces smashed through Israel's defensive Bar-Lev Line, only the strategic depth of the Sinai gave Israel the necessary time to mobilize her forces in time to launch a state-saving counterattack and retake the area. Israel agreed to return the Sinai Peninsula when it signed a peace treaty with Egypt. The agreement also calls for complex troop limitations on Egyptian forces in the Sinai. Because of its strategic importance connecting Africa to Asia, the Sinai Peninsula has been invaded by more than 50 different armies.

675. Sharm El-Sheikh   Located on the southern tip of the Sinai Peninsula, Sharm El-Sheikh overlooks the Straits of Tiran, the transit point between the Gulf of Eilat and the Red Sea. After the War of Independence, in violation of international law, Egypt used the location to block shipping to the Eilat port. In 1956, Israel captured the area and destroyed the Egyptian weapons aimed at the Straits. Upon Israel's withdrawal from Sinai, a United Nations force was stationed at Sharm El-Sheikh to guarantee the right of Israeli shipping through the Straits. In 1967, the international force withdrew upon Nasser's demand. Egypt immediately halted Israeli shipping, contributing to the outbreak of Six-Day War. Today Sharm El-Sheikh is a world-famous scuba diving resort known for its beautiful Ras Mohammed and Tiran reefs.

676. Eilat   Located at the southernmost tip of Israel, Eilat is a picturesque tourist destination with beautiful beaches surrounded by desert. On most days, standing atop nearby mountain peaks, one has a panoramic view of Israel, Egypt, Jordan, and Saudi Arabia. Eilat is warm all year around; even in the winter, the ocean temperature during the day hovers around 70 degrees F

(21 degrees C). During the summer, the temperature often exceeds 100 degrees F. The coral reefs in Eilat are the most northern reefs in the world and are part of the Coral Beach Nature Reserve. Eilat sits along the only land bridge between Africa and Europe and is an ideal place to watch one of the world's largest bird migrations during the fall and spring months.

677. Dimona   Located in the Negev 21.5 miles southeast of Beersheba, Dimona was established in 1955 to house immigrants and employees of the Sodom Dead Sea Works. Israel's nuclear facility is located just outside of the city. The reactor was built in the late 1950s with assistance from France. The city is also known for being the home of the Black Hebrews.

678. Gaza   Located on the southern plain of Israel, Gaza covers 140 square miles. Most Jews left the area between 1916 and 1917 because of anti-Jewish Arab disturbances. Egypt gained control of Gaza during the War of Independence and lost it to Israel in the Sinai Campaign. Israel withdrew from Gaza in 1956, recapturing it during the Six-Day War. Today, the Arab population of Gaza is just under one million. On August 22, 2005, the last Jews were evacuated from Gaza as part of Israel's unilateral disengagement. At the time of the disengagement, some 8,500 Jews lived in 21 settlements in Gaza.

WAR AND PEACE

Israel at War

679. Arab-Israel Conflict   Casualties in Arab-Israeli violence since 1940 are estimated at more than 70,000 killed.

680. Israel's War Casualties   More than 20,000 Israelis died in wars and miscellaneous engagements between Novermber 1947 and May 2005. These include 6,373 killed in the 1948 War of Independence, 776 in the 1967 Six-Day War, 2,688 in the 1973 Yom Kippur War, and 1,216 in the Lebanon War (1982–1985).

681. Tax of the Yishuv (*Kofer Ha-Yishuv*)   In November 1938 a voluntary levy was established to help finance the Haganah's activities defending the Jewish community.

682. Post-Partition Fighting   On November 30, 1947, one day after the United Nations voted for the partition of Palestine, Palestinian Arabs, joined by irregular forces arriving from Arab countries, attacked Jewish settlements. Communication and transportation between Jewish cities and towns was severed. Armed convoys used to reinforce and supply Jewish centers were under frequent attack. Jerusalem was under siege. The Haganah, with its arsenal of 15,000 rifles, a handful of machine guns, 3-inch mortars, hand grenades, and some Sten guns, was the primary force defending Jewish communities. The Irgun's 5,000 and Lehi's 1,000 men operated independently of the Haganah. By April, the tide of battle shifted and Jewish forces took the offensive. Operation Nahshon temporarily relieved the siege of Jerusalem. Haifa, Jaffa, Safed, Tiberias, and almost 100 Arab villages were captured. During this period the Haganah grew significantly, receiving boatloads of new immigrants and weapons supplied by Czechoslovakia (including antitank and antiaircraft guns).

683. Operation Nahshon   Initiated on April 6, 1948, and lasting until April 15, this operation succeeded in opening the road to Jerusalem long enough to push through three large convoys of food and weapons. In one of the largest operations of the War of Independence, 1,500 soldiers fielded by the Haganah attacked five different locations. The name "Operation Nahshon" was derived from Nahshon Ben Aminadav who was the first to jump into the Red Sea during the biblical account of the Jewish exodus from Egypt. The operation was led by Yitzhak Rabin.

684. The Burma Road   In response to the passing of the UN partition plan in November 1947, Jerusalem, then Israel's most populous city, was under siege. Unable to use existing roads to supply Jerusalem with a steady supply of food and other crucial materials, the Jews dug a new, makeshift road winding through the mountains surrounding Jerusalem. The road, opened in July 1948, broke the siege of Jerusalem and was nicknamed the Burma Road after the supply route used by the Allies in World War II.

685. War of Independence   On May 15, 1948, shortly after declaring independence, Israel was attacked by the combined might of five neighboring Arab states: Egypt, Iraq, Transjordan, Syria, and Lebanon (Saudi Arabia and Yemen supported the war effort by sending some forces). Heavily outgunned and outnumbered by the regular armies they faced, the newly formed Israel Defense Forces was on the defensive. *Kibbutzim* and Jewish outposts were overrun by Jordanian and Egyptian forces. The Arab advances were eventually halted, and Jewish forces won back much of the territory they lost and captured additional territory. A truce brokered by Count Folke Bernadotte lasted from June 11 to July 9. The truce favored the Israelis, who used the time to step up training and arms procurement.

686. Hill of the Twenty-Eight   The Haganah needed to capture a British fort that overlooked the entire Hula Valley. When efforts to dynamite the building failed, the group's commander strapped the dynamite to his back, ignited it, and threw himself at a weak point in the wall. A total of twenty-eight fighters died taking the stronghold.

687. War of Independence–Part II   When hostilities resumed after the truce ended in July, the Jews went on the offensive on all fronts. After ten days of fighting another truce went into effect on July 18. This truce, marked by frequent violations, soon broke down. On January 8, 1949, five British jet fighters flying over Israeli positions were shot down; Churchill led a number of parliament members in criticizing the British government's interference in the war. On February 24, Israel signed an armistice agreement with Egypt. This was followed by agreements with Lebanon (March 23), Transjordan (April 3), and Syria (July 20), ending the war. The armistice lines left Israel in control of 7,700 square miles, 2,500 square miles more than the UN partition plan had allotted for a Jewish state. Israel suffered 6,373 casualties—equivalent to about 1 percent of the original entire population.

688. Operation Yoav   The Egyptians, in violation of an agreement, blocked passage of Israeli convoys to the Negev, seized territory beyond the truce lines, and attacked IDF forces, setting the stage for Israeli retaliation. On October 15, 1949, Israeli forces launched Operation Yoav, a seven-day coordinated land and air operation that captured Beersheba and opened the supply routes to the Negev.

689. Tripartite Declaration   On May 25, 1950, the United States, France, and England issued a joint declaration called the Tripartite Declaration Regarding the Armistice Borders. The declaration was aimed at strengthening the armistice agreements signed by Israel and the Arab states, and to contain the conflict by controlling the introduction of weapons into the region. The parties agreed to work together to ensure the integrity of the agreed-upon armistice lines.

690. Arab Refugees   Large numbers of Arabs fled their homes before, during, and after the War of Independence. The total number of Arab refugees is in dispute, but was between 520,000–800,000. These Arabs, instead of being absorbed into the population of neighboring countries, were herded into refugee camps where many of them and their descendants have remained. A confluence of reasons prompted the Arabs to flee, including: encouragement by the Arab states to clear the way for their armies (with the expectation that the inevitable Arab victory would permit their return), Arab propaganda warning of Jewish massacres against Arab populations (the attack at Deir Yassin, albeit a rare instance, fueled this perception), encouragement by Jewish commanders (some Jewish commanders pleaded with local Arabs to remain), and expulsion.

691. Jewish Refugees   Following the establishment of Israel, some 800,000–900,000 Jews left Arab lands, many fleeing persecution and violence. Approximately 600,000 of the Jewish refugees settled in Israel, where they were quickly absorbed into the population. Most of the remainder went to Europe or the United States.

692. Undeclared War   Between 1951 and 1955, 400 Israelis were killed and 900 were injured as a result of approximately 3,000 attacks or infiltrations into Israel by Arab soldiers and terrorists.

693. *Fedayeen*   In 1955, Egyptian President Nasser introduced a new form of warfare to the Arab-Israeli conflict: terrorists called *fedayeen* (one who sacrifices himself). Nasser trained and equipped the *fedayeen* to engage in hostile action on the border and infiltrate Israel to commit acts of sabotage and murder. The *fedayeen* operated mainly from bases in Jordan so that Egypt would not bear the brunt of Israel's inevitable retaliations. The terrorist attacks violated the armistice agreement provision that prohibited the initiation of hostilities by paramilitary forces.

694. Khan Yunis   A city in Gaza where an Egyptian military installation was attacked by Israeli forces in August 1955 in retaliation for *fedayeen* attacks in Israel. Eighty Egyptian soldiers and one Israeli paratrooper were killed.

695. Kalkilya   Following a spurt of terrorist attacks launched from Jordanian territory that left 20 dead, Israel reacted by raiding a Jordanian police station at Kalkilya on October 11, 1956, killing eighty-eight Jordanian soldiers. Eighteen Israelis died in the assault.

696. Golan Heights   Responding to numerous Syrian attacks originating from the Golan Heights, the IDF struck a Syrian military outpost on December 11, 1955, killing more than fifty Syrian soldiers and capturing thirty. Four Israeli soldiers died in the action.

697. Sinai Campaign (October 29–November 5, 1956)   In 1955, Egypt procured large arms shipments from Czechoslovakia. A joint military command under Egyptian leadership was created by Egypt, Jordan, and Syria in October 1956. Egypt closed the Straights of Tiran to Israeli shipping (the Suez Canal was already closed) and assumed an offensive military posture in the Sinai. Egypt's recent nationalization of the Suez Canal played into Israeli hands, and Israel responded with a preemptive strike. Britain and France, in secret coordination with the IDF, planned the attack. Israeli forces invaded the Sinai, halting ten miles short of the Suez Canal on November 2, in compliance with a joint British and French "demand" for the cessation of hostilities and withdrawal from the Suez region by both sides. Egypt refused to withdraw from the region, and Franco-British paratroops secured the Suez Canal. Under intense international pressure, Britain, France, and Israel withdrew from the captured territories. United Nations forces were stationed in the Sinai to guarantee free shipping into the Gulf of Eilat.

698. Prisoner Exchange I   Following the Sinai Campaign, Israel freed 5,850 Egyptians in return for four Israelis.

699. First MIG-Mirage Dogfight   Four Syrian MIGs and four IAF Mirages engaged in the first MIG-Mirage aerial dogfight in history on November 13, 1964. One Syrian MIG was downed.

700. The Six-Day War (June 5–10, 1967)   The Arab nations surrounding Israel began preparations for war in 1967. Egypt closed the Straits of Tiran after successfully demanding the evacuation of United Nations' forces stationed in the Sinai. Arab leaders publicly declared their intention to "throw the Jews into the sea." Egypt mobilized some 100,000 troops and 1,000 armored vehicles into the Sinai. Rather than wait for an impending attack, Israel launched a preemptive air strike against the air forces of Egypt, Syria, Jordan, and Iraq. The Israeli Air Force destroyed 452 Arab aircraft in under three hours. On the first day of the war Israel told King Hussein bin Talal that if Jordan stayed out of the war Israel would not attack Jordan. Ignoring the warning, Jordanian troops opened fire on Israeli positions. The war, which pitted Israel against Egypt, Syria, Jordan, and Iraq, began on June 5, 1967, and ended 132 hours and 30 minutes later. Fighting on the Egyptian front lasted only four days; fighting on the Jordanian front ended in three days. By war's end, Israel controlled the entire West Bank (captured from Jordan), Gaza Strip and Sinai Peninsula (from Egypt), and the Golan Heights (from Syria). Israeli casualties totaled 777 dead, 2,586 wounded, 15 captured. Arab losses equaled roughly 15,000 dead and over 5,000 prisoners. Moshe Dayan dubbed the conflict the Six-Day War because he believed that just as God created the world in six days, the six days of war resulted in making permanent the creation of the State of Israel.

701. Liberation of the Western Wall On June 7, 1967, under the leadership of Colonel Motta Gur, Israeli forces captured the Old City of Jerusalem and the Western Wall. Rabbi Major-General Shlomo Goren reached the Wall with Israeli troops and blew a shofar to commemorate the event.

702. The *Liberty* On the fourth day of the Six-Day War, June 8, 1967, the Israeli Air Force responded to intelligence reports of Israeli troops being fired upon from a boat off the coast of El Arish by attacking a ship located fourteen miles off the Sinai coast. The ship attacked turned out to be the USS *Liberty*. Thirty-four members of the *Liberty*'s crew were killed and 171 were wounded. Israel had reason to believe the ship belonged to a hostile country. An Egyptian vessel had been in the same location a day before. Also, just days earlier the United States had publicly declared that U.S. naval forces were operating in the field of battle. Ten official U.S. investigations and three official Israeli inquiries conclusively established that the attack was a tragic error. Israel issued an apology for the attack and paid some $13 million in reparations to the United States and the families of the sailors who died.

703. Operation Refugee In the wake of the Six-Day War, Israel permitted every Arab who fled because of the war to return to the territories captured by Israel. Only 14,056 refugees accepted the offer.

704. Three No's In August 1967, in the aftermath of the Six-Day War, an Arab summit was held in Khartoum during which the Arabs enunciated their policy toward Israel with three no's: no negotiation, no recognition, no peace.

705. Arab Legion Barracks   The barracks, located in a stone quarry in al-Azariyyah, were constructed by the Jordanian army with Jewish grave stones hauled from the Mount of Olives (even the latrines were built with tombstones). Tombstones from the Jewish cemetery were also used by the Jordanians to pave a road running through the cemetery and one leading to the Intercontinental Hotel.

706. The *Eilat*   An Israeli destroyer that was sunk by Egyptian missile boats on October 21, 1967. Forty-seven sailors were killed.

707. The Bar-Lev Line   A 100-mile string of underground forts and minefields along the Israeli-controlled side of the Suez Canal created by and named after General Haim Bar-Lev. Completed in March 1969, the line was originally intended to serve as a trip-wire force in the event of an Egyptian attack. The undermanned and overestimated defensive line offered no effective resistance to the advancing Egyptian army during the Yom Kippur War.

708. War of Attrition   As early as July 1, 1967, Egypt began shelling and sniping Israeli positions near the Suez Canal. On October 21, 1967, Egypt sank the Israeli destroyer *Eilat*, killing 47. Less than one year later, Egyptian artillery began to shell Israeli positions along the Suez Canal. Nasser believed that because most of Israel's army consisted of reserves, it could not withstand a lengthy war of attrition. He believed that Israel would be unable to endure the economic burden and that the constant stream of casualties would undermine Israeli morale. The War of Attrition lasted nearly two years. Israel lost fifteen combat aircraft, most shot down by antiaircraft guns and missiles. The Israeli death toll between June 15, 1967, and August 8, 1970, was 1,424 soldiers and more than 100 civilians. Another 2,000 soldiers and 700 civilians were wounded. From March 1969 to April 1970, violence along the Suez Canal front caused Israeli losses of 152 dead and 726 wounded. During the same time period, Egypt suffered 2,500 killed and 7,000 injured.

709. Paving Swamps   During the War of Attrition, engineers from the Technion developed a technique to build and pave roads over swampland. Within three months, 29 kilometers of road were paved over swamps near the Suez Canal. The new technique was eventually adopted worldwide.

710. Stolen Egyptian Radar   On the eve of December 26, 1969, Israeli soldiers conducted a raid on an island in the Suez Canal, disassembled one of Egypt's Russian-built modern radar installations, and brought the unit to Israel.

711. MIG-Mirage Dogfight II   In September 1973, Israeli jets downed thirteen Syrian MIGs and lost only one IAF Mirage jet.

712. The Yom Kippur War (October 6–23, 1973)   On October 6, 1973, on Yom Kippur, the most solemn and holy day in Judaism, Egypt and Syria launched a joint surprise attack against Israel. Along the Suez Canal, the

Egyptian army faced an Israeli force of fewer than 500 defenders. In the Golan Heights, Israel's 180 tanks were attacked by a Syrian force of some 1,400. Finding itself on the defensive during the first two days of fighting, Israel lost almost 150 airplanes and hundreds of soldiers. Israel mobilized its civilian army and struggled to mount counterattacks. The Arab armies were resupplied by the Soviet Union while the United States began a massive airlift of military supplies to Israel. Two weeks later, Israeli forces were routing Egyptian and Syrian forces, driving toward Cairo and Damascus. The Security Council adopted Resolution 338 on October 22, calling for "all parties to the present fighting to cease all firing and terminate all military activity immediately." Despite the Israel Defense Forces' ultimate success on the battlefield, the heavy price paid for victory caused most Israelis to consider the war a diplomatic and military failure. Prime Minister Golda Meir resigned amid the furor of Israel's near defeat. A total of 2,688 Israeli soldiers were killed, compared to Arab casualties of some 8,500.

713. Valley of Tears   A stretch of valley in the northern Golan Heights where an Israeli force of 100 tanks was decimated by the invading Syrian army in 1973. Only seven tanks survived, but they continued to fight. Thanks to similar courage in the southern Golan, the Syrians were routed within four days and nearly 600 Syrian tanks were left in ruins in the Valley of Tears.

714. U.S. Airlift   Answering Russian efforts to resupply Egypt with military equipment during the Yom Kippur War, President Nixon ordered an airlift to resupply Israel with weapons and material. Starting on October 14, 1973, and lasting for over four weeks, the United States flew 566 resupply missions carrying 22,000 tons of material to Israel. America also provided $2.2 billion in emergency aid to Israel.

715. UJA and the Yom Kippur War   On October 7, 1973, the second day of the war, the United Jewish Appeal raised $30 million.

716. No Fly Zone   Foreign airlines, with the exception of Air France and Sterling (Denmark), suspended flights to and from Israel during October 1973.

717. Separation of Forces   Negotiations for the separation and disengagement of forces between Israel and Syria following the Yom Kippur War were held in February and March 1974, when Israeli and Syrian representatives came to Washington and presented their respective initial positions to U.S. Secretary of State Henry Kissinger. The secretary then spent the month of May in the Middle East, shuttling between Jerusalem and Damascus. On May 31, senior military officers of both sides signed the disengagement agreement in Geneva.

718. Prisoner Exchange II   In the aftermath of the Yom Kippur War, an agreement was reached whereby Israel released 8,031 Egyptian soldiers in exchange for 241 Israelis. Agreement was also reached with Syria whereby Israel exchanged 410 Syrian soldiers for 67 Israeli soldiers.

719. Elizabeth Taylor   The famed actress raised money for casualties of the Yom Kippur War by embarking on a fund-raising tour, stopping in Rome, Hamburg, Amsterdam, Los Angeles, and New York.

720. Oil Embargo   Reacting to American support of Israel, Saudi Arabia, Abu Dhabi, Libya, Algeria, Kuwait, Qatar, and Bahrain enacted an oil embargo against the United States on October 19, 1973. The embargo led to substantial price hikes in oil and gasoline. A world oil shortage ensued, causing long lines at gas stations, rocking world economies, and leading to the rationing of gasoline.

721. U-2 Golan   In the aftermath of the 1973 Yom Kippur War, the United States agreed to help Jerusalem and Damascus stabilize the border. Every week since then, an American U-2 reconnaissance plane has flown over the Golan Heights, taking photos of Israeli and Syrian positions in the limited forces zones established in the 1974 disengagement agreement. These photos are given to Israel and Syria, supplementing their own intelligence and providing each state with another means to verify that the other is not planning a surprise attack. The information allows the two countries to defuse potentially flammable issues before they reach the crisis stage.

722. Operation Litani   In March 1978, PLO terrorists infiltrated Israel. After murdering an American tourist walking near an Israeli beach, they hijacked a civilian bus. The terrorists shot through the windows as the bus traveled down the highway. When Israeli troops intercepted the bus, the terrorists opened fire. A total of 34 hostages died in the attack. In response, an Israeli force numbering some 25,000 crossed into Lebanon and overran terrorist bases in the southern part of that country, pushing the terrorists away from the border. The Israel Defense Forces (IDF) withdrew after two months, allowing United Nations forces to enter, but UN troops were unable to prevent terrorists from reinfiltrating the region and introducing new, more dangerous arms.

723. Prisoner Exchange III   In exchange for releasing 76 Palestinian terrorists on March 14, 1979, Israel won the freedom of one Israeli soldier.

724. First F-15-MIG Dogfight   In the first aerial dogfight between American-made F-15s and Russian-made MIGs, Israeli Air Force F-15s downed five Syrian MIG-21s on June 27, 1979.

725. Osirak Nuclear Reactor   With French assistance, Iraq built a nuclear reactor capable of producing nuclear weapons in Osirak, near Baghdad. Prime Minister Menachem Begin decided that Israel would not permit Iraq to attain nuclear weapon capability and ordered an attack on the Iraqi reactor. On June 7, 1981, eight Israeli jets flew over 1,100 kilometers and destroyed the reactor in an attack that lasted just one minute and twenty seconds.

The United States joined the other members of the United Nations Security Council in condemning the Israeli attack. In the aftermath of the Persian Gulf War, many American commentators—and then U.S. Secretary of Defense Dick Cheney—praised the Israeli attack as an act that, in retrospect, prevented Iraq from possessing and utilizing nuclear technology against American troops. No nation retracted or apologized for their UN condemnation.

726. Operation Peace for Galilee   In the late 1970s and early 1980s, terrorism increased along Israel's border with Lebanon. The frequency of terrorist and rocket attacks forced thousands of Israeli residents to leave their homes or to spend significant time in bomb shelters. The PLO had some 15,000 men, hundreds of tanks and thousands of weapons ensconced in Southern Lebanon. Palestinian attacks were becoming frequent and brazen, culminating with a June 1982 assassination attempt of Israel's ambassador to Great Britain. On June 6, 1982, the IDF invaded Lebanon with the aim of clearing Southern Lebanon of terrorists in Operation Peace for Galilee. The initial success of the Israeli operation led to the attempt to expel the PLO from all Lebanese territory and lure Lebanon into signing a peace agreement with Israel. The IDF drove to the outskirts of Beirut and laid siege to Yasser Arafat and PLO forces. Through negotiations, Israel allowed Arafat and many of his followers to leave Lebanon. Meanwhile, increasing casualties provoked intense debate within Israel. For the first time in Israel's history, a consensus for war did not exist (though it did at the outset). Prime Minister Menachem Begin resigned amid the political turmoil, and a national coalition government that took office in 1984 ordered the withdrawal of Israeli troops from Lebanon, leaving behind a small force to help the South Lebanese Army secure a zone along Israel's border. Though the war did drive the PLO out of Lebanon, terrorism continued. The war was also costly: 1,216 soldiers died between June 5, 1982, and May 31, 1985.

727. Sabra and Shatila   On September 16, 1982, during the Lebanon War, Israeli forces allowed members of the allied Lebanese Christian Phalangist militia to enter the Sabra and Shatila refugee camps and search for PLO forces. Over a two-day period, the militia massacred residents of the camps, killing between 460 to 800 people. The massacre was in response to the recent murder of Lebanese President Bashir Gemayel, which the Christian Phalangists blamed on Palestinian forces.

728. Kahan Commission   The Israeli government established the Kahan Commission of Inquiry to explore Israel's role in the Sabra and Shatila massacres. The commission found that Israel was indirectly responsible for the deaths for its failure to anticipate Phalangist atrocities. As a result of the commission's findings and recommendations, Defense Minister Ariel Sharon and Army Chief of Staff General Raful Eitan were dismissed.

729. Lebanon Security Zone   After Israel's 1985 withdrawal from Lebanon, officials sought to prevent the reinfiltration of terrorists into the area along Israel's border. Therefore, a 1,000-man force was stationed in a swath of Lebanese territory extending eight miles into Southern Lebanon to keep towns and villages in northern Israel beyond the range of rocket attacks.

730. Lebanon Violence   Between 1985 and 1999, nine Israeli civilians were killed and 248 wounded on the Lebanese border.

731. Operation Grapes of Wrath   In April 1996, the IDF launched Operation Grapes of Wrath to halt Hezbollah katyusha rocket attacks on Israeli towns along the Lebanese border. During the sixteen-day operation, Israeli artillery mistakenly hit a UN outpost in Kafr Kana, killing nearly 100 Lebanese civilians. Afterward, a Joint Monitoring Group, including American, French, Israeli, Syrian, and Lebanese representatives, was created to prevent attacks on civilian populations and the use of civilians as shields for terrorist activities.

732. Withdrawal from Lebanon   Eighteen years after Israel invaded Lebanon in Operation Peace for Galilee, Israel withdrew completely from Lebanese territory. The withdrawal took place on May 24, 2000, with the removal of all forces from all Israel Defense Force and South Lebanon Army outposts and bases. The United Nations coordinated the withdrawal with Israel and officially verified that Israel was in compliance with Security Council Resolution 425 (1978) that called for Israeli withdrawal from Lebanon.

733. Prisoner Exchange IV   In November 1983, Israel and the PLO engaged in a prisoner exchange in which 4,500 Arab prisoners were released in return for six Israelis held by the PLO.

734. Prisoner Exchange V   In May 1985, Israel freed 1,150 Arabs, including over 150 convicted of murder, in exchange for three Israeli soldiers held by the PLO.

735. The Intifada   On December 6, 1987, an Israeli was killed by a Palestinian in the Gaza Strip. The following day, four Palestinians were killed in a traffic accident by an Israeli driver. Amid rumors that the Palestinian deaths were part of a revenge killing, rioting broke out in Jabalya. On December 9, during continued rioting, an Israeli soldier shot and killed a 17-year-old Palestinian who was throwing a Molotov cocktail. News of the shooting death spread and Palestinian protests and riots spread throughout the West Bank, Gaza, and Jerusalem. This uprising became known as the Intifada. In the first four years of the Intifada, the Israel Defense Forces reported that Palestinians perpetrated more than 4,000 attacks with guns, Molotov cocktails, hand grenades, and other explosives. Sixteen Israeli civilians and eleven soldiers were killed, while more than 1,400 Israeli civilians and 1,700 Israeli soldiers were injured. Approximately 1,000 Palestinians died in clashes with Israelis. The Intifada waned with the onset of the Gulf crisis and ended shortly afterward.

736. The Intrafada Throughout the uprising, Palestinian-on-Palestinian violence was perpetrated in the name of executing collaborators with Israel or killing women for immoral behavior. Between 1989 and 1992, almost 1,000 Palestinians were killed by other Palestinians.

737. Temple Riot On October 8, 1990, Arabs standing atop the Temple Mount stoned Jews praying at the Western Wall below. Israeli police entered the Temple Mount and clashed with the Arabs, resulting in the deaths of seventeen Palestinians. Israel was blamed for its handling of the matter.

738. Israel's POW/MIAs A number of Israeli soldiers remain prisoners or MIAs. Most famous among them is Ron Arad, an Air Force navigator downed over Lebanon in 1986. The rallies for his release and appeals by world leaders for his cause have not yet secured his freedom.

739. The Gulf War On August 2, 1990, Iraq invaded Kuwait. The United States responded by launching Operation Desert Shield under the command of General Norman Schwarzkopf. The first phase of the operation was to get U.S. troops into Saudi Arabia to defend the kingdom in the event that Iraqi forces were to push beyond Kuwait. The second objective was to establish a sufficient force to deter Iraq from attacking the Saudis. By October, the United States had mobilized sufficient force in Saudi Arabia and the Gulf to shift the emphasis from a defensive to an offensive posture. Over the course of five months, President Bush succeeded in building a coalition of three dozen nations, though the bulk of the military forces was American (roughly 75 percent of the total), British, and French. On January 17, 1991, coalition forces launched Operation Desert Storm by firing Tomahawk cruise missiles. The missiles were followed by F-117 Stealth planes dropping laser-guided smart bombs on Iraqi communications centers. After Iraq ignored another ultimatum to withdraw, the coalition began the ground campaign, Operation Desert Sword, on February 24, 1991. Military operations ceased on February 28, 1991, just 100 hours after the ground war began. On April 6, Iraq accepted a cease-fire and agreed to pay reparations to Kuwait, destroy its stockpiles of biological and chemical weapons, and dismantle nonconventional weapons production facilities.

740. Israel Stays Out A critical element in maintaining an international coalition against Iraq was preventing the conflict from engulfing Israel. For decades, Iraq had been one of the leaders of the Arab rejectionist front against Israel, and Israel was frustrated because it appeared that the United States did not take seriously Saddam's threats to attack Israel. The Bush administration was convinced the Arab states would not support a war with Iraq if Israel was involved in the conflict. On January 19, Iraq fired its first Scud missiles at Israel. Israel desperately wanted to respond and had plans in place to destroy the Iraqi missile sites. President Bush pressured Israeli Prime Minister

Yitzhak Shamir to let the coalition forces handle the problem. Israel held its fire and was applauded by American officials for showing restraint.

741. Raining Scuds During the Gulf War, between 38 and 42 Iraqi Scud missiles hit Israel. Two people died directly from the attacks, and eleven more died of heart attacks or improper usage of gas masks. More than 200 people were wounded, and thousands of homes and buildings were destroyed.

742. Patriots To partially compensate Israel for its decision to hold its fire after coming under attack from Iraqi Scud missiles, President Bush sent Patriot missiles to Israel in January 1991. During the course of the Gulf War, however, the Patriots failed to intercept a single missile.

743. Al-Aksa Intifada On September 28, 2000, opposition Likud leader Ariel Sharon entered the Temple Mount. That event marked the beginning of the Al-Aksa Intifada, so named because the Al-Aksa Mosque stands on the Temple Mount. From the onset of the Al-Aksa Intifada until the end of 2004, more than 700 Israeli citizens and 300 Israeli soldiers were killed in some 150 suicide and other bombing attacks, 13,750 shooting attacks, and over 300 rocket attacks. Since April 2002, the IDF has killed some 1,000 suspected terrorists and arrested more than 6,000. Palestinians have long argued that Sharon's entrance to the Temple Mount was a desecration of a Muslim holy place and that his visit sparked the violence. However, the Palestinian Authority communications minister admitted that "it [the uprising] has been planned since Chairman Arafat's return from Camp David, when he turned the tables on the former U.S. President and rejected the American conditions." On November 7, 2000, a fact-finding mission chaired by former U.S. Senator George Mitchell reported that "the Sharon visit did not cause the 'Al-Aksa Intifada.'"

744. Prisoner Exchange VI In February 2004, Israel and Hezbollah agreed to a prisoner exchange whereby Hezbollah released a kidnapped Israeli citizen and the bodies of three Israel soldiers in exchange for 462 prisoners, including Sheikh Abdel Karim Obeid and Mustafa Dirani, both of whom were kidnapped from Lebanon by Israeli forces ten years earlier.

The War on Terrorism

745. Birth of the PLO The Palestine Liberation Organization was created by the Arab League and established in June 1964 at a conference of the Palestinian National Council in the Ambassador Hotel in Sheikh Jarrah, Jerusalem.

746. First PLO Terrorist Attack On January 1, 1965, the PLO attempted to perpetrate its first terrorist attack, targeting Israel's recently opened National Water Carrier. The attack failed because the explosive never detonated. One terrorist was captured.

747. EL AL Hijacking On July 23, 1968, Palestinian terrorists hijacked an EL AL plane that was flying from Rome to Tel Aviv. The plane was forced to land in Algeria where all the non-Jews were released. On August 31, Algeria freed the plane and her remaining Jewish hostages.

748. Israeli Hijacking Response In retaliation to a spate of PLO attacks on EL AL airplanes, Israeli paratroopers seized International Beirut Airport on December 29, 1968, and destroyed all fourteen planes at the airport. No civilians died in the attack.

749. Bazooka Attack on Children On May 22, 1970, terrorists fired bazooka rockets at a bus carrying children, killing twelve of the children and wounding nineteen.

750. Ephraim Elon On May 17, 1971, Israel's consul general in Istanbul, Turkey, Ephraim Elon, was kidnapped from his residence. The kidnappers, believed to be a Turkish underground organization, killed Elon when their demands for a prisoner release went unmet.

751. Sabena Hijacking On May 8, 1972, a Sabena flight heading from Brussels to Tel Aviv was hijacked by Palestinian terrorists. The hijackers demanded that hundreds of PLO prisoners be released by Israel. Under the cover of night, Israeli troops siphoned off the jet's fuel and took the air out of the tires. Israeli troops boarded the plane disguised as airport technicians and regained control of the aircraft. Two terrorists and one passenger were killed. Benjamin Netanyahu was led by Ehud Barak in the daring rescue.

752. Lod Airport Attack On May 30, 1972, terrorists from the Japanese Red Star Organization flew to Israel aboard an Air France flight. Upon landing at Lod Airport they fired Kalishnikovs and threw grenades at passengers in the terminal. Twenty-five people were killed and seventy-two wounded.

753. Munich Massacre On September 5, 1972, during the Munich Olympic Games, Arab terrorists entered the competitors' compound and killed eleven Israeli athletes and coaches. Some of the terrorists were killed by German security forces. The Olympic Games were suspended for one day. Some athletes withdrew from the competition in light of the bloodshed. Israel responded by attacking terrorist bases in Lebanon. On September 10, the Security Council voted on a resolution to condemn the Israeli raids—no mention of the terrorist attack was included in this or any other UN resolution. The United States cast a veto to defeat the motion. On October 29, bowing to the demands of terrorists who hijacked a Lufthansa plane, West Germany released the three remaining imprisoned perpetrators of the Munich attack. After the murder of its athletes at the Olympics, Israeli forces attacked PLO bases in Syria and Lebanon, killing more than 200 PLO members and downing three Syrian jet fighters. Israel also sent agents to kill those responsible for planning and executing the attack. The story of the agents sent to kill the Munich terrorists is retold in the book *Vengeance*. A TV movie was *Sword of Gideon*, based on the book.

754. Botched Hit   On July 21, 1973, Mossad agents in Norway mistakenly killed Ahmed Boushiki, a waiter in a local restaurant. Boushiki was mistaken for one of the masterminds of the attack on the Israeli delegation to the Munich Olympics.

755. Operation Aviv Neurim   On April 9, 1973, in response to a PLO attack on the home of Israel's ambassador to Cyprus, IDF commandos infiltrated PLO headquarters in Beirut and killed PLO leaders in their sleep. Those killed included Abu Yussuf, Arafat's deputy, and Lamal Nasser, spokesman for the PLO. Ehud Barak participated in the assault.

756. Kiryat Shemonah Attack   On April 11, 1974, a PLO force killed sixteen people, mostly women and children, in the city of Kiryat Shemonah. Israel called on the United Nations to condemn the attack. When the UN failed to condemn the attack, Israel's delegation walked out of the Security Council in protest.

757. Archbishop Hilarion Capucci   On August 18, 1974, East Jerusalem's Greek Catholic patriarchal vicar was arrested for smuggling weapons into Israel on behalf of terrorists. An Israeli court sentenced him to twelve years in prison. Capucci was freed on November 6, 1977, in response to a request for clemency made by Pope Paul VI.

758. Ma'alot Hostage Situation   On May 15, 1974, PLO terrorists infiltrated Israel from Lebanon and seized a school in Ma'alot, taking more than 100 children hostage. Israeli troops entered the school and killed the terrorists. One Israeli soldier died in the firefight. Twenty-one children were killed and seventy wounded during the event.

759. Savoy Hotel   On March 5, 1975, eight PLO terrorists landed on a Tel Aviv beach and seized the Savoy Hotel. The terrorists issued demands that included the freeing of Archbishop Hilarion Capucci and others imprisoned by Israel. All the terrorists and three Israeli soldiers were killed when IDF forces stormed the hotel.

760. Operation Redemption (renamed Operation Jonathan)   On June 27, 1976, an Air France airliner flying from Israel to France was hijacked by four Palestinian terrorists. After being diverted to Entebbe, Uganda, the hijackers released 155 of the 258 passengers (only those believed to be Jewish or Israeli were held) and demanded the release of 53 imprisoned Palestinians located in Israel, Kenya, and West Germany. When France failed to act, Israel stepped in. On July 3, Israel dispatched a volunteer military unit aboard four Hercules C-130h cargo planes escorted by Phantom fighter jets. On July 4, after flying some 2,500 miles, the Israeli force landed, rescued the hostages, and left—all within one hour. As a result of the action, seven terrorists, twenty

Ugandan soldiers, three hostages, and one soldier (Col. Yoni Netanyahu, brother of former Prime Minister Benjamin Netanyahu) were killed and eleven Ugandan planes were destroyed. The crew of the Air France plane refused to leave their Jewish passengers, an act that won them Israel's highest civilian award and worldwide respect. The heroics of the operation were depicted in the films *Operation Thunderbolt* (which received an Oscar nomination for Best Foreign Language Film in 1977) and *Raid on Entebbe* (which starred Charles Bronson).

761. Syrian Espionage Ring   On December 8, 1972, twenty Arabs and four Jews were arrested in Israel for spying on behalf of Syria. One of those arrested was a reserve corporal in the IDF.

762. Hebron Murders   On May 2, 1980, Palestinian gunmen in Hebron killed six Jews returning from Sabbath prayers. Israel responded to the attack by exiling the Kadi of Hebron and the mayors of Hebron and Halhul.

763. Bus 300   On April 12, 1984, an Israeli bus traveling from Ashkelon to Tel Aviv was hijacked by terrorists. Israeli soldiers stormed the bus. A commission established to investigate the incident revealed that two of the terrorists were captured alive, only to be beaten to death by Israeli security forces.

764. Jewish Terror Ring   In 1984, authorities uncovered a Jewish underground responsible for attacking mosques, bombing Arab buses, and targeting Arab mayors in the West Bank. Several of the members who were sentenced to jail were eventually pardoned.

765. Bombing of PLO Headquarters   On October 1, 1985, Israeli F-15 jets flew over 1,200 miles and bombed PLO headquarters in Tunis. The IAF operation was carried out in response to a PLO attack targeting Israeli tourists in Cyprus.

766. Abu Jihad Hit   On April 16, 1988, Israeli special forces killed Abu Jihad, one of Yasser Arafat's deputies. Abu Jihad was killed in his Tunis home.

767. Kidnapping Sheikh Obeid   On July 29, 1989, Israeli commandos kidnapped Hezbollah leader Sheikh Obeid in Lebanon.

768. Argentina Explodes   On March 17, 1992, a car bomb exploded next to the Israeli embassy in Argentina. The attack killed 29, wounded more than 200, and destroyed the embassy.

769. Jewish Terror   On February 25, 1994, Baruch Goldstein, a Jewish settler from Kiryat Arba, entered the Tomb of the Patriarchs and shot dead twenty Arabs while they were praying. Goldstein was killed by Arabs in the vicinity.

770. The Engineer's Bad Connection   On January 5, 1996, Yihyeh Ayash, known as "the Engineer" because of his skill in building bombs for terrorists, was killed by Israeli operatives who planted an explosive device in his cell phone.

771. Crazed Soldier   On March 13, 1997, a Jordanian soldier shot and killed seven Israeli girls who were on a school trip to Naharayim, an island in the Jordan River that is known as the "Island of Peace." King Hussein of Jordan visited the families of the victims and sent each a personally signed check for $1 million.

772. Mash'al Affair   On September 25, 1997, Hamas leader Halid Mash'al was poisoned in Jordan. Two Mossad agents involved in the action were arrested by Jordanian security forces. In exchange for the release of the Mossad agents, Israel gave Mash'al the antidote for the poison and also released Hamas founder Sheikh Yassin from an Israeli prison.

773. Disco Bombing   On June 1, 2001, a suicide bomber killed twenty-one people and wounded 120 outside a disco in Tel Aviv. Most of the victims were Russian teenagers who were recent immigrants to Israel.

774. Sbarro Pizzeria Bombing   On August 9, 2001, fifteen people were killed, including seven children, and about 130 were injured when a suicide bomber detonated a bomb packed with nails, screws, and bolts inside a Jerusalem pizzeria.

775. Assassination of Cabinet Minister   On October 15, 2001, Minister of Tourism and former IDF Major-General Rechavam Ze'evy was assassinated on the steps of the Jerusalem Hyatt Hotel. Just hours earlier, Ze'evy, who served as adviser to Prime Minister Yitzhak Rabin on antiterrorism and intelligence, had resigned from the cabinet of Prime Minister Ariel Sharon because of the latter's failure to fight terrorism.

776. *Karine A*   On the evening of January 3, 2004, Israeli special forces seized the ship *Karine A* in the Red Sea about 310 miles (500 kilometers) from Israel. More than 50 tons of weaponry were found on board headed to the Gaza Strip. The captain of the ship was a PLO member, and the boat was purchased by the Palestinian Authority. The arms, valued at some $15 million, were bought through an Iranian organization.

777. Passover Attack   On March 27, 2002, timed to coincide with the eating of the Jewish Passover holiday *seder*, a HAMAS terrorist entered the Park Hotel in Netanya and blew himself up, killing thirty and wounding more than sixty.

778. Operation Defensive Shield   Approximately 135 Israelis were killed in various terrorist attacks in March 2002. By March 28, in the largest mobilization since the 1982 Lebanon War, the IDF mobilized 20,000 military reservists and launched an operation throughout the West Bank designed to destroy the terrorist infrastructure. Violent fighting occurred in Jenin and in a standoff at Church of the Nativity when Palestinian gunmen took refuge in the church and were surrounded by Israeli forces. Some 216 Palestinians and twenty-nine Israeli soldiers were killed in the operation, which ended on May 10, 2004.

779. Ashdod Port Bombings   On March 15, 2004, a double suicide bombing at the port in Ashdod killed eight victims and wounded sixteen. The port is a guarded strategic asset in Israel, and the attack raised questions as to the security of strategic Israeli installations.

780. HAMAS Leadership killed   Sheikh Ahmed Yassin, the spiritual leader and a cofounder of HAMAS, was killed on March 23, 2004, by an IAF gunship missile attack as he left a mosque. About 150,000 mourners from across the Palestinian political spectrum gathered to take part in his funeral procession. On April 19, 2004, less than a month after taking over the leadership of HAMAS, cofounder Abdel Aziz Rantisi was killed by an Israeli air strike.

781. Attack on Israeli Soldiers   Over a two-day period in May 2004, eleven soldiers were killed in Palestinian attacks on Israeli armored personnel carriers. These attacks highlighted the increased sophistication and ability of Palestinian groups to attack Israeli soldiers.

782. Operation Days of Penitence   This operation was launched in October 2004 to end the rain of rockets fired from the Gaza Strip toward Israeli towns and cities. The IDF thrust nine kilometers—the maximum range of a Qassam rocket—into northern Gaza. Approximately 138 Palestinians were killed in the operation.

Israel Defense Forces (IDF) and the Mossad

783. Israel Defense Forces   On May 26, 1948, the provisional government of Israel transformed the Haganah into the Israel Defense Forces. Irgun and Lehi forces were absorbed into the new army, creating a 51,500-strong force. The Hebrew name of the IDF (*Zeva Haganah le-Israel*) includes the term Haganah to mark the role of the Haganah in the creation of the state and army. The three Hebrew letters of the IDF correspond to the first letter of all three Jewish underground organizations.

784. Israel Defense Budget   In 2004, Israel spent some $9 billion on defense, equaling almost 9 percent of its GDP. The United States' defense budget is only 3.5 percent of its GDP.

785. Mossad (*Hamossad Le'mode'in U'le'tafkidim Meyuchadim*)   Israel's famous intelligence agency uses agents to collect intelligence and to conduct covert operations and counterterrorism. The Mossad maintains relations with its counterparts around the world and has especially close ties to the American Central Intelligence Agency. The agency is involved in psychological warfare and propaganda and has mounted clandestine operations, including assassinations and sabotage, against targets viewed as threats to Israeli national security.

786. Israel's Strategic Doctrine   The basic principles of Israel's military strategy are that the nation cannot afford to lose a single war; that the country has no territorial ambitions and would prefer to avoid war by political means and a credible deterrent posture; that the outcome of any war be decided quickly and decisively; and that terrorism must be combated.

787. The IDF Draft   In Israel, all physically capable citizens are drafted into the Israel Defense Forces at the age of eighteen. Arabs are exempt from the draft so as not to require them to fight against fellow Arabs. Additionally, students studying in yeshiva may opt for an army exemption. Women may choose national service (*Sherut Leumi*), which includes working in schools, hospitals, clinics, and day care centers to fulfill their army service. The IDF may defer military service when a student studies a subject of particular interest. Thus, a student of medicine may finish his or her studies prior to entering the Medical Corps. Men under the age of twenty-nine must undergo a minimum of three years of military service and unmarried women under the age of twenty-six must serve up to twenty-one months. After the initial draft, males are required to serve in reserve units until the age of fifty-one.

788. Religious Exemptions   As part of a compromise with religious parties when the state was founded, David Ben-Gurion agreed to exempt yeshiva students from army service. At first, only a handful of people claimed exemptions from the IDF due to religious study. By 1999, some 28,000 yeshiva students—over 7 percent of all military-eligible men—were claiming religious exemptions. Growing public anger over the large number of yeshiva students seeking to avoid military service has sparked a public outcry. The Tal Commission was established by the government to help draft legislation that will limit the number of religious exemptions.

789. Equal Opportunity   Ten Israelis with Down's syndrome were inducted into the army in 2000 and were assigned reserve duty at a northern base.

790. IDF Deserter   In 1998, the longest-term alleged deserter was brought to trial. Private Meir Golan was charged with having eluded the army from the day of his induction, August 24, 1977, until the military police arrested him on March 28, 1997, a total of 7,150 days. Golan denied he was a deserter, saying he had actually been discharged. His trial lasted one day, and he was given a two-year prison sentence on the reduced charge of absence without leave.

791. Soldiers of Humanity   Special units of the Israel Defense Forces have been dispatched around the world on humanitarian missions to aid in disaster relief. Some of their activities have included rescue work after devastating earthquakes in Mexico City in 1985 and Armenia in 1988; medical teams sent to aid refugees in war-torn Rwanda in 1994 and Macedonia in 1999; firefighting equipment sent to fight fires in Turkey in 1997; a search-and-rescue team sent to find survivors after terrorists blew up the U.S. embassy in Kenya in 1998; assisting in the rescue effort after the World Trade Center attacks in 2001; and medical personnel and relief goods to Sri Lanka and Thailand in the Asian tsunami disaster in 2004. Israel offered to send humanitarian assistance to Iran following an earthquake that killed more than 20,000. Iran refused Israeli assistance, saying, "The Islamic Republic of Iran accepts all kinds of humanitarian aid from all countries and international organizations with the exception of the Zionist regime."

792. Women Soldiers   Women played a vital role in the underground struggle for Israel's independence, including participation in signaling and combat units in the Haganah, Irgun, and Lehi. A Women's Corps was founded on May 16, 1948. Within a year, however, the Women's Corps was restructured and female soldiers were dispersed throughout various units. All women between the ages of 18 and 26, who are physically fit, unmarried, have not borne children, and have not objected on grounds of religion or conscience, must fulfill their military obligation. Women perform compulsory military service for a period of one year and nine months. Though women can serve in support and combat support roles in the IDF, they have, until recently, been prohibited from engaging in actual combat. This policy was changed following a Supreme Court ruling and in 1999 the IDF started training women for combat roles. On June 29, 2001, Lieutenant Roni Zuckerman became the first female fighter pilot in Israel (and the fourth to complete the IAF pilot course). As of 2004, hundreds of women had already been trained for and were serving in combat roles along with their male counterparts. Women who serve in combat roles are required to serve in the military for thirty months.

793. Mahal (*Mitnaddvei Huz la-Aretz*—Foreign Volunteers)   Mahal is the IDF branch in charge of foreigners who volunteer to serve in the army. Men between the ages of eighteen and twenty-three serve fourteen and a half months in the IDF. Roughly 3,500 volunteers from 43 countries, including both Jews and non-Jews, served in Mahal during the War of Independence. Today, Mahal only accepts Jews into the program.

794. Yeshivot Hesder   Institutions that allow Israelis to serve in the armed forces while simultaneously learning in a yeshiva. The five-year program roughly splits a student's time between religious studies and military service. Some of the more renowned Yeshivot Hesder are Keren B'Yavneh, Shaluvim, Har Etzion, Kiryat Arba-Hebron, and Hakotel.

795. Nahal (*Noar Halutzi Lohem*—Pioneering Fighting Youth)   The mission of this special branch of the IDF is to establish agricultural settlements in regions considered dangerous that will later be turned over to civilian communities. The soldiers in this unit combine military and agricultural training. Nahal has helped to establish some 108 settlements and helped to develop many more. Nahal units remain extremely active and have assumed a growing security-related role for settlements in outlying areas. Nahal has increased its capability to meet an ever-growing demand for its units.

796. Sayeret Matkal   Also known as General Staff Reconnaissance, Sayeret Matkal's Unit 269 is one of Israel's elite counterterrorism forces. Operatives from this unit have led or been instrumental in almost every notable counterterrorist operation since 1957. Sayeret Matkal is also responsible for hostage rescue missions within Israel and intelligence gathering behind enemy lines.

797. Military Intelligence   Aman, or *Agaf Hamodi'in* in Hebrew, is the intelligence branch of the IDF. It produces comprehensive national intelligence briefings for the prime minister and the cabinet, daily intelligence reports, risk-of-war estimates, target studies on nearby Arab countries, and communications intercepts. It also handles cross-border operations. The organization uses reconnaissance commando teams behind enemy lines, aerial reconnaissance, and military attachés stationed in overseas embassies to gather intelligence.

798. Israel Air Force   Formerly the Jewish Aviation Force, the IAF was established on May 21, 1948. Israeli aircrews operate cutting-edge weapons systems with precision accuracy. The fighter forces include the F-15, F-15I, and the state-of-the-art F-16I fighter jets. By 2008, Israel will have a fleet of over 100 F-16I's. The air force arsenal also includes attack helicopters such as the Apache, Cobra, Blackhawk, and the CH-30. Sikorsky and Bell helicopters transport troops and equipment while performing assault, medevac, and rescue missions in both war and peace. The transport fleet includes the Boeing 707 and Hercules C-130 aircraft. The Air Force has become the military's principal strike force and is considered one of the best in the world.

799. Israel's Ace   The Israeli Air Force's greatest "ace" is Giora Aven, who downed seventeen enemy aircraft. Twelve of his kills took place during the Yom Kippur War; eight of them within a span of 26 hours. Originally, Aven was not allowed to undergo pilot training due to medical reasons. After leaving the army, Aven reapplied to the IAF and was admitted to flight training.

800. U.S. Pilots   Only about a half-dozen Americans who served in the U.S. Air Force have tried to fly in the Israel Air Force. One of them, Yoel Aronoff, is credited with helping to train Israeli pilots in how to avoid surface-to-air missiles that were decimating the air force during the 1973 war. No other foreign-trained jet pilots have been accepted in the IAF.

801. Israeli Navy   The Israeli Navy deploys its ships into the Mediterranean Sea from the Ashdod and Haifa ports, and into the Red Sea from the port in Eilat. The sea corps operates Dolphin-class submarines. During the Yom Kippur War, the navy sank eight enemy ships without sustaining any losses.

802. Flotilla 13   Israel's underwater commando unit, Flotilla 13, is responsible for carrying out amphibious attacks and sabotage.

803. Shavit II On July 6, 1961, Israel launched its first domestically built missile, the Shavit II.

804. The Uzi Israel Military Industries introduced the Uzi submachine gun in 1954. Named after its inventor Uzi Gal, the weapon became one of the most famous submachine guns in history.

805. First Israeli Fighter In 1975, Israel's first domestically produced fighter, the Kfir, was unveiled.

806. Lavi Fighter In February 1980, Israel began developing the Lavi, a jet fighter intended to be designed and built domestically, thereby reducing Israel's dependence on foreign military equipment. The United States participated in the effort to develop the Lavi by supplying mature technologies and contributing some two billion dollars. Despite the production of three Lavi prototypes, the project was canceled in August 1987 due to budget constraints. As a result of the cancellation of the project, Israel Aircraft Industries fired some 5,000 employees.

807. Air Tragedy On February 4, 1997, in the most deadly accident in IDF history, two military helicopters crashed into each other, killing seventy-three soldiers.

Toward Peace

808. Rogers Plan In December 1969, U.S. Secretary of State William Rogers gave a speech in which he made a number of proposals for a Middle East settlement, including detailing potential borders and other issues. The section of the speech dealing with the Middle East became known as the Rogers Plan. The essence of the plan was that Israel would withdraw from disputed lands and the Arabs would agree to make peace, but not be required to sign a formal treaty normalizing relations. He also raised the issue of Palestinian refugees and suggested that Israel and Jordan should share in the civic, economic, and religious life of Jerusalem. Rogers declared U.S. policy to be balanced between the Arabs and Israelis.

809. First Peace Conference On December 21, 1973, foreign ministers of Israel, Jordan, and Egypt arrived in Geneva, Switzerland, for peace talks sponsored by the Russian foreign minister, American secretary of state, and United Nations president. Syria refused to attend. All the parties agreed in advance that the meeting would be largely ceremonial. When the conference convened, the Israeli and Arab delegates were in the same room, but the Arabs refused to have direct contact with Israelis; they would not shake hands, address the Israelis directly, or attend a joint cocktail party.

810. Sadat Goes to Israel After Egyptian President Anwar Sadat said he would be willing to go even to Jerusalem to pursue peace with Israel, he received an invitation to do so from Prime Minister Menachem Begin. Sadat accepted, arrived in Israel on November 19, 1977, and addressed the Knesset the next day. In his speech Sadat called for the establishment of a Palestinian state; Israeli withdrawal from the West Bank, Golan Heights, and Arab East Jerusalem; recognition of Israel; and the recognition of every states' right to security. Though the substance of the speech showed little willingness to compromise, his presence in the Israeli capital broke a psychological barrier between the Egyptian and Israeli people that made future peace possible.

811. Camp David Peace Accords   The first peace agreement between the State of Israel and a neighboring Arab country was signed at Camp David on September 17, 1978, by Menachem Begin, Anwar Sadat, and Jimmy Carter, after twelve days of secret negotiations. Two agreements were signed. The first dealt with the future of the Sinai and peace between Israel and Egypt, to be concluded within three months. The second established a format for conducting negotiations for the establishment of an autonomous regime in the West Bank and Gaza Strip. The Israel-Egypt agreement clearly defined the future relations between the two countries, all aspects of withdrawal from the Sinai, military arrangements in the peninsula such as demilitarization, and a supervision mechanism. The framework agreement regarding the future of Judea, Samaria, and Gaza was less clear and was later interpreted differently by Israel, Egypt, and the United States.

812. Knesset Accords Vote   On September 27, 1978, the Knesset ratified the Camp David Accords by a vote of 84 to 19.

813. Egypt-Israel Peace Treaty   The final treaty between Egypt and Israel was similar to the Camp David Accords, but changes were made because both the Palestinians and Jordanians refused to participate in the negotiations. The treaty, signed in Washington on March 26, 1979, contains nine articles, a military annex, an annex dealing with the relation between the parties, and agreed minutes interpreting the main articles of the treaty. The issue of Palestinian autonomy was also addressed in a letter written by President Sadat and Prime Minister Begin to President Carter. In a separate Israel-U.S. Memorandum of Agreement, concluded on the same day, the United States spelled out its commitments to Israel in case the treaty is violated, the role of the UN, and the future supply of military and economic aid to Israel.

814. Knesset Treaty Vote   On March 20, 1979, the Knesset opened debate on the Israel-Egypt Peace Treaty. The debate raged through the night and a vote was held on March 22 at 3:00 am. The treaty was ratified by a margin of 95 to 18.

815. Alma Oil Field   By turning over the Sinai to Egypt as part of the peace agreement, Israel ceded an opportunity to become energy-independent. The Alma oil field in the southern Sinai, discovered and developed by Israel, was transferred to Egypt in November 1979. When Israel gave up the field it had become the country's largest single source of energy, supplying half the country's energy needs. Israel, which estimated the value of untapped reserves in the Alma field at $100 billion, had projected that continued development there would have made the country energy self-sufficient by 1990.

816. Yamit   After the Six-Day War, the Labor government encouraged the development of Jewish settlements in parts of the territories captured by Israel. One of these settlements was the town of Yamit, which was built in the Sinai. Yamit became the largest Jewish community in the Sinai, boasting a population of some 7,000 residents. In 1982, the citizens of Yamit were forcibly removed by Israeli soldiers and the town was destroyed prior to the return of the region to Egypt as part of the Israel-Egypt peace agreement.

817. Taba   Israel built a resort in what had been a barren desert area along the Red Sea. Taba's status was not resolved by the Camp David Accords, and Israel resisted Egyptian demands to withdraw from the area. When an international arbitration panel ruled in Cairo's favor on September 29, 1988, Israel turned the town over to Egypt.

818. Multinational Force and Observers (MFO)   The largest and most visible U.S. peacekeeping mission is the Multinational Force and Observers. Charged with observing the demilitarized Sinai peninsula, the MFO was born out of the 1979 Egyptian-Israeli peace treaty. Broad Arab and Soviet opposition to the agreement made it impossible for the UN to assume its traditional peacekeeping role, so the United States organized an alternate monitoring force free of the highly politicized UN. Composed of a large military monitoring force and a much smaller civilian observer unit, the MFO has almost 2,700 personnel, about half of whom are Americans.

819. Nobel Peace Prize I   Menachem Begin and Anwar Sadat were jointly awarded the prize in 1978 for their achievements in forging peace between Egypt and Israel.

820. Lebanese Peace Agreement   In May 1983, Lebanese President Amin Gemayel signed a peace treaty with Israel. A year later Syria forced Gemayel to renege on the agreement. He was later assassinated.

821. Madrid Conference   On October 30, 1991, the United States and Russia cosponsored the opening session of a peace conference in Madrid, Spain. The conference was designed to serve as an opening forum for the participants and inaugurated two separate, parallel negotiating tracks—a bilateral track and a multilateral track. The first ever bilateral negotiations between Israel and Syria, Lebanon, and a joint Jordanian-Palestinian delegation took place in Madrid on November 3, immediately following the Madrid Conference. The multilateral negotiations were broken up into five separate working groups covering the most important and difficult issues faced by the parties.

The groups, which met first in Moscow in January 1992 and were supposed to meet periodically in different countries, dealt with water, the environment, arms control and regional security, refugees, and regional economic development. After a three-year hiatus, the multilateral talks resumed in Moscow on January 31, 2000, and were suspended again indefinitely.

822. Rabin-Arafat Letters   After almost two years of secret bilateral talks that took place in Oslo, Norway, the Palestine Liberation Organization agreed to recognize Israel and renounce terrorism. On September 9, 1993, in letters to Israeli Prime Minister Rabin and Norwegian Foreign Minister Holst, Yasser Arafat committed the PLO to cease all violence and terrorism against Israel. Rabin wrote to Arafat on the same date that "in light of the PLO commitments . . . the Government of Israel has decided to recognize the PLO as the representative of the Palestinian people and commence negotiations with the PLO within the Middle East peace process." This mutual recognition paved the way for the Oslo Accords that were established by the Declaration of Principles.

823. Oslo Accords/The Declaration of Principles (DOP)   Days after the Rabin-Arafat letters were sent, a joint Declaration of Principles was signed on September 13, 1993, outlining an interim self-governing arrangement for the Palestinians. The agreement, which was signed during a ceremony at the White House, called for immediate Palestinian self-rule in Gaza and Jericho, early empowerment for the Palestinians in parts of the West Bank, an agreement on self-government and the election of a Palestinian Council, and extensive economic cooperation between the two parties.

824. Gaza to the Palestinians   Shortly after the signing of the Declaration of Principles (DOP), Israeli and Palestinian negotiators began to discuss the implementation of the first stage of the interim agreement—the Israeli withdrawal from Gaza and Jericho. On May 4, 1994, Israel and the Palestinians signed the interim agreement transferring authority over Gaza and Jericho from the Israeli Civil Administration to a Palestinian Authority.

825. Nobel Peace Prize II   Yitzhak Rabin, Shimon Peres, and Yasser Arafat were awarded the prize in 1994 for their efforts in signing a peace agreement between the PLO and Israel. One member of the Nobel committee resigned in protest over the awarding of the Nobel Peace Prize to Arafat.

826. Peace with Jordan   On October 26, 1994, Prime Minister Yitzhak Rabin and the prime minister of Jordan convened at the White House and signed a peace treaty.

827. Talks With Syria   Between 1994 and 1996, Israeli and Syrian representatives met in Washington, D.C., under the guidelines established in the Madrid Conference. During the discussions, Israel accepted the principle of withdrawing from the Golan Heights within the framework of a comprehensive peace agreement that would include normalization of relations, an overall security arrangement, and a detailed plan for a staged withdrawal linked to progress in the process of a complete normalization of relations. The two countries did not meet again until 1999. No Israeli–Syrian negotiations have taken place since the death of Syrian President Hafez Assad in June 2000.

828. Oslo Accords II/Interim Agreement   On September 28, 1995, Israel and the Palestinian Authority signed an agreement that expanded Palestinian autonomy to Bethlehem, Hebron, Nablus, Jenin, Ramallah, Tulkarm, Qalqilya, and hundreds of Arab villages in the West Bank.

829. Hebron Protocol   On January 17, 1997, Israel and the Palestinians signed the Hebron Protocol in which terms were laid out for the Israeli withdrawal from Hebron as part of the redeployment of Israeli troops agreed upon in the Israeli–Palestinian Interim Agreement (Oslo II) of 1995.

ISRAEL AND AMERICA

830. The Special Relationship   The unique relationship between the United States and Israel dates to the days preceding the establishment of Israel. Over the years, a broad range of agreements have been forged that have made the alliance stronger with each passing decade. Nearly every U.S. government agency has a cooperative agreement with its counterpart in Israel. The two countries have a close strategic relationship. A series of binational foundations support joint research projects. More than 10,000 U.S. companies do business in or with Israel. Every U.S. state does business with Israel, and many have their own specific agreements for cooperation with Israel. Academic institutions also have a variety of arrangements with their Israeli counterparts, and scholars engage in many types of exchanges and collaborative research.

831. America's Opinion of Israel   "In the Middle East situation, are your sympathies more with Israel or with the Arab nations?" is the most consistently asked question about the Middle East. In more than 130 surveys by major polling organizations dating back to 1967, on average 46 percent of Americans say their sympathies are with Israel and 12 percent the Arabs/Palestinians. In January 1991, at the time of the Gulf War, sympathy for Israel reached a record high of 64 percent, according to Gallup. Meanwhile, support for the Arabs dropped to 8 percent and the margin was a record 56 points.

832. Americans Honored in Israel   Americans are honored throughout Israel. In Tel Aviv, Abraham Lincoln and Woodrow Wilson have streets named after them. George Washington Street is in Jerusalem and Martin Luther King has a street and memorial in his honor in the Galilee. A statue of Lincoln is in Ramat Gan and a replica of the Liberty Bell was built in Jerusalem's Liberty Bell Garden. A special memorial to John Kennedy is located in the Jerusalem Forest.

833. America–Israel UN Voting   Israel votes with the United States more than 90 percent of the time at the United Nations. The only country with a better record is Micronesia. By comparison, U.S. allies such as Britain and France usually vote with the United States less than 80 percent of the time. Arab "allies" such as Saudi Arabia, Egypt, and Jordan vote *against* the United States roughly 70 percent of the time.

834. AIPAC   The American Israel Public Affairs Committee (AIPAC) is the organization that lobbies the U.S. government on behalf of Americans who believe in a strong U.S.-Israel relationship. Originally called the American Zionist Committee for Public Affairs, AIPAC was founded in 1951 by I. L. (Sy) Kenen to circumvent State Department opposition and appeal directly to Congress for legislation to provide aid to Israel. As recently as the late 1960s the organization, which is now considered the most powerful foreign policy lobby in Washington, was essentially a one-man operation run by Kenen. Today, AIPAC has 100,000 members, approximately 160 employees with 11 regional offices, and a budget of approximately $40 million. The organization lobbies the executive branch as well as the legislative branch of government. Because of its name, AIPAC is sometimes mistakenly thought to be a political action committee (PAC), but the organization does not rate, endorse, or financially support political candidates.

835. First Aid   In 1914, the *North Carolina* became the first U.S. ship to arrive in Palestine. It brought aid from the American Jewish community.

836. Congress Backs Balfour   On September 21, 1922, the U.S. Congress approved the following resolution in support of the Balfour Declaration: "That the United States of America favors the establishment in Palestine of a national home for the Jewish people, it being clearly understood that nothing shall be done which will prejudice the civil and religious rights of Christian and all other non-Jewish communities in Palestine, and that the holy places and religious buildings and sites in Palestine shall be adequately protected."

837. Arms Embargos   President Truman imposed an arms embargo on the Middle East in 1948 in a failed effort to prevent bloodshed. Since the Arabs had no trouble getting weapons from the British and others, the U.S. embargo only harmed the Jewish state. President Johnson also imposed an embargo in 1967, partly in the hope of avoiding war and partly because Israel had eschewed his admonition not to initiate hostilities. Once again, the impact was disproportionate since Israel had no other reliable arms suppliers (Israel's other main source of arms, France, also embargoed arms), while the Arab nations continued to receive an unimpeded flow of weapons from their allies.

838. Second Aid In January 1949, the United States announced it would provide a $100 million loan to Israel. This was the first economic aid from the United States to the new state. Israel eventually became the leading recipient of U.S. economic and military assistance.

839. First Ambassadors James G. McDonald was appointed by President Truman to be the first U.S. ambassador to Israel. The first Israeli ambassador to the United States was Eliyahu Eilat.

840. Two Timer Israel has had fourteen different ambassadors to the United States. Zalman Shoval is the only person to serve in the post twice (1990–1993 and 1998–1999).

841. Israel Proves Worth Israel first proved its strategic value in 1957 when it allowed British paratroopers to overfly its territory on their way to Jordan to save the monarchy. In 1970, Israel acted more directly when the United States asked for help in bolstering King Hussein's regime. Israel's willingness to aid Amman and mobilize troops along the Jordanian border persuaded Syria to withdraw the tanks it had sent into Jordan to support PLO forces during the Black September uprising. In addition, the Soviets knew that all the squadron leaders of the Sixth Fleet landed in Israel to coordinate activities.

842. First U.S. Arms to Israel In 1962, Israel received its first major weapons system from the United States when President Kennedy agreed to sell HAWK antiaircraft missiles to Israel. The sale was opposed by the State Department, but Kennedy completed the sale after he failed to dissuade Egyptian President Nasser from escalating the arms race and after he learned that the Soviet Union had supplied Nasser with long-range bombers.

843. America Becomes Israel's Armorer The United States avoided becoming Israel's principal arms supplier for twenty years to reduce the risk of a United States–Soviet Union confrontation in the Middle East. At the end of 1968, however, President Johnson agreed to sell Israel Phantom jets. It was the largest single arms deal signed to that point by Israel. From that point on, the United States became Israel's principal arms supplier and began to guarantee Israel a qualitative arms advantage over its neighbors.

844. BSF The United States–Israel Binational Science Foundation (BSF) is a grant-awarding institution that promotes research cooperation between scientists from the United States and Israel. It was established by the two governments in 1972 and has awarded more than 2,500 research grants involving more than 2,000 scientists from more than 400 institutions located in forty-two states. BSF's income is derived from interest on an endowment of $100 million. Each government contributed $30 million in 1972 and added another $20 million each in 1984. The benefits to the United States from

BSF-sponsored studies include the extension and elaboration of research to achieve milestones that might not have been reached otherwise; the introduction of novel thinking and techniques that led American researchers to move in new directions; confirmation, clarification, and intensification of research projects; access to Israeli equipment and facilities unavailable elsewhere; and early access to Israeli research results that sped American scientific advances. BSF has documented more than seventy-five new discoveries that probably would not have been possible without foundation-supported collaboration.

845. Nixon in Israel   In 1974, Richard Nixon became the first sitting American president to visit Israel.

846. F-15s Arrive   The first U.S.-made F-15 fighters arrived in Israel in December 1976. A firestorm of protest by the religious parties erupted because they landed after the start of the Sabbath. The IAF's F-15s have downed 40 Syrian planes.

847. BIRD   The Binational Industrial Research and Development Foundation, or BIRD, was established by the United States and Israel in 1977 to fund joint U.S.-Israeli teams in the development and subsequent commercialization of innovative, nondefense technological products from which both Israeli and American companies can derive benefits commensurate with the investments and risks. Most grant recipients are small businesses involved with software, instrumentation, communications, medical devices, and semiconductors. Since its inception, BIRD has funded more than 500 joint high-tech projects. Products developed from these ventures have generated sales of $5 billion, tax revenues of more than $700 million in both countries, and created an estimated 20,000 American jobs.

848. America Fights the Boycott   In 1977, Congress prohibited U.S. companies from cooperating with the Arab boycott of Israel. When President Carter signed the law, he said the "issue goes to the very heart of free trade among nations" and that it was designed to "end the divisive effects on American life of foreign boycotts aimed at Jewish members of our society." Contrary to claims that the bill would lead to a drastic reduction in American trade with the Arab world, imports and exports increased substantially. Broader diplomatic and cultural relations also improved. Nevertheless, certain U.S. companies were blacklisted for their relations with Israel.

849. Coca-Cola   In April 1966, the Coca-Cola Company caved in to demands from consumers, restaurateurs, and distributors from around the country and opened a plant in Israel. Rival Pepsi, however, adhered to the boycott and did not sell products in Israel until 1992.

850. BARD   The Binational Agricultural Research and Development Fund (BARD) was created in 1978 with equal contributions by the United States and Israel. Since its inception, BARD has funded more than 900 projects in 42 states. BARD-sponsored research has led to new technologies in drip irrigation, pesticides, fish farming, livestock, poultry, disease control, and farm equipment.

851. MERC   The Middle East Regional Cooperation Program (MERC) was created in 1979 to promote cooperation between Israeli, Egyptian, and American scientists. Since 1989, projects have expanded to include other Arab nations. MERC focuses on projects in human and animal health, marine technology, water management, pest control, sustainable development, and agriculture. Any project of joint interest to Israel and an Arab country (Egypt, Morocco, Tunisia, and the Palestinian Authority) is eligible, but the emphasis is on solving economic and social development problems, and developing or advancing shared economic and social development opportunities.

852. Strategic Cooperation   On November 31, 1981, Israel and the United States signed a Memorandum of Understanding (MOU) termed "strategic cooperation." The agreement was diluted by opposition from the Pentagon and State Department and did not provide for joint exercises or a regular means of cooperation. Still, for the first time, Israel was formally recognized as a strategic ally and, by the end of Ronald Reagan's term, the United States had prepositioned equipment in Israel, regularly held joint training exercises, began codevelopment of the Arrow Anti-Tactical Ballistic Missile, and was engaged in a host of other cooperative military endeavors.

853. JPMG and JSAP   In 1983, Israel and the United States signed a second strategic Memorandum of Understanding (MOU) that created the Joint Political-Military Group (JPMG). The JPMG was originally designed to discuss means of countering Soviet threats, but it almost immediately focused more on bilateral concerns. The same MOU also created a group to oversee security assistance, the Joint Security Assistance Planning Group (JSAP). The JSAP was formed in response to Israel's economic crisis in the mid-1980s and focused primarily on Israel's military procurement needs.

854. JEDG   The economic relationship between Israel and the United States grew more interdependent in 1984 when Secretary of State George Shultz suggested the creation of an American-Israeli Joint Economic Development Group (JEDG) to work continuously on Israel's economic challenges. The JEDG played a pivotal role in the formulation of Israel's ambitious stabilization plan in 1984.

855. Free Trade   Israel was the first country to have a free trade agreement with the United States. The agreement was signed in 1985. Since then, trade between the two nations has increased more than 320 percent.

856. Iran-Contra Affair   According to the Report of the Congressional Committees Investigating the Iran-Contra Affair issued in November 1987, the sale of U.S. arms to Iran through Israel began in the summer of 1985, after receiving the approval of President Reagan. Israel's involvement was stimulated by separate overtures in 1985 from Iranian arms merchant Manucher Ghorbanifar and National Security Council (NSC) consultant Michael Ledeen, the latter working for National Security Adviser Robert McFarlane. When Ledeen asked Prime Minister Shimon Peres for assistance, the Israeli leader agreed to sell weapons to Iran at America's behest, providing the sale had high-level U.S. approval. By December 1985, the president had decided future sales to the Iranians would come directly from U.S. supplies. According to the committees' report, NSC aide Lt. Col. Oliver North first used money from the Iran operation to fund the Nicaraguan resistance in November 1985.

857. Pollard Affair   In November 1985, the FBI arrested Jonathan Pollard, a U.S. Navy intelligence analyst, on charges of passing sensitive information to Israel. Pollard was tried and sentenced to life in prison. His wife was convicted of aiding her husband and was handed a five-year prison term. Israel confirmed that Pollard was working as an Israeli agent and apologized for the incident. Pollard claims that the information he passed to Israel was improperly being withheld by the Pentagon. His life sentence is the longest prison term ever given to someone convicted of spying for an ally and is longer than the average term imposed for spying for the Soviet Union.

858. Almost NATO   In 1987, Congress designated Israel as a Major Non-NATO ally, which allowed Israeli industries to compete equally with NATO countries and other close U.S. allies for contracts to produce a significant number of defense items.

859. Cooperative Development Program (CDP)   The United States created CDP in 1988 to fund training and technical assistance projects run by Israel in Latin America, Asia, Africa, and Eastern and Central Europe and, increasingly, with Israel's neighbors. Past areas of emphasis included arid-lands agriculture, livestock, exotic crops, and irrigation. In addition, dozens of courses are taught in Israel on agriculture; rural development; community development; cooperation and labor studies; education; and health, medicine, and management. Projects are run out of Israel by MASHAV, Israel's foreign assistance agency, with limited U.S. involvement.

860. Loan Guarantees I   After the Soviet Union opened its gates, Russian immigration to Israel increased from less than 13,000 people in 1989 to more than 185,000 in 1990. As a result, Israel asked for assistance from the United States, which responded in 1990 by approving $400 million in loan guarantees to help Israel absorb its newcomers. The United States cosigned loans for Israel that gave bankers confidence to lend Israel money at more favorable terms—lower interest rates and longer repayment periods.

861. Israel and Desert Storm   During the Gulf War the United States benefited from the use of Israeli-made Have Nap air-launched missiles on its B-52 bombers. The navy, meanwhile, used Israeli Pioneer pilotless drones for reconnaissance in the Gulf. Israel provided mine plows that were used to clear paths for allied forces through Iraqi minefields. Mobile bridges provided by Israel were employed by the U.S. Marine Corps. Israeli recommendations led to several software changes that made the Patriot a more capable missile defense system. Night-vision goggles used by U.S. forces were supplied by Israel. A low altitude warning system produced and developed in Israel was utilized on Blackhawk helicopters. Israel offered the United States the use of military and hospital facilities. U.S. ships utilized Haifa port shipyard maintenance and support on their way to the Gulf. Since Israel's military intelligence has focused on Iraq much more carefully over the years than has the U.S. intelligence community, the Israelis were able to provide Washington with detailed tactical intelligence on Iraqi military activities.

862. Loan Guarantees II Realizing immigration demands exceeded its resources, Israel asked the United States for an additional $10 billion in guarantees. In 1992, Congress authorized the president to provide guarantees in annual increments of $2 billion over five years. The president was empowered to reduce the annual loan guarantees by the amount equal to the estimated value of Israeli settlement activities in the West Bank and Gaza Strip undertaken the previous year. He was also given the option of waiving some of this amount for security reasons. The State Department determined that Israel spent just under $1.4 billion for settlement activity from 1993 to 1996 and the president determined that $585 million could be offset for security reasons, so the final reduction was just under $774 million.

863. USISTC Recognizing the potential for greater cooperation, in March 1993 President Clinton established a U.S.-Israel Science and Technology Commission. Its mission is to encourage high-tech industries in both countries to engage in joint projects, to foster scientific exchanges between universities and research institutions, to promote development of agricultural and environmental technologies, and to assist in the adaptation of military technology to civilian production.

864. Embassy Relocation Act The Jerusalem Embassy Act of 1995 recalls several previous congressional resolutions calling for the city to remain united. The act states that the official policy of the United States toward Jerusalem is that it should remain a united city in which the rights of every ethnic and religious group are protected; that it should be recognized as the capital of the State of Israel; and that the U.S. Embassy should be established there no later than May 31, 1999. The act also allowed the president to waive provisions in the act if he determines it is necessary to protect the national security interests of the United States. Since it was enacted, every president has used waivers to prevent the act from being implemented.

865. TRIDE   To encourage economic cooperation as a pillar of the peace process, the United States, Jordan, and Israel launched TRIDE as a pilot program in 1996. The program, based on the model of the U.S.-Israel Binational Industrial Research and Development (BIRD) Foundation, supports joint venture projects by private-sector firms from the three countries. TRIDE grants promote research and development, manufacturing, and marketing of new products and technologies. Jordan, Israel, and the United States agreed to contribute equally toward a $1 million fund for the pilot program. Like BIRD, the companies involved will pay 50 percent of the costs to develop the product while TRIDE will provide a matching grant for the remaining 50 percent. The BIRD Foundation administers the program in cooperation with Jordan's Investment Promotion Corporation. Together, they will identify potential joint ventures and facilitate three-way strategic partnerships.

866. Joint Stamps   The United States and Israel each issued the same Chanukah stamp in 1996.

867. Letter of 81   On April 6, 1998, eighty-one U.S. senators wrote to President Clinton after reports were published of a disagreement between the administration and Israel regarding the peace process. The letter expressed opposition to the idea of the United States publicly presenting a peace proposal that would be unacceptable to Israel. The senators wrote: "American Middle East diplomacy, as you know and have shown so well, has always worked best when pursued quietly and in concert with Israel. We strongly urge you to continue our critical role as facilitator of a process that can ultimately succeed only through the direct negotiations by the parties themselves." This rebuke of Clinton's policy eased pressure on the Israeli government.

868. Security MOA   On October 31, 1998, the United States and Israel signed a Security Memorandum of Agreement to enhance Israel's defensive and deterrent capabilities and upgrade the framework of the U.S.-Israeli strategic and military relationships, as well as the technological cooperation between them.

869. Strategic Policy   The United States and Israel agreed in 1999 to establish the Strategic Policy Planning Group, composed of senior representatives of the national security entities of both countries, to bolster Israel's defense and deterrence capabilities.

870. Counterterror Group   In 1994, the two countries signed an agreement concerning counterterrorism research and development, and in 1996 they signed another general agreement on counterterrorism cooperation. In July 1999, a U.S.-Israel Working Group on Counter-terrorism was established to "share intelligence assessments, and prepare plans for cooperation in the development of technological means for counter-terrorism."

871. Cooperative Development Research Program (CDR)   The United States funds the CDR program to help scientists from target countries in Africa, Asia, Latin America, Eastern Europe, and the Balkan states obtain Israeli technology and collaborate with Israeli researchers. CDR provides funding for Israeli and developing country scientists to cooperate in joint research on significant development problems, while strengthening the future ability of the non-Israeli scientists to do such research themselves. CDR seeks innovative research ideas in natural sciences and engineering that aim to solve serious development problems. The program emphasizes areas in which Israeli technology and expertise could be particularly valuable to target countries, such as arid-lands and saline agriculture, irrigation and hydrology, biological control of insects, development of appropriate medical technology, solar energy, and desalination.

872. Joint Weapons   Israel is a world leader in the development of military technology. Using the lessons learned from a history of fighting for its survival without enormous resources from which to draw, Israeli engineers have designed military equipment that is extremely cost-effective. By teaming with American defense industries, Israeli defense companies have become a significant provider of military equipment to the U.S. Armed Forces. For example, U.S. Air Force bombers now have a supply of Israeli-designed missiles that can be fired from long ranges. U.S. Army soldiers in some units are now safer because their infantry vehicles have Israeli-designed armor attached to the sides and American commanders on the ground can now locate enemy units through the use of high-flying unmanned aircraft, the use of which has been pioneered by the Israel Defense Forces for more than a decade. These systems are all being jointly manufactured in the United States and Israel as a result of these industrial partnerships. The Arrow antitactical ballistic missile program is one of the centerpieces of the U.S.-Israel strategic relationship. One of the most advanced missile defense systems in the world, the Arrow offers Israel an essential capability against ballistic missiles and provides the U.S. with key research and technology for other theater missile defense programs.

873. NASA and Israel   The United States and Israel have cooperated extensively in space-related research. This cooperation includes: an Israeli astronaut aboard the *Columbia* in 2003; an experiment on the space shuttle *Endeavor* in 1992 that investigated the effects of near-zero gravity; and the AERONET program, established in 1992 with Ben-Gurion University of the Negev, which studied the relation between atmospheric and surface properties in desert transition areas. In 1996, NASA and International Space Agency (ISA) signed an agreement calling "for cooperation in the peaceful use of space" and the development of cooperative programs. This cooperation was highlighted in 1999 with the opening of NASA's regional Earth Observing System Data and Information System (EOSDIS) center, located at Tel Aviv University.

874. Firefighters   Beginning in 1987, the United States Forest Service (USFS) and the Jewish National Fund (JNF) have cooperated in fire-fighting and conservation efforts. The relationship was forged when Israel was suffering one of the worst fire seasons in its history. Terrorists were setting the country's precious forests ablaze, and Israel urgently needed to modernize its fire-fighting systems to cope with the widespread arson. Since that time, USFS and Israeli firefighters and conservationists have had regular exchanges to share their knowledge and experience.

875. Internet II   The United States included Israel in the Internet II project, a consortium of academic research centers, high-tech companies, and government agencies working to create a new, faster information highway.

876. U.S. Aid to Israel, 1949–1973   Israel has received more direct aid from the United States since World War II than any other country. Between 1949 and 1973, the United States provided Israel with an average of about $122 million a year, for a total of $3.1 billion (more than $1 billion of the total was loans for military equipment in 1971–1973). Prior to 1971, Israel received a total of only $277 million in military aid, all in the form of loans as credit sales. The bulk of the economic aid took the form of loans, not grants.

877. U.S. Aid to Israel, 1974–2005   Since 1974, Israel has received approximately $90 billion in assistance, including three special aid packages. Starting with fiscal year 1987, Israel received $1.2 billion in grants for economic aid. In 1998, Israel offered to voluntarily reduce its dependence on U.S. economic aid. According to an agreement reached with the Clinton administration and Congress, the $1.2 billion economic aid package is reduced each year so that it will be phased out in ten years. By 2008, military aid will increase from $1.8 billion to $2.4 billion and economic aid will cease. For 2005, Congress approved $2.22 billion in military assistance, $360 million in economic assistance, and $50 million to help resettle refugees.

878. Military Aid to Israel   U.S. military aid to Israel is provided through the Foreign Military Financing (FMF) program. Roughly one-fourth of what Israel receives can be spent in Israel for military procurement. The remaining three-fourths must be spent in the United States purchasing military equipment from American firms to generate profits and jobs. More than 1,000 companies in 47 states, the District of Columbia, and Puerto Rico have signed contracts worth billions of dollars through this program.

879. Hoover on Palestine   "Palestine which, desolate for centuries, is now renewing its youth and vitality through enthusiasm, hard work, and self-sacrifice of the Jewish pioneers who toil there in a spirit of peace and social justice."—President Herbert Hoover

880. Truman on Israeli Independence   "I had faith in Israel before it was established; I have faith in it now."—President Harry Truman granting de facto recognition to the new Jewish State eleven minutes after Israel's proclamation of independence.

881. Eisenhower on Israel   "Our forces saved the remnant of the Jewish people of Europe for a new life and a new hope in the reborn land of Israel. Along with all men of good will, I salute the young state and wish it well."—President Dwight Eisenhower

882. LBJ on Israel   "The United States and Israel share many common objectives . . . chief of which is the building of a better world in which every nation can develop its resources and develop them in freedom and peace. Our society is illuminated by the spiritual insights of the Hebrew prophets. America and Israel have a common love of human freedom and they have a common faith in a democratic way of life."—President Lyndon Johnson

883. Nixon on Israeli Values   "Americans admire a people who can scratch a desert and produce a garden. The Israelis have shown qualities that Americans identify with: guts, patriotism, idealism, a passion for freedom. I have seen it. I know. I believe that."—President Richard Nixon

884. Ford on America's Commitment   "[The American] commitment to the security and future of Israel is based upon basic morality as well as enlightened self-interest. Our role in supporting Israel honors our own heritage."—President Gerald Ford

885. Carter on Israeli Survival   "The survival of Israel is not just a political issue, it is a moral imperative. That is my deeply held belief and it is the belief shared by the vast majority of the American people. . . . A strong, secure Israel is not just in Israel's interest. It's in the interest of the United States and in the interest of the entire free world."—President Jimmy Carter

886. Reagan on Israeli Stability   "In Israel, free men and women are every day demonstrating the power of courage and faith. Back in 1948 when Israel was founded, pundits claimed the new country could never survive. Today, no one questions that Israel is a land of stability and democracy in a region of tyranny and unrest."—President Ronald Reagan

887. Bush on Friendship with Israel   "The friendship, the alliance between the United States and Israel is strong and solid, built upon a foundation of shared democratic values, of shared history and heritage, that sustains the life of our two countries. The emotional bond of our people transcends politics. Our strategic cooperation . . . is a source of mutual security. And the United States' commitment to the security of Israel remains unshakeable. We may differ over some policies from time to time, individual policies, but never over the principle."—President George Bush

888. Clinton on Israel's Fiftieth Birthday   "The United States admires Israel for all that it has overcome and for all that it has accomplished. We are proud of the strong bond we have forged with Israel, based on our shared values and ideals. That unique relationship will endure just as Israel has endured."—President Bill Clinton (from a letter to Israeli Prime Minister Netanyahu from President Bill Clinton on the occasion of Israel's 50th birthday)

889. Bush on Standing with Israel   "We will speak up for our principles and we will stand up for our friends in the world. And one of our most important friends is the State of Israel."—President George W. Bush

ISRAEL AND THE WORLD

Israel and the Arab World

890. Hajj Amin Al-Husseini (1893–1974)   Haj Amin al-Husseini was the uncontested leader of the Arab Palestinian community from 1921 until 1948. He was born in Jerusalem to a wealthy and influential Arab family; both his father and brother served as Mufti of Jerusalem. During World War I, al-Husseini served as an officer in the Turkish army. Upon returning to Palestine after being released from the army, he galvanized anti-British and anti-Jewish feelings in the Arab community. The British sentenced him to a ten-year prison term for inciting riots, whereupon he fled to Transjordan to avoid prison. A year later, in 1921, when his brother Mufti Kamel died, he was pardoned and appointed Grand Mufti of Jerusalem by British High Commissioner Sir Herbert Samuel. He was responsible for the deadly attacks against Jewish settlements in 1929 and 1936. Following the 1936 riots, the British removed al-Husseini from his post and he left Palestine. During World War II the Mufti met with Adolf Hitler and actively supported the Nazis. His influence waned following Israel's victory in the War of Independence. Hajj Amin al-Husseini raised the funds to have the dome of the Dome of the Rock overlaid with gold.

891. Egypt   With a population of over 76 million, Egypt is the most populous Arab country and possesses the strongest military in the Arab world. Located in northern Africa, Egypt borders the Mediterranean Sea and is sandwiched between Libya and Israel. Egypt, along with other Arab countries, attacked Israel in 1948 in an effort to prevent the establishment of the Jewish State. Egypt maintained a state of belligerence with Israel, sponsored terrorist attacks, and blocked the Straits of Tiran to Israeli shipping, all of which contributed to Israel's decision to join Britain and France in attacking Egypt in the 1956 Suez campaign. Israel was forced to withdraw from the territory it conquered in that war, but the Egyptians again blocked Israel's shipping lanes and prepared to attack Israel. On June 6, 1967, Israel launched a preemptive strike and wiped out the Egyptian air force. At the end of six days, Israel had cap-

tured the Sinai Peninsula. The fighting did not end for long. Egypt soon began shelling Israeli positions in what became a two-year (1968–1970) war of
attrition. In conjunction with Syria, Egypt launched a surprise attack against
Israel on October 6, 1973. Though Israel won the war, the success of the Egyptians in surprising the Israelis and inflicting heavy casualties helped restore
Egypt's pride and prestige in the Arab world. The result, combined with Anwar Sadat's decision to shift from an alliance with the Soviet Union to one
with the United States, paved the way for his historic trip in November 1977
to Jerusalem, which was followed, in 1979, by the signing of the Camp David
Accords. Egypt's peace with Israel has been termed a "cold peace" because relations have not expanded and normalized to the degree expected by Israel;
nonetheless, Sadat's bold move to make peace with Israel ultimately eased the
path for other Arab nations to negotiate peace agreements with Israel.

892. Gamal Abdul Nasser (1918–1970)   Served as president of Egypt
and was the leader of Pan-Arabism, an ideology espousing the unification of
the Arab world under a single leadership. As an officer in the army he fought
against Israel in the War of Independence and participated in the successful
1952 coup against King Farouk. After assuming the presidency in 1954, Nasser
nationalized the press, moved decisively into the Russian orbit, procured large
quantities of Soviet arms, nationalized the Suez Canal, and actively supported
fedayeen attacks on Israel. These actions contributed to the decision of Britain,
France, and Israel to attack Egypt in 1956. Nasser's closing of the Gulf of Eilat
to Israeli shipping and mobilization of forces along Israel's borders led to the
Six-Day War. After military defeat in the conflict, he resigned, only to return
within hours after mass demonstrations demanded his leadership. Nasser's support extended beyond Egypt to the Arab masses; he founded Nasserism, a pan-
Arabist movement under his leadership.

893. Muhammed Anwar al-Sadat (1918–1981)   Succeeded Nasser
as president of Egypt and forged a peace treaty with Israel. Sadat supported
Germany during World War II, praising Hitler, and assisted German prisoners
of war in escaping from Allied prison territory. He served five years as an officer in the army, participated in the overthrow of King Farouk in 1952, and succeeded Nasser as president in October 1970. After expelling some 20,000 Soviet advisers in 1972, Sadat orchestrated the surprise attack against Israel during
the 1973 Yom Kippur War. In a bold move, Sadat went to Jerusalem in November 1977. This trip set in motion the events that led to the signing of the
Camp David Peace Accords between Egypt and Israel. On October 6, 1981,
while reviewing a parade celebrating Egypt's participation in the Yom Kippur
War, Sadat was assassinated by Islamic fundamentalists.

894. Hosni Mubarak (1928–)   A former fighter pilot and chief of staff in
the Egyptian Air Force, Mubarak succeeded Anwar Sadat as president of Egypt in

1981 and has served ever since. He pledged to maintain the peace with Israel and has done so. Mubarak endured a ten-year-long exile from the Arab League due to Egypt's peace agreement with Israel. He has done little to strengthen ties with Israel and often encourages other Arab countries to take a hard line in talks with Israel rather than encouraging them to make concessions for peace. Mubarak's only trip to Israel was for Rabin's funeral in November 1995.

895. Syria   Located on Israel's northern frontier and bordering the Mediterranean Sea between Turkey and Lebanon, Syria was administered by the French until independence in 1946. In 1948, Syria joined the other Arab nations that attacked Israel. The two countries had a number of border skirmishes in the 1960s, and Syrian artillery shelled Israeli farms in the Galilee. After Syria joined in an alliance with Egypt and threatened to attack, Israel launched a preemptive strike in 1967, capturing the Golan Heights. Syria tried to regain the area and destroy Israel with its surprise attack in 1973 but ended the war with less territory than when it began. Since 1967, Syria has been in an official state of war with Israel; however, no large-scale combat between the two countries has occurred since 1973. From 1976 to 2005, Syrian troops occupied Lebanon. Syria demands the return of the Golan Heights but will not say what steps it will take toward normalizing relations with Israel in return. Israel has expressed a willingness to return most, if not all, of the territory if it is in exchange for a peace treaty similar to those signed with Egypt and Jordan. Syria has a population of just over eighteen million, 10 percent of whom are Christian.

896. Hafez Assad (1930–2000)   Assad was a general in the Syrian army and was serving as defense minister when he led a coup against the government in 1970 and installed himself as president in 1971. A member of the minority Alawite sect of Islam, Assad ruled Syria by maintaining a tight grip on power and quashing dissent. In one of the most brutal examples of his willingness to violently suppress opposition, he sent troops to raze the town of Hama in 1982, killing as many as 10,000 of his own citizens. Assad aspired to create a Greater Syria and took effective control of Lebanon in 1976 when he sent 30,000 troops into the country under the pretext of ending Lebanon's civil war. In the 1990s, Assad opened negotiations with Israel but refused to make concessions regarding ending the state of war with Israel without first getting back the entire Golan Heights. He never negotiated directly with an Israeli official.

897. Bashar Assad (1965–)   After Hafez Assad's death, his son and handpicked successor took power. Bashar Assad became president of Syria in 2000. Educated in England as an eye doctor, he assumed power because his older brother, who was the heir apparent, was killed in a car crash in 1994.

898. Syria's Jews   Roughly 30,000 Jews lived in Syria in 1946, the year that Syria became independent. That same year, Jewish emigration was banned and Jews were subject to physical attack and economic boycotts. In 1947, in Aleppo, where the Jewish community continued uninterrupted for some 2,500 years, Jews were killed and buildings were destroyed. Jews remained trapped in Syria, subject to persecution. Few Jews were allowed to leave Syria until 1994 when 1,262 Syrian Jews came to Israel. Following the Madrid peace conference, the Jewish community was permitted to immigrate. Today, fewer than 200 Jews live in Syria.

899. Hashemite Kingdom of Jordan   Located east of the Jordan River and bordering the nations of Israel, Syria, Iraq, and Saudi Arabia, Trans-Jordan was established in 1921 when the territory was shorn from the Palestinian Mandate and ceded to Abdullah in return for his efforts in fighting the Turks in World War I. This region covers some 92,000 square kilometers, equaling approximately three-fourths of the entire Palestinian Mandate. In 1946, Jordan achieved independence and King Abdullah, who traces his lineage directly to Muhammad, assumed the throne, establishing the Hashemite Kingdom. In 1948, it was Jordan's British-trained Arab Legion that did most of the fighting against Israel, capturing the Old City and the eastern half of Jerusalem, as well as the West Bank. Jordan's annexation of the West Bank in 1950, recognized by only England and Pakistan, prompted the government to change its name from Transjordan to Jordan. In its nineteen-year reign over that area, it never accepted any Palestinian claim to the territory. After fighting began in the region in 1967, Israel urged Jordan to stay out of the war, but King Hussein opted to attack Israel and ultimately lost both Jerusalem and the West Bank. After the Six-Day War, although they were technically at war, Israel and Jordan maintained cordial relations. In 1970, Israel came to Hussein's aid and prevented a Syrian-Palestinian takeover of his country. Jordan signed a formal peace treaty with Israel in 1994. Unlike Israel's treaty with Egypt, the treaty with Jordan has led to greater cooperation and warmer relations. A majority of Jordan's population of 5.6 million is Palestinian. About 6 percent of the country is Christian.

900. King Abdullah's Death   On July 20, 1951, King Abdullah was assassinated while leaving Friday morning prayers at the Al-Aksa Mosque. The King's secret meetings with Golda Meir and Moshe Dayan contributed to his assassination.

901. King Hussein (1935–1999)   Prior to his death at age 63 on February 7, 1999, King Hussein bin Talal was the longest-serving executive head of state in the world. He was able to trace his ancestry directly to Muhammad, a span of 42 generations. Born in Amman, Hussein was with his grandfather, King Abdullah, when the king was assassinated in 1951. Originally, King Abdullah's eldest son, King Talal, assumed the throne, but he was determined to be mentally incapacitated and was quickly replaced by his eldest son, Hussein, who was proclaimed King on August 11, 1952.

Hussein did not officially take power until after turning eighteen in 1953. He survived numerous assassination attempts and held many covert meetings with Israeli officials. Ignoring Israeli warning to stay out of the Six-Day War, Hussein ordered an attack on Israel and subsequently lost control of the West Bank. Always reluctant to move ahead of others in the Arab world, Hussein moved quickly to sign a peace treaty with Israel in 1994 only after the Israelis had first negotiated the Oslo agreement with the Palestinians. King Hussein was viewed as a moderate Arab leader who frequently allied himself with American interests.

902. King Abdullah bin al-Hussein (1962–)   On February 7, 1999, the day his father, King Hussein, passed away, Abdullah bin al-Hussein was crowned monarch of the Hashemite Kingdom of Jordan. Abdullah was educated in American and British secondary schools and studied at the Royal Military Academy Sandhurst and at Oxford University. Returning to Jordan, Abdullah pursued a military career. In June 1994, he became the commander of the Jordanian Special Forces, holding the rank of brigadier general. In 1997 he led the Special Operations Command, and just one year later achieved the rank of major general.

903. Israel-Jordan Relations   Formal peace between Israel and Jordan has only existed since 1994, but the level of hostility between the two countries was never as great as that between Israel and the other Arab countries, and secret contacts were maintained for more than twenty years. In addition to the treaty itself, the two countries have signed more than fifteen agreements covering such issues as economic trade, scientific cooperation, and cultural understanding. Jordan withdrew from the Arab boycott of Israel, and a fairly open border policy prevails.

904. Palestine Liberation Organization (PLO)   Founded in 1964 during a meeting known as the Palestinian Congress in an effort to give a voice to the large number of Palestinians living in refugee camps in Lebanon. The group splintered into various factions, most notable of which are the Popular Front for the Liberation of Palestine (PFLP), Popular Democratic Front for the Liberation of Palestine, Popular Democratic Front for the Liberation of Palestine-General Command, and al-Fatah. Each of these factions remained under the umbrella of the PLO. For the next decade, the organization pursued its goals primarily through terrorist means. In 1974, the PLO altered its focus from being a purely terrorist organization to one that would pursue its goals on the political front as well. This decision caused a further split in the organization, as certain factions remained committed to the liberation of Palestine through violent means alone. By 1988, PLO leader Yasser Arafat, seeking greater diplomatic recognition, particularly from the United States, announced his acceptance of the right of the State of Israel to exist and renounced terrorism. This was the first step in a process that led to the inclusion of the PLO in the peace process and the eventual signing of the Oslo peace agreement. Two groups under the PLO umbrella, the PFLP and the Democratic Front for the Liberation of Palestine-Hawatmeh faction (DFLP-H), suspended their participation in the PLO in protest of the agreement and continued their campaign of violence. Despite this renunciation, the PLO continued committing terrorism. Upon the implementation of the Oslo peace agreement, the PLO became the overwhelmingly dominant player in the newly established Palestinian Authority, the government of the Palestinians in the West Bank and Gaza Strip. The only two elected leaders of the Palestinian Authority, Yasser Arafat and Mahmoud Abbas, hailed from the PLO.

905. Yasser Arafat (1929–2004)   Yasser Arafat was born Mohammed Yasser Abdul-Ra'ouf Arafat al-Qudwa al-Husseini, in Cairo, Egypt, to Palestinian parents. When Arafat was five years old, his mother died and he went to live with an uncle in Jerusalem. He returned to Egypt a few years later, and eventually attended King Fuad University in Egypt, where he received a bachelor's degree in civil engineering in 1956. He was a member of the Muslim Brotherhood while a student. In 1958, he left Egypt for Kuwait, where he worked as an engineer. In Kuwait, he discussed the idea of establishing "Fatah," the Palestinian National Liberation Movement. He then returned to Palestine and met with a group of Palestinian activists and founded the Fatah Movement on January 1, 1965. Arafat stayed in Jerusalem until 1967 before moving to Jordan. In 1969 he became the third person to be elected chairman for the Executive Committee of the PLO. In the aftermath of the September 1970 war in Jordan, he fled to Lebanon and remained there until 1982. In 1982, as a result of Israel's invasion of Lebanon, Arafat left Beirut for Tunisia. In 1974, he became the first person representing a nongovernmental organization to address the UN General Assembly at a plenary session. During his address, he wore a gun on his hip and compared himself to George Washington and Abraham Lincoln. On September 13, 1993, Yasser Arafat signed the Declaration of Principles agreement in Washington, D.C., with Israeli Prime Minister Yitzhak Rabin. On May 4, 1994, Arafat signed the Cairo agreement with Rabin. On July 1994, he returned to Gaza after a twenty-seven-year absence from Israel and the territories. Arafat was awarded the Nobel Peace Prize, which he shared with PM Yitzhak Rabin and Shimon Peres. On January 20, 1994, Arafat was elected president of the Palestinian National Authority with 83 percent of the vote. No other votes were held by the Palestinian Authority during Arafat's lifetime, and he remained the president of the Authority until November 11, 2004, when he died in a French hospital.

906. Mahmoud Abbas (1935–)   Also known as Abu Mazen, Mahmoud Abbas was elected president of the Palestinian Authority on January 9, 2005, with

62 percent of the popular vote. His election was just the second election for PA president and the first since the death of Yasser Arafat. Abbas was born in 1935 in the city of Safed. He fled to Syria in 1948 as a result of the Arab-Israel conflict. Abbas received a PhD from a Russian school and later returned to the Middle East, where he became one of the founders of the PLO's largest faction, Fatah. He served on the PLO Executive Committee and was elected to be the secretary general of the committee in 1996. Abbas led the Palestinian delegation involved with the secret negotiations with Israel at Oslo, and he signed the 1993 Oslo Accords as a representative of the PLO. While Arafat was serving as president, Abbas held numerous top political posts, including being named the first prime minister of the Palestinian Authority in 2003. He resigned as prime minister as a result of not being given enough authority by Yasser Arafat.

907. Black September   After the defeat of the Arab armies during the Six-Day War, the PLO established itself in Jordan and built an extensive terrorist infrastructure that included some 20,000 armed members. The increasing influence of the PLO within Jordan and the frequent military strikes by Israel on PLO targets within Jordanian territory increasingly threatened the stability of King Hussein bin Talal's regime. The king moved against the Palestinians on September 9, 1970, and fighting continued until September 29. PLO losses numbered some 8,000 dead and tens of thousands wounded. PLO forces, expelled from Jordan, fled to Lebanon. Amidst the fighting, Syrian forces briefly invaded northern Jordan but were forced to pull out when PLO forces were trounced and Israel indicated that it would not stand idly by and watch Syria invade Jordan.

908. Lebanon   Located on Israel's northern border between the Mediterranean Sea and Syria, Lebanon—a country of 3.8 million people—has been torn apart by internal conflict for much of its history. The country gained its independence from the French in 1943 and quickly became the "Paris of the Middle East." It was governed by a constitution that crafted a balance of power between the various religious groups, based largely on their population. In the early 1970s, the PLO established itself in southern Lebanon, building an armed force and launching terrorist attacks against Israel from Lebanese territory. By 1975, Palestinian refugees in Southern Lebanon numbered some 300,000. That same year, the country was plunged into a bloody sixteen-year civil war between Christians and Muslims due in part to the changing religious demographics and the Christian refusal to share power with the Muslims. The Christian population, which is now about 39 percent of the country, used to be a majority and once dominated the political scene, but with the growth of the Muslim population from minority to majority status, the balance of power shifted. The civil war ended in 1989 when Syria sent thousands of troops into the country, ostensibly to keep the peace. Lebanese politics has been dominated by Syria ever since. It is estimated that more than 100,000 Lebanese were killed during the civil war. Repeated attacks from Palestinian terrorists provoked Israel to launch large-scale counterattacks. In 1982, Israel invaded Lebanon with the intention of finally ending the Palestinian threat to its northern border. Israel succeeded in driving the Palestinian leadership out but maintained a security zone to insure quiet. This did not work out as planned, as other terrorists took up where the PLO left off and kept up attacks against Israeli forces and their southern Lebanese Christian allies. Finally, in 2000, Israel unilaterally withdrew to the internationally recognized border. The Good Fence is a border crossing in northern Israel where some Lebanese are allowed to enter Israel for work and medical care. The name originated in 1976, when a Lebanese child was allowed to come to Israel for medical treatment. In just five months in 1976, Israel treated over 11,000 Lebanese who sought medical care in Israel. In May 2000, when Israel withdrew from Lebanon, some 6,500 Lebanese entered and settled in Israel by passing through the fence.

909. Iraq   Bordering the Persian Gulf between Iran and Kuwait, this country of twenty-five million has no border with Israel; nevertheless, it has been one of Israel's staunchest enemies, sending troops to fight in the wars of 1948 and 1967. Iraq gained its independence in 1932 and was run by a series of dictators from 1958 until 2004, when the United States removed Saddam Hussein from power. In 1980, seeking to seize land, Iraq initiated what became an eight-year war with Iran that cost the lives of approximately one million people. In 1981, Israel bombed Iraq's Osirak nuclear facility, destroying Iraq's ability to produce nuclear weapons. Iraq invaded Kuwait in 1990, and the United States led an international coalition to liberate Kuwait in the Gulf War. In an attempt to fracture the coalition, Iraq bombarded Tel Aviv with some forty Scud missiles and four Israeli lives were lost. Israel did not retaliate against Iraq during the war.

910. King Hassan (1929–1999)   Crowned in 1961, King Hassan served as the king of Morocco for almost forty years. Hassan was an ally of the United States during the Cold War and took a conciliatory position vis-à-vis Israel. Morocco was the site of many discreet meetings between Israeli and Arab diplomats, and Hassan played a key role in facilitating the negotiations between Israel and Egypt in the 1970s. King Hassan died in 1999 and was succeeded by son Sidi Mohammed.

911. Saudi Arabia   In 1902, Abdul al-Aziz Ibn Saud began a campaign that conquered and unified the Arabian peninsula under one banner. In the 1930s, the discovery of oil made the Saudi kingdom an important player on the world stage. Over the years, oil revenue helped make the Saudis rich and politically influential. Saudi Arabia sent troops to fight against Israel in 1947,

1967, and 1973. In 1973, Saudi Arabia organized the oil embargo against countries that supported Israel. The embargo was lifted in 1974 after Israel signed cease-fire agreements with Egypt and Syria. Saudi Arabia hosted American troops during the Gulf War. Though it has no territorial dispute with Israel, Saudi Arabia has remained in a formal state of war with Israel and is one of the few Arab countries that continues to enforce the Arab boycott against Israel. Today, Saudi Arabia possesses the largest oil reserves in the world (25 percent of proved reserves) and has a population of over twenty million citizens.

912. The Arab Boycott   The Arab League Council announced on December 2, 1945, that "Jewish products and manufactured goods shall be considered undesirable to the Arab countries." In establishing the boycott, the council called upon the Arab world "to refuse to deal in, distribute, or consume Zionist products or manufactured goods." The boycott, which was established before the State of Israel came into existence, eventually contained three elements: a primary boycott against direct trade with Israel, a secondary boycott against companies that do business with Israel, and a tertiary boycott against companies that do business with other companies that do business with Israel.

913. The Boycott Crumbles   Egypt ceased adhering to the boycott of Israel when the two countries signed a peace treaty. On September 30, 1994, the six Persian Gulf states declared that they too would cease adhering to the secondary boycott of Israel. In February 1995, Egyptian, American, Jordanian, and Palestinian trade leaders signed a declaration calling for "efforts to end the boycott of Israel." The boycott has continued to weaken.

International Relations

914. Diplomatic Ties   Israel has relations with 160 countries. It has full diplomatic relations with three Arab countries: Jordan, Egypt, and Mauritania. Morocco, Tunisia, and Oman severed relations in 2000; Niger did so in 2002.

915. Czechoslovakia   Between 1948 and 1950, while the United States, Britain, and the other Western nation adhered to an arms embargo against Israel, Israel purchased arms from Czechoslovakia, which provided tens of thousands of rifles, twelve German Messerschmitt planes, and twenty British Spitfires.

916. Holland   The first country to establish diplomatic representation in Jerusalem, Holland has allied itself with Israeli interests. When the USSR severed relations with Israel, Holland represented Israeli interests to the Soviet government. Holland also voted in the UN for the establishment of Israel, fought against Arab aggression and the boycott of Israel, and actively supported Israeli participation with the European Economic Community. Holland has always played an active role assisting Jews, be it during the Holocaust or in response to oppression in the Soviet Union or Arab countries.

917. Doctor's Plot   In January 1953, Josef Stalin "exposed" a cabal of doctors intent on murdering top Russian officials. This exposé served as the pretext for a purge of Stalin's enemies in the Russian government. Seven of the nine doctors named were Jewish, and the Russian media was overtly anti-Semitic. On February 9, a bomb detonated in the Russian Embassy injured four staff members. Despite official Israeli apologies, Russia suspended relations with Israel for a few months.

918. U Nu (1907–1995)   In 1955, the prime minister of Burma, U Nu, became the first head of state to visit Israel.

919. Bulgaria   A Bulgarian Air Force jet shot down an EL AL plane flying from Paris to Israel that had veered off course and entered Bulgarian airspace on July 29, 1955.

920. Libyan Airplane   Israel downed a civilian Libyan airliner when it errantly flew over the Sinai on February 21, 1973. One hundred and five passengers and the crew were killed in the incident.

921. African Relations   Between November 25, 1973, and November 13, 1974, twenty-six African states severed diplomatic relations with Israel as a result of Arab political pressure in the aftermath of the 1973 war.

922. Embassies in Jerusalem   Only two countries have embassies in Jerusalem—Costa Rica and El Salvador. Of the nearly 200 nations with which America has diplomatic relations, Israel is the only nation whose capital is not recognized by the United States and for which the U.S. embassy is not in the capital. The U.S. embassy, like most other embassies, is located in Tel Aviv.

923. German War Reparations   In 1951, Israel asked the four powers occupying Germany for $1.5 billion in reparations for the Holocaust. The following year, Germany signed an agreement with Israel to pay war reparations to recompense partially for the atrocities and losses visited on the Jews by the Nazis. The offer of monetary reparations by Germany set off a heated debate within Israeli society and in the Knesset, marked by the temporary expulsion of MK Menachem Begin from the Knesset because of his outbursts and behavior opposing the reparations. The agreement resulted in the payment of $820 million to Israel. Additionally, Germany distributed $468 million to Jews residing in Israel. To date, Germany has paid more than $80 billion in compensation to Holocaust victims worldwide.

924. German Reconciliation   In 1965, Israel and West Germany exchanged ambassadors for the first time. Even two decades after the Holocaust, the move was controversial. Today, Germany is Israel's largest trading partner in

Europe, importing over $138 million worth of Israeli goods and exporting to Israel over $282 million in 2004.

925. France Ends Embargo   After more than two decades, France resumed shipping arms to Israel in 1989. The French had been Israel's principal supplier for nearly twenty years before Charles de Gaulle imposed an arms embargo in 1967.

THE UNITED NATIONS

926. League of Nations   This forerunner of the United Nations was established in 1920 and dissolved in April 1946 to make room for the formation of the United Nations. On July 24, 1922, the League granted Britain the task of placing Palestine "under such political, administrative, and economic conditions as will secure the establishment of the Jewish National Home." The refusal of the United States, one of the original architects of the institution, to join the League crippled the organization from the outset. The start of World War II prevented the League from taking up any further action regarding Palestine.

927. United Nations   The United Nations has played a prominent role in Israel's history starting with the partition plan. Only after extended debate and two separate applications for consideration was Israel granted membership on May 11, 1949. For decades, Israel was frozen out of numerous spheres of UN participation. Additionally, for forty-five years Arab states moved to expel Israel from the UN and walked out of sessions addressed by Israelis. The combination of the Arab and communist blocs influenced the UN into a consistently anti-Israel bias, condemning Israeli reprisals while ignoring Arab military and terrorist attacks. In the 1948, 1956, 1967, and 1973 wars, the United Nations stepped in to broker cessation of hostilities only after Israel achieved dominance on the battlefield. Important resolutions include 181, 242, and 338, and the Zionism is Racism resolution and subsequent repeal. Each year, numerous anti-Israel resolutions are introduced and many are adopted by the General Assembly. The United States has cast more Security Council vetoes to kill one-sided resolutions criticizing Israel than on any other issue.

928. WEOG   On May 30, 2000, after being excluded from UN bodies for fifty years, Israel was invited to become a member of the Western European and Others regional group (WEOG). Although Israel belongs in the Asian group geographically, Arab states have prevented Israel's participation. The geopolitical WEOG includes 27 members: all West European states, Australia, Canada, New Zealand, and the United States. Membership allows Israel to sit on the Security Council and on other UN bodies from which it was previously excluded. However, because the membership is limited, Israel can only participate in the New York office, which excludes it from discussions on a number of issues handled at other offices, including racism and human rights. Although change in status marks improvement, Israel still hopes to gain membership in the Asian group and participate in other UN offices.

929. UN Posting   In February 2003, Israeli David Govrin was elected to serve on the UN General Assembly Working Group on Disarmament, giving Israel its first committee posting in over forty years. Iran and several Arab states voted in favor of Israel's posting.

930. UNSCOP (United Nations Special Committee on Palestine)   At British request, representatives of eleven member-states (Australia, Canada, Czechoslovakia, Guatemala, India, Iran, Netherlands, Peru, Sweden, Uruguay, and Yugoslavia) were empowered by the United Nations General Assembly in 1947 to explore possible resolutions for the Palestine Mandate. The Palestinian Arabs boycotted the commission, which met with some Arabs as well as Jewish community representatives. After completing its work in Palestine, the committee presented two options to the General Assembly. The majority report recommended that Palestine be partitioned into Arab and Jewish states, with international administration of Jerusalem, and that all three be linked in an Economic Union. The minority report recommended the creation of a federal unitary state, with Jerusalem as its capital. The majority's recommendation was subsequently adopted.

931. The United Nations Partition Plan (Resolution 181)   The idea of dividing Palestine into Jewish and Arab states was brought before the General Assembly on November 29, 1947. By a vote of thirty-three for (Australia, Belgium, Bolivia, Brazil, Belorussia, Canada, Costa Rica, Czechoslovakia, Denmark, Dominican Republic, Ecuador, France, Guatemala, Haiti, Iceland, Liberia, Luxemburg, Netherlands, New Zealand, Nicaragua, Norway, Panama, Paraguay, Peru, Philippines, Poland, Soviet Union, Sweden, Ukraine, Union of South Africa, United States, Uruguay, Venezuela), thirteen against (Afghanistan, Cuba, Egypt, Greece, India, Iran, Iraq, Lebanon, Pakistan, Saudi Arabia, Syria, Turkey, Yemen), and ten abstentions (Argentina, Chile, China, Colombia, El Salvador, Ethiopia, Honduras, Mexico, United Kingdom, Yugoslavia), the UN passed a resolution recommending the partition of Palestine into Jewish and Arab states, with Jerusalem falling under international auspices. Under this plan, Israel was to be roughly 5,200 square miles. The Partition Plan vote represented the first time that the United States and the Soviet Union agreed on a UN resolution. In response, the British announced that they would not participate in the implementation of the plan and would unilaterally withdraw all forces and personnel by May 15, 1948. Arab leaders and Arab states denounced the vote and vowed to solve the issue through the use of force.

932. Israel Admission to the United Nations   On May 13, 1949, exactly one year after the declaration of the State of Israel, Israel became the fifty-first country to join the international body.

933. Arafat Addresses the UN   On November 13, 1974, during the twenty-ninth session of the General Assembly, Yasser Arafat spoke at the United Nations General Assembly. With a pistol strapped to his side, Arafat claimed that the Jewish invasion, beginning in 1881, interfered with the Arab nation-building then taking place in Palestine.

934. Resolution 242   Adopted by the Security Council on November 22, 1967, following the Six-Day War, this resolution outlined guidelines for establishing "a just and lasting peace in the Middle East." The resolution called for the "withdrawal of Israeli armed forces from territories occupied" during the Six-Day War and for the Arab states to recognize the right of all states "to live in peace within secure and recognized boundaries free from threats or acts of force." The issue of Israeli control over the Golan Heights and parts of the West Bank and Gaza Strip is addressed in the phrase in the resolution that requires the "withdrawal of Israeli armed forces from territories occupied in the recent conflict." In the resolution, Israeli withdrawal is contingent upon a reciprocal Arab recognition of secure borders for the State of Israel. Furthermore, the clause does not say that Israel must withdraw from "all the" territories occupied after the Six-Day War. The Soviet Union and Arab members wanted to include this language in the text of the resolution because without it, the resolution means "that part of these territories can remain in Israeli hands." The United Nations rejected the insertion of this language precisely to indicate that Israel is not obligated to withdraw from "all the territories." The U.S. ambassador who helped draft Resolution 242, Arthur Goldberg, said that the resolution "in no way refers to Jerusalem, and this omission was deliberate. . . . Jerusalem was a discrete matter, not linked to the West Bank."

935. Resolution 338   Adopted by the Security Council on October 22, 1973, in the aftermath of the Yom Kippur War, Resolution 338 serves as a reaffirmation and continuation of Resolution 242. The resolution also called for all parties to immediately cease all hostilities and enter into direct negotiations.

936. "Zionism Is Racism" Resolution   Resolution 3379, labeling Zionism a "form of racism and racial discrimination," was adopted by the General Assembly on November 10, 1975, by a vote of 72 to 35 (with thirty-two abstentions and three delegations absent). Twenty of the seventy-two supporting votes were cast by Arab states. In response to the resolution, the United States withheld funds for UNESCO and withdrew from the international labor organization for two years because of the organization's anti-Israel bias. In December 1991, by a vote of 111 to 25 (with thirteen abstentions), the General Assembly voted to revoke the "Zionism is Racism" resolution. The result was the culmination of an intensive, behind-the-scenes lobbying effort spearheaded by the United States. The vote marked only the second time in UN history that the General Assembly repealed a previously passed resolution.

937. UN Boulevard   The road running past the Bahai Shrine to the top of Mount Carmel in Haifa is known as *Sedorot Hatziyonut,* Zionism Boulevard. Originally the street was named UN Boulevard in honor of the international body's role in the creation of Israel. After the UN adopted its resolution equating Zionism with racism in 1975, the name was changed.

938. UNTSO   When Palestinian Arabs initiated hostilities following Israel's declaration of independence in May 1948, the United Nations called for a cease-fire and decided that military observers should supervise the truce. These military observers, the first peacekeeping force in the region, came to be known as the United Nations Truce Supervision Organization (UNTSO). Since that time, UNTSO has supervised armistice agreements on all four of Israel's borders and has maintained relations with Israel, Egypt, Jordan, Lebanon, and Syria. It currently operates with a force of approximately 150 military observers and 100 civilian personnel. Since its inception, it has suffered forty-one fatalities.

939. UNDOF   The Israeli-Syrian disengagement agreement of 1974 provided for an area of separation with two equal zones of limited forces and armaments on both sides of that area, as well as the establishment of a United Nations observer force to supervise its implementation. In order to fulfill this last provision, the UN Security Council passed Resolution 350 to create the United Nations Disengagement Observer Force (UNDOF). The mandate of UNDOF is renewed every six months and has a budget exceeding $43 million. Roughly 1,000 troops provided by Austria, Canada, Japan, Nepal, Poland, and the Slovak Republic are supported by some 200 civilian personnel and military observers. The force has suffered forty fatalities.

940. UNIFIL   The early 1970s saw an increase in tension along the Israel-Lebanon border, particularly after the PLO was driven out of Jordan. Palestinian terrorist attacks against Israel provoked reprisals that led in March 1978 to an Israeli invasion. The Lebanese government, which did nothing to rein in the terrorists, protested to the UN, and on March 19, the Security Council adopted a resolution calling on Israel to withdraw its forces from Lebanon and another resolution creating the United Nations Interim Force in Lebanon (UNIFIL). For three years, until Israel invaded Lebanon in 1981,

UNIFIL remained behind the Israeli lines and had the limited role of providing some degree of protection and humanitarian assistance to the local population. UNIFIL's mandate is renewed every six months, and it operates on an annual budget that now exceeds $97 million. UNIFIL has approximately 2,000 troops provided by France, Ghana, India, Ireland, Italy, Poland, and Ukraine who are supported by more than 350 civilian personnel and military observers. UNIFIL has suffered 250 casualties.

NOTABLE QUOTATIONS

Zionism

941. I really wish the Jews again in Judea an independent nation.—**President John Adams**, 1819

942. It truly is monotonous and uninviting, there is no sufficient reason for describing it as being otherwise. Of all the lands there are for dismal scenery, I think Palestine must be the prince. The hills are barren, they are dull of color, they are unpicturesque in shape. The valleys are unsightly deserts fringed with feeble vegetation that has an expression about it of being sorrowful and despondent. The Dead Sea and the Sea of Galilee sleep in the midst of a vast stretch of hill and plain wherein the eye rests upon no pleasant tint, no striking object, no soft picture dreaming in a purple haze or mottled with the shadow of clouds. . . . It is a hopeless, dreary, heartbroken land. Palestine sits in sackcloth and ashes. Over it broods the spell of a curse that has withered its fields and fettered its energies. . . . Nazareth is forlorn. About that ford of Jordan where the hosts of Israel entered into the Promised Land with songs of rejoicing, one finds only squalid camps of fantastic Bedouins of the desert. Jericho the accursed lies a smoldering ruin today. . . . Renowned Jerusalem itself, the stateliest name in history, has lost all its ancient grandeur and has become a pauper village. . . . Palestine is desolate and unlovely. . . . Palestine is no more of this workaday world.—**Mark Twain**, describing his 1867 visit to Palestine in his book *The Innocents Abroad*

943. In Judea it is hardly an exaggeration to say that for miles and miles there was no appearance of life or habitation.—English cartographer **Arthur Pehrhyn Stanley**, *Sinai and Palestine*, 1881

944. We are here to lay the foundation stone of the house which is to shelter the Jewish nation. . . . Zionism is the return of the Jews to Judaism even before their return to the Jewish land. We seek to awaken the Jewish people to self-help . . . to create a permanent organ which the Jewish people has lacked until now.—**Theodor Herzl**, opening remarks at the First Zionist Congress, Basle, Switzerland, 1897

945. Jerusalem was the capital of our country when London was a marsh.—**Chaim Weizmann**, 1906, explaining to Lord Arthur Balfour why the Zionist movement rejected Britain's proposal that Uganda, not Palestine, become the Jewish homeland

946. I know that with the issue of this Declaration I shall please one group and displease another. I have decided to please your group because you stand for a great idea.—**British Prime Minister David Lloyd George** to Chaim Weizmann on his approval of the Balfour Declaration

947. There is no such thing as "Palestine" in history, absolutely not.—Princeton University Professor **Philip Hitti**, testifying against partition before the Anglo-American Committee in 1946

948. If you will it, it is no fairytale.—**Motto** of Theodor Herzl's book Altneuland (Old New Land), referring to the Zionist dream of returning the Jewish people to Israel. The phrase became a rallying cry of the Zionist movement.

949. In Basle I founded the Jewish state. . . . Maybe in five years, certainly in fifty, everyone will realize it.—**Theodor Herzl** wrote this in his diary after the First Zionist Congress in 1897. His prediction was off by only one year.

950. The Jews are in Palestine by right, not sufferance.—**Winston Churchill**, White Paper, 1922

951. A Jewish state on both sides of the Jordan.—**The rallying cry** of the Revisionists, articulating their opposition to the 1922 separation of Transjordan from the Palestine Mandate

952. The Arab charge that the Jews have obtained too large a proportion of good land can not be maintained. Much of the land now carrying orange groves was sand dunes or swamp and uncultivated when it was purchased. . . . There was at the time of at least the earlier sales little evidence that the owners possessed either the resources or training needed to develop the land.—**British Peel Commission**, 1937

953. I do not deny that (if a Jewish state is established) . . . the Arabs of Palestine will necessarily become a minority in the country of Palestine. What I do deny is that is a hardship. It is not a hardship on any race, any nation, possessing so many National States now and so many National States in the future. One fraction, one branch of that race, and not a big one, will have to lie in someone else's state. . . . I fully understand that any minority would prefer to be a majority. It is quite understandable that the Arabs of Palestine would also prefer Palestine to be the Arab State number 4, number 5, number 6 . . . but when the Arab claim is confronted with our Jewish claim to be saved, it is like the claims of appetite versus the claims of starvation.—**Zev Jabotinsky**, testifying before the Peel Commission, 1937

954. Ninety percent of Zionism may consist of tangible settlement, and only ten percent of politics; but those ten percent are the precondition of success.—**Zev Jabotinsky**, arguing that no Jewish state in Palestine can be realized under Britain's anti-Zionist rule

955. The Nazis meant to eradicate Judaism from Germany and they will succeed. Nobody loves the Jews, nobody wants them and yet we are pledged to give them a homeland. Instead we slam the door in their faces just at the moment when it should be wide open. . . . The action of His Majesty's Government in Palestine is very near to that of Hitler in Germany. They may be more subtle, they are certainly more hypocritical, but the result is similar—insecurity, misery, exasperation and murder.—**Colonel Richard Meinertzhagen**, British chief of intelligence in the Middle East during World War I and chief political officer, Palestine (1919), in his Middle East Diary

956. There are now two sorts of countries in the world, those that want to expel the Jews and those that don't want to admit them.—**Chaim Weizmann**, commenting on the world during World War II

957. We must assist the British in the war as if there were no White Paper and we must resist the White Paper as if there were no war.—**Ben-Gurion**, defining the position of the Zionist movement toward the British during World War II

958. The Jewish Underground now operating in Italy for the sole purpose of assisting emigration to Egypt and Palestine is one of the most efficient underground organizations with which this writer has ever come in contact.—*Illegal Immigration in and through Italy*, **Vincent La Vista**, U.S. National Archives

959. Palestine will become a Communist puppet within three years.—**CIA report** to President Truman claiming that if a Jewish state is established it will go communist

960. We are thinking of a refuge for Jews who do not wish or are unable to remain where they are, not of an asylum for criminals.—**Ben-Gurion** on why Dr. Robert Soblen, who arrived in Israel after jumping bail in the United States on charges of espionage on behalf of the Soviet Union, was expelled from Israel

961. When people criticize Zionists, they mean Jews. You're talking anti-Semitism.—**Martin Luther King**, quoted in Seymour Martin Lipset, "The Socialism of Fools—the Left, the Jews and Israel," *Encounter* (December 1969)

962. For the first time in history, thousands of black people are being brought to a country not in chains but in dignity, not as slaves but as citizens.—**William Safire**, describing Operation Moses in the *New York Times* (January 7, 1985)

War and Peace

963. It is good to die for our country.—**Last words** of Joseph Trumpeldor, who died leading the defense of Tel-Hai in 1920. These words, engraved on a monument of a roaring lion, mark the graves of the Jewish defenders.

964. All our efforts to find a peaceful solution to the Palestine problem have failed. The only way left for us is war. I will have the pleasure and honor to save Palestine.—**Transjordan's King Abdullah**, April 26, 1948

965. The representative of the Jewish Agency told us yesterday that they were not the attackers, that the Arabs had begun the fighting. We did not deny this. We told the whole world that we were going to fight.—**Jamal Husseini**, speaking to the Security Council on April 16, 1948

966. This will be a war of extermination and a momentous massacre which will be spoken of like the Mongolian massacres and the Crusades. —**Azzam Pasha**, Secretary-General of the Arab League

967. Early in January, the first detachments of the Arab Liberation Army began to infiltrate into Palestine from Syria. Some came through Jordan and even through Amman. . . . They were in reality to strike the first blow in the ruin of the Arabs of Palestine.—British commander of Transjordan's Arab Legion, **John Bagot Glubb**

968. The best we can tell you is that we have a 50–50 chance.—Chief of operations **Yigal Yadin** to David Ben-Gurion on Israel's chances of winning the War of Independence

969. Let us not be intoxicated with victory. To many people and not only among ourselves, it would appear to be a miracle: a small nation of 700,000 persons (at the outset of the campaign there were only 640,000) stood up against six nations numbering 30 million. However, none of us knows whether the trial by bloodshed has yet ended. The enemy forces in the neighboring countries and in the world at large have not yet despaired of their scheme to annihilate Israel in its own land or at least to pare away its borders, and we do not yet know whether the recent war, which we fought in the Negev and which ended in victory for the IDF, is the last battle or not, and as long as we cannot be confident that we have won the last battle, let us not glory.—**David Ben-Gurion**, 1948

970. The Arab nations should sacrifice up to 10 million of their 50 million people, if necessary, to wipe out Israel. Israel to the Arab world is like a cancer to the human body, and the only way of remedy is to uproot it, just like a cancer.—**King of Saudi Arabia**, 1954

971. Of all the beautiful gifts and birthday greetings, I enjoy Canada's gift the most.—**Ben-Gurion**, September 1956, after Canada agreed to sell twenty-four Saber jets to Israel

972. The problem presently before the Arab countries is not whether the port of Eilat should be blockaded or how to blockade it—but how to totally exterminate the State of Israel for all time.—**Gamel Abdel Nasser** in an address to the Egyptian National Assembly, May 25, 1967

973. The Temple Mount is in our hands.—IDF Major-General **Rabbi Shlomo Goren**, upon witnessing the liberation of the Western Wall on June 7, 1967

974. By the time they come to save Israel, there won't be an Israel. —Attributed to **Golda Meir**

975. I can forgive you for killing my sons, but I cannot forgive you for forcing me to kill your sons.—**Golda Meir** after the Six-Day War

976. I should have listened to the warnings of my heart and ordered a call up. . . . I shall live with this terrible knowledge for the rest of my life.—Excerpt from **Golda Meir's** *My Life*, referring to the surprise attack launched against Israel in the Yom Kippur War

977. Jordan is ours, Palestine is ours, and we shall build our national entity on the whole of this land.—**Yasser Arafat**, speaking at the United Nations, November 13, 1974

978. I am ready to go to the ends of the earth if this will prevent a soldier or an officer of my sons from being wounded—not being killed, but wounded. Israel will be astonished when it hears me saying now before you that I am ready to go to their house.—This single statement made by Egyptian leader **Anwar Sadat** in a nationwide broadcast on November 9, 1977, marked Egypt's first public peace overture to Israel and led to the Camp David Peace Accords

979. No more war, no more bloodshed.—Coined by **Anwar Sadat** in 1977, the phrase has been repeated ever since by those arguing for further negotiations with Arab entities

980. May God guide our steps towards peace, let us end suffering for all mankind.—Inscription entered into Yad Vashem's guest book by **Anwar Sadat** after his visit to the Holocaust memorial, November 20, 1977

981. The truth is that Jordan is Palestine and Palestine is Jordan.—**King Hussein bin Talil of Jordan**, December 26, 1981, *Al-Nahar Al-Arabi*, an Arab newspaper in Paris

982. I want all of Palestine . . . Haifa, Acre, Jaffa, Galilee, Nazareth—all of these are parts of Palestine.—**Intifada leader**, February 9, 1988, on 48 Hours

983. The conflict between the Arab nation and Zionism is over existence, not borders.—Syrian Defense Minister **Mustafa Tlas**, Damascus Television Service, March 7, 1990

984. [I] look onto the West Bank and say to myself, "If I'm the Chief of Staff of the Israel Defense Forces, I cannot defend this land without this terrain." . . . And I don't know about politics, but if you want me to defend this country and you want me to defend Jerusalem, I've got to hold that ground.—Lieutenant-General **Thomas Kelly**, director of operations for the Joint Chief of Staffs (U.S.) during the Persian Gulf War, November 7, 1991

985. Barak made a proposal that was as forthcoming as anyone in the world could imagine, and Arafat turned it down. If you have a country that's a sliver and you can see three sides of it from a high hotel building, you've got to be careful what you give away and to whom you give it.—U.S. Defense Secretary **Donald Rumsfeld,** quoted in *Yediot Aharonot,* August 7, 2002

986. Our position is clear: all of Palestine. Every inch of Palestine belongs to the Muslims.—**Mahmoud Zahar,** senior leader of Hamas, quoted in the *Jerusalem Post,* November 14, 2003

Politics

987. I should not have a prize coming to me for having done my duty to my country.—**David Ben-Gurion,** rejecting the Israel Prize in 1968

988. Because it is right.—**President Lyndon Johnson** replying to Soviet Premier Aleksei Kosygin, who asked why the United States supports Israel when there are eighty million Arabs and only three million Israelis

989. [This] issue goes to the very heart of free trade among nations. . . . End the divisive effects on American life of foreign boycotts aimed at Jewish members of our society.—**President Jimmy Carter,** 1977, upon signing legislation making it illegal for American companies to adhere to the Arab boycott of Israel

990. Shalom Have—Good-bye, Friend.—**President Bill Clinton,** in a nationally televised eulogy for assassinated Prime Minister Yitzhak Rabin. The phrase became a potent political slogan and was seen on signs and bumper stickers around Israel by supporters of Rabin's negotiations with the PLO.

991. Shalom Haverim—Good-bye, Friends.—Shortly after Rabin's assassination and the proliferation of the slogan Shalom Haver, terrorist attacks claimed the lives of scores of Israelis. In response, those opposed to the policies of Prime Minister Peres rallied around the slogan *Shalom Haverim,* saying good-bye to all those killed in the murderous attacks.

Miscellaneous

992. We are investing and continue to invest in our research and development in Israel. . . . Israel has become a place which the biggest technology companies recruit high-tech brilliance.—**Bill Gates,** founder and chairman of Microsoft

993. He who saves one life is considered as having saved the whole universe.—Phrase engraved on the silver medal sent by Yad Vashem to Righteous Gentiles to honor their bravery and heroism. The term originates from *Pirkei Avot* (Ethics of our Fathers).

994. Since we long ago resolved never to be servants to the Romans, nor to any other than to God Himself, who alone is the true and just Lord of mankind, the time has now come that obliges us to make that resolution true in practice. . . . We were the very first that revolted, and we are the last to fight against them; and I cannot but esteem it as a favor that God has granted us, that it is still in our power to die bravely, and in a state of freedom.—**Elazar ben Yair**'s last speech at Masada before he and the other Zealots committed suicide in 73 C.E. according to Josephus, *War of the Jews*

995. But for the decision of the United Nations, the State of Israel would not have arisen; but even after the UN decision, had it not been for our courage in proclaiming independence and our capacity to defend it, the decision would never have been implemented.—**Moshe Sharett**, *Davar*, Independence Day, 1965

996. The people of Israel in the Land of Israel according to the Bible of Israel.—**Motto** of Mizrachi, coined by Rabbi Meir Berlin Bar-Ilan.

997. I can live as a Jew outside Israel but not without Israel.—**Elie Wiesel**

998. Through a historical catastrophe—the destruction of Jerusalem by the emperor of Rome—I was born in one of the cities in the Diaspora. But I always deemed myself a child of Jerusalem, one who is in reality a native of Jerusalem.—**S. Y. Agnon**, upon receiving the Nobel Prize for literature, 1966

999. The hand that controls the faucet rules the country.—A *Jerusalem Post* (July 16, 1994) headline stating the strategic importance of Israel's water supply

1,000. Pray for the peace of Jerusalem.—Psalms 122:6

1,001. Here is a place whose atmosphere is peace, where political and religious jealousies can be forgotten and international unity fostered and developed.—Inscription in Hebrew, English, and Arabic at the entrance to the Jerusalem YMCA, quoting from remarks made by Lord Allenby at its grand opening

Bibliography

Allon, Yigal. *The Making of Israel's Army*. New York: Universe Books, 1970.

Atkinson, Rick. *Crusade*. New York: Houghton Mifflin, 1993.

Aumann, Moshe. *Land Ownership in Palestine, 1880–1948*. Jerusalem: Academic Committee on the Middle East, 1976.

Avineri, Shlomo. *The Making of Modern Zionism: Intellectual Origins of the Jewish State*. New York: Basic, 1981.

Avneri, Arieh. *The Claim of Dispossession*. New Brunswick, N.J.: Transaction, 1984.

Bard, Mitchell. *The Complete Idiot's Guide to the Middle East Conflict*. New York: Macmillan, 1999.

———. *The Water's Edge and Beyond*. New Brunswick, N.J.: Transaction, 1991.

Becker, Jillian. *The PLO*. New York: St. Martin's, 1985.

Begin, Menachem. *The Revolt*. New York: Dutton, 1978.

Bell, J. Bowyer. *Terror out of Zion*. New Brunswick, N.J.: Transaction, 1996.

Ben-Ami, Yitshaq. *Years of Wrath, Days of Glory: Memoirs from the Irgun*. New York: Shengold, 1996.

Ben-Gurion, David. *Rebirth and Destiny of Israel*. New York: Philosophical Library, 1954.

Benvenisti, Meron. *City of Stone: The Hidden History of Jerusalem*. Berkeley: University of California Press, 1996.

———. *Intimate Enemies: Jews and Arabs in a Shared Land*. Berkeley: University of California Press, 1995.

———. *Jerusalem, the Torn City*. Minneapolis: University of Minnesota Press, 1977.

Bernadotte, Folke. *To Jerusalem*. London: Hodder and Stoughton, 1951.

Boutros-Ghali, Boutros. *Egypt's Road to Jerusalem: A Diplomat's Story of the Struggle for Peace in the Middle East*. New York: Random House, 1997.

Buehrig, Edward. *The UN and the Palestinian Refugees*. Bloomington: Indiana University Press, 1971.

Burrell, David, and Yehezkel Landau. *Voices from Jerusalem: Jews and Christians Reflect on the Holy Land*. New York: Paulist, 1991.

Carter, Jimmy. *Keeping Faith: Memoirs of a President*. Fayetteville: University of Arkansas Press, 1995.

Churchill, Randolph S., and Winston S. Churchill. *The Six Day War*. New York: Penguin, 1967.

Cobban, Helena. *The Palestine Liberation Organisation*. Cambridge: Cambridge University Press, 1984.

Cohen, Aharon. *Israel and the Arab World*. New York: Funk and Wagnalls, 1970.

Collins, Larry, and Dominique Lapierre. *O Jerusalem!* New York: Simon & Schuster, 1972.

Cordesman, Anthony. *After the Storm*. Boulder, Colo.: Westview, 1993.

Cordesman, Anthony, and Abraham Wagner. *The Lessons of Modern War*. Vol. 2, *The Iran-Iraq War*. Boulder, Colo.: Westview, 1990.

Cull, Brian, Shlomo Aloni, and David Nicolle. *Wings over Suez*. London: Grub Street, 1996.

Curtis, Michael, ed. *The Palestinians*. New Brunswick, N.J.: Transaction, 1975.

———, ed. *Religion and Politics in the Middle East*. Boulder, Colo.: Westview, 1981.

Degani, Nissan. *Exodus Calling*. New York: Herzl, 1996.

Dimont, Max. *Jews, God, and History*. New York: Mentor, 1994.

Dupuy, Trevor. *Elusive Victory: The Arab-Israeli Wars, 1947–1974*. Dubuque, Iowa: Kendall/Hunt, 1992.

Eban, Abba. *Heritage: Civilization and the Jews*. New York: Summit, 1984.

———. *My Country: The Story of Modern Israel*. New York: Random House, 1972.

Erlich, Avi. *Ancient Zionism: The Biblical Origins of the National Idea*. New York: Free Press, 1994.

Friedman, Thomas. *From Beirut to Jerusalem*. New York: Farrar, Straus & Giroux, 1989.

Gilbert, Martin. *Exile and Return: The Struggle for a Jewish Homeland*. Philadelphia: Lippincott, 1978.

Glubb, John Bagot. *A Soldier with the Arabs*. London: Staughton and Hodder, 1957.

———. *The Story of the Arab Legion*. New York: Da Capo, 1976.

Goitein, S. D. *Jews and Arabs*. New York: Schocken, 1974.

Granott, Abraham. *The Land System in Palestine*. London: Eyre and Spottiswoode, 1952.

Halpern, Ben. *The Idea of a Jewish State*. Cambridge, Mass.: Harvard University Press, 1969.

Harkabi, Yehoshofat. *Arab Attitudes to Israel*. New Brunswick, N.J.: Transaction, 1974.

———. *The Arab-Israeli Conflict on the Threshold of Negotiations*. Princeton, N.J.: Princeton University Press, 1992.

———. *Israel's Fateful Hour*. New York: HarperCollins, 1989.

———. *Palestinians and Israel*. Portland, Ore.: Valentine Mitchell, 1981.

Hertzberg, Arthur. *The Zionist Idea*. Philadelphia: Jewish Publications Society, 1997.

Herzl, Theodore. *The Diaries of Theodore Herzl*. New York: Peter Smith, 1987.

———. *The Jewish State*. Mineola, N.Y.: Dover, 1989.

Herzog, Chaim. *The Arab-Israeli Wars*. New York: Random House, 1984.

———. *War of Atonement: The Inside Story of the Yom Kippur War*. Philadelphia: Stackpole, 1998.

Hirst, David. *The Gun and the Olive Branch*. London: Faber & Faber, 1977.

Horowitz, David. *State in the Making*. Westport, Conn.: Greenwood, 1981.

Israeli, Raphael, ed. *PLO in Lebanon*. New York: St. Martin's, 1983.

Jabotinsky, Z'ev. *The War and the Jew*. New York: Altalena, 1987.

Johnson, Paul. *A History of the Jews*. New York: HarperCollins, 1988.

Katz, Samuel. *Battleground—Fact and Fantasy in Palestine*. New York: SPI, 1986.

Kimche, Jon. *The Second Arab Awakening*. New York: Henry Holt, 1973.

———. *The Secret Roads: The "Illegal" Migration of a People, 1938–1948*. New York: Hyperion, 1976.

———. *There Could Have Been Peace: The Untold Story of Why We Failed with Palestine and Again with Israel*. New York: Dutton, 1973.

Kirk, George. *A Short History of the Middle East*. New York: Frederick Praeger, 1964.

Kissinger, Henry. *The White House Years*. Boston: Little, Brown 1979.

———. *Years of Renewal*. New York: Simon & Schuster, 1999.

Kollek, Teddy. *Jerusalem*. Washington, D.C.: Washington Institute for Near East Policy, 1990.

Laqueur, Walter. *A History of Zionism*. New York: Fine Communications, 1997.

———. *The Road to War*. London: Weidenfeld and Nicolson, 1968.

Laqueur, Walter, and Barry Rubin. *The Israel-Arab Reader*. New York: Penguin, 1995.

Lenczowski, George. *American Presidents and the Middle East*. Durham, N.C.: Duke University Press, 1990.

———. *The Middle East in World Affairs*. New York: Cornell University Press, 1980.

Livingstone, Neil C., and David Halevy. *Inside the PLO*. New York: Morrow, 1990.

Lorch, Netanel. *One Long War*. New York: Herzl, 1976.

Lukacs, Yehuda. *The Israeli-Palestinian Conflict: A Documentary Record*. New York: Cambridge University Press, 1992.

———. *Israel, Jordan, and the Peace Process*. New York: Syracuse University Press, 1997.

Mandel, Neville. *The Arabs and Zionism before World War I*. Berkeley: University of California Press, 1977.

McDowall, David. *Palestine and Israel: The Uprising and Beyond*. Berkeley: University of California Press, 1990.

Meinertzhagen, Richard. *Middle East Diary, 1917–1956*. London: Cresset, 1959.

Meir, Golda. *My Life*. New York: Dell, 1975.

Miller, Aaron. *The Arab States and the Palestine Question*. Greenwood, Conn.: Praeger, 1986.

Moore, John. ed. *The Arab-Israeli Conflict*. Princeton, N.J.: Princeton University Press, 1974.

———, ed. *The Arab-Israeli Conflict: The Difficult Search for Peace (1975–1988)*. Parts 1 and 2. Princeton, N.J.: Princeton University Press, 1992.

Neff, Donald. *Warriors at Suez*. New York: Simon & Schuster, 1981.

Netanyahu, Benjamin. *A Place among Nations: Israel and the World*. New York: Warner, 1998.

Nixon, Richard. *RN: The Memoirs of Richard Nixon*. New York: Touchstone, 1990.

O'Brien, Conner Cruise. *The Siege: The Saga of Israel and Zionism*. New York: Touchstone, 1986.

Oesterreicher, John, and Anne Sinai, eds. *Jerusalem*. New York: John Day, 1974.

Patai, Ralph, ed. *Encyclopedia of Zionism and Israel.* New York: McGraw-Hill, 1971.

Penkower, Monty Noam. *The Holocaust and Israel Reborn: From Catastrophe to Sovereignty.* Urbana-Champaign: University of Illinois Press, 1994.

Quandt, William B. *Camp David: Peacemaking and Politics.* Washington, D.C.: Brookings Institution, 1986.

———, ed. *The Middle East: Ten Years after Camp David.* Washington, D.C.: Brookings Institution, 1988.

Rabin, Yitzhak. *The Rabin Memoirs.* Berkeley: University of California Press, 1996.

Randal, Jonathan. *Going All the Way: Christian Warlords, Israeli Adventurers, and the War in Lebanon.* New York: Vintage Books, 1983.

Roth, Cecil, and Geoffrey Wigoder, eds. *Encyclopedia Judaica.* 18 vols. Philadelphia: Coronet, 1972–1991.

Roumani, Maurice. *The Case of the Jews from Arab Countries: A Neglected Issue.* Tel Aviv: World Organization of Jews from Arab Countries, 1977.

Rubenstein, Amnon. *The Zionist Dream Revisited: From Herzl to Gush Emunim and Back.* New York: Schocken, 1987.

Sachar, Abram Leon. *History of the Jews.* New York: Random House, 1982.

Sachar, Howard. *A History of Israel: From the Rise of Zionism to Our Time.* New York: Alfred A. Knopf, 1998.

Safran, Nadav. *Israel the Embattled Ally.* Cambridge, Mass.: Harvard University Press, 1981.

Schechtman, Joseph B. *European Population Transfers, 1939–1945.* New York: Russell & Russell, 1971.

———. *The Life and Times of Jabotinsky.* 2 vols. Silver Spring, Md.: Eshel, 1986.

———. *The Refugee in the World.* New York: A. S. Barnes, 1963.

Schiff, Ze'ev. *Israel-Syria Negotiations: Lessons Learned, 1993–1996.* Washington, D.C.: Washington Institute for Near East Policy, 1997.

Schiff, Ze'ev, and Ehud Ya'ari. *Intifada.* New York: Simon & Schuster, 1990.

———. *Israel's Lebanon War.* New York: Simon & Schuster, 1984.

Schoenberg, Harris. *Mandate for Terror: The United Nations and the PLO.* New York: Shapolsky, 1989.

Segev, Tom. *1949: The First Israelis.* New York: Henry Holt, 1988.

Shipler, David. *Arab and Jew.* New York: Penguin, 1987.

Silverberg, Robert. *If I Forget Thee O Jerusalem: American Jews and the State of Israel.* New York: Morrow, 1970.

Spiegel, Steven. *The Other Arab-Israeli Conflict.* Chicago: University of Chicago Press, 1985.

Stone, I. F. *Underground to Palestine.* New York: Random House, 1979.

Sykes, Christopher. *Crossroads to Israel: 1917–1948.* Bloomington: Indiana University Press, 1973.

Teveth, Shabtai. *Ben Gurion: The Burning Ground, 1886–1948.* New York: Houghton Mifflin, 1987.

———. *Ben-Gurion and the Palestinian Arabs: From Peace to War.* London: Oxford University Press, 1985.

———. *Moshe Dayan, the Soldier, the Man, the Legend.* New York: Houghton Mifflin,

1973.

Truman, Harry. *Years of Trial and Hope*. Vol. 2. New York: Doubleday, 1956.

Twain, Mark. *The Innocents Abroad*. London: Chatto & Windus, 1881.

Vance, Cyrus. *Hard Choices: Critical Years in America's Foreign Policy*. New York: Simon & Schuster, 1983.

Weizmann, Chaim. *Trial and Error*. New York: Greenwood, 1972.

Wigoder, Geoffrey, ed. *New Encyclopedia of Zionism and Israel*. Madison, N.J.: Fairleigh Dickinson University Press, 1994.

Yaniv, Avner. *National Security and Democracy in Israel*. Boulder, Colo.: Rienner, 1993.

———. *PLO*. Jerusalem: Israel Universities Study Group of Middle Eastern Affairs, August 1974.

Ye'or, Bat. *The Dhimmi*. London: Associated University Press, 1985.

WEBSITES

Bar-Ilan University	www.biu.ac.il
Ben-Gurion University of the Negev	www.bgu.ac.il
CIA World Fact Book	www.cia.gov/cia/publications/factbook
Daily newspaper *Haaretz*	www.haaretz.com
Dead Sea region	www.deadsea.co.il
Foreign Ministry of the State of Israel	www.mfa.gov.il/mfa
Hadassah Hospital	www.hadassah.org.il
Hadassah Medical Organization	www.hadassah.org.il/english
Hashemite Kingdom	www.kinghussein.gov.jo
Hebrew University	www.huji.ac.il/huji/eng
Israel Defense Forces	www.idf.il
Israeli-Weapons	www.israeli-weapons.com
Jewish Agency for Israel	www.jafi.org.il
Knesset	www.knesset.gov.il
Shaare Zedek Medical Center	www.szmc.org.il
Technion Israel Institute of Technology	www.technion.ac.il
Tel Aviv University	www.tau.ac.il
United Nations	www.un.org
University of Haifa	www.haifa.ac.il
Weizmann Institute	www.weizmann.ac.il
Yad Sarah	www.yadsarah.org
Yad Vashem	www.yadvashem.org

About the Authors

Mitchell Bard, Ph.D., is executive director of the nonprofit American-Israeli Cooperative Enterprise (AICE), webmaster for the Jewish Virtual Library (www.JewishVirtualLibrary.org), and a foreign policy analyst who lectures frequently on U.S. Middle East policy. For three years he was the editor of the *Near East Report*, a weekly newsletter on U.S. Middle East policy. Bard is the author of several books, including *The Water's Edge and Beyond: Defining the Limits to Domestic Influence on U.S. Middle East Policy, Forgotten Victims: The Abandonment of Americans in Hitler's Camps, The Complete Idiot's Guide to World War II* and *The Complete Idiot's Guide to Middle East Conflict*, and the *Encyclopedia of the Holocaust*. Bard holds a doctorate in political science from the University of California, Los Angeles, and a master's degree in public policy from the University of California, Berkeley. He received his bachelor of arts in economics from the University of California, Santa Barbara.

Moshe Schwartz is an analyst for the U.S. government. He worked for the Israeli government at the Permanent Mission of Israel to the United Nations and at the Consulate General of Israel in New York. For three years he served as an assistant district attorney in Brooklyn. Subsequently, he was vice president of KCSA Public Relations Worldwide, where he represented a number of leading Israeli high-tech companies. Schwartz has lectured on the Middle East throughout North America and has led two fact-finding trips to Israel. He studied at Yeshivat Hakotel and Hebrew University, both located in Jerusalem. Schwartz holds a juris doctorate from Yeshiva University Cardozo School of Law, an MBA from the Carnegie Mellon Tepper School of Business, and a master's degree in public policy management from the Carnegie Mellon H. John Heinz III School of Public Policy and Management.